Praise for

ROMANTIC VIOLENCE: MEMOIRS OF AN AMERICAN SKINHEAD

"Christian's journey exemplifies how hate and violence are unsustainable, and tolerance, forgiveness, and love are the only way forward. If Christian can change, there is hope for all humankind—a compelling and extraordinary story."
—**JANE ROSENTHAL, Co-Founder, Tribeca Film Festival**

"*Romantic Violence* takes the reader into the depths of the hate movement and sheds a valuable light on the mindset of those who can be lured into this dark world. Christian's astonishing change of heart is a testament to our endless capacity for personal transformation."
—**LONNIE NASATIR, Regional Director, Anti–Defamation League**

"*Romantic Violence* is a very hard book to put down. Though the tale often takes the reader into disturbing territory, the storyteller's voice is filled with a beautiful, unwavering honesty. There have been countless sociological texts and documentaries devoted to the exploration of American neo-Nazi skinhead culture, but this book starts at the very beginning. Christian Picciolini was one of the first foot soldiers (and eventual leaders) of that movement, and though he has long since renounced those racist beliefs, there is a riveting emotional immediacy to his depiction of the process and mindset that led him down the white power path. The issues and events dominating today's headlines are reminders that the roots *Romantic Violence* exposes are eminently germane. This memoir is not, however, merely a one-of-a-kind historical account. It is, first and foremost, the story of a human being who looks back on his earlier self with shock and horror, but it is told from the vantage point of one who refused to let his past define him. Though he will be forever haunted by deeds he cannot change, he lives with the joy of one who now understands the preciousness of every life—including his own."
—**DON DE GRAZIA, author of *American Skin***

"Upon reading *Romantic Violence*, you will learn and understand how the average person—even your next-door neighbor—can be drawn into a hate movement. At the same time, reading this book will make you wish that you were lucky enough to have someone like Christian Picciolini as that neighbor. *Romantic Violence* by Christian Picciolini is powerful, honest, and insightful. A no-holds-barred look into how nearly a decade of hate transformed a man and allowed him to create a life of strength, love, kindness, and tolerance."
—**FRANK MEEINK, author of *Autobiography of a Recovering Skinhead* and Founder, Harmony Through Hockey**

ROMANTIC VIOLENCE

ROMANTIC VIOLENCE

MEMOIRS OF AN AMERICAN SKINHEAD

CHRISTIAN PICCIOLINI

GOLDMILL GROUP
CHICAGO

Published in association with GOLDMILL GROUP LLC
917 W. Washington Boulevard, Suite 213
Chicago, Illinois 60607
www.goldmill.com

For information about special discounts for educational, business, fundraising,
or sales promotional use bulk purchases, please contact Goldmill Group special sales: orders@goldmill.com

Printed in the United States of America

Hardcover design and illustrations by Nick Colella / Great Lakes Tattoo, Chicago, Illinois (www.GreatLakesTattoo.com)
Paperback and e-book cover design by James T. Egan / Bookfly Design LLC (www.BookflyDesign.com)
Interior layout by James T. Egan / Bookfly Design LLC
Photography (author headshot) by Mark Seliger (www.MarkSeligerPhotography.com)
Interior Photography (chapter photos) by Various
Edited by Michael Mohr (www.MichaelMohrWriter.com)
Proofread by Jill Bailin Rembar

ISBN:
978-0-9862404-2-3 (paperback)
978-0-9862404-3-0 (e-book)

First Edition: May 2015

10 9 8 7 6 5 4 3 2 1

Publisher's Cataloging-in-Publication data

Romantic violence : memoirs of an American Skinhead / Christian Picciolini.
p. cm.
ISBN 978-0-9862404-2-3 (pbk.)
ISBN 978-0-9862404-3-0 (e-book)

1. Picciolini, Christian. 2. Skinheads—United States—Biography. 3. Neo-Nazis—United States—Biography.
4. White supremacy movements—United States. 5. Ex-gang members—United States. I. Title.

HV6439.U5 P53 2015
320.5/6—dc23   2015900837

For more information on *Romantic Violence: Memoirs of an American Skinhead*, please visit:
www.RomanticViolence.com

To contact Christian Picciolini for speaking engagements:
www.ChristianPicciolini.com / Twitter: @cpicciolini
christian@christianpicciolini.com

A portion of the proceeds from the sale of this book will be donated to LifeAfterHate.org to help counter racism and promote compassion.

To my Buddy, my boys, and my Britton

Any intelligent fool can make things bigger, more complex, and more violent. It takes a touch of genius—and a lot of courage— to move in the opposite direction.
—E.F. Schumacher, *Small is Beautiful*

TABLE OF CONTENTS

FOREWORD BY JOAN JETT

T HE UNIVERSAL STRUGGLE FOR IDENTITY AND BELONGING is what binds us all together. It is this search, ultimately, that makes us human; that makes us, especially as children, vulnerable.

When I was in The Runaways, the first American all-female rock band ever, in the 1970s, as a woman I experienced all types of prejudice and bigotry. Sometimes it was all I could do to not give up altogether. But my guitar, along with my pen and my voice, led me out of that hollow fear and into a long and successful rock and roll career—one that, thankfully, I am still riding the powerful wave of today.

Thanks in large part to Kenny Laguna, my producer, manager, close friend, and lifetime confidante, I have arrived at this level of commercial success and have been able to carve out a life of music. Kenny was then and still is very much a mentor to me. Without his direction and aid, I would not be where I am today. He believed in me when most others didn't.

I met Christian Picciolini in 1996 while on tour in Chicago. I did not know about Christian then what I know now. We needed an opener and when I saw his punk band, Random55, warming up on stage, I saw something special in their style and knew from some place

Christian Picciolini and Joan Jett, 1996

deep inside that they were the right ones. I approached Christian, who seemed down and withdrawn, backstage after the set. He seemed sad for some reason, and I talked with him for a little while, throwing my arm around his shoulder, trying to assuage his fears. Like me as a struggling teenager, I sensed that Christian, too, was in a dark place searching for identity and belonging—acceptance. He needed someone to believe in him.

Random55 ended up going out with us on the road that year, becoming our opening act for a string of shows. Christian and I had many more meaningful conversations, and I like to think that some of what I had to say helped him cope with whatever he was going through. I will always recall his dedication to music and his drive. I could tell, at that time, that he was seeking something from life, from his soul. And now he has written this incredible memoir, detailing and forcing out the truth, after all these years. And in doing so, he has hopefully released his inner demons for good.

Compassion is an important human quality, and we all have the ability to tap into it. I have it for Christian's former, younger, troubled self. He was not a bad kid, but a kid trying desperately to belong to a group; to do something that mattered; to understand his loneliness and sense of rejection and abandonment. Hating the LGBT community, non-white minorities, Jews, and others when he was involved with the white power skinhead movement is tantamount to a disgusting and blind allegiance to hatred. And yet, Christian was able to pick his head up from the muck of that ideology and see the error of his ways, to steer the ship in the other direction, and to get out. He not only left and at last denounced the movement in the late '90s, he became an active voice against hatred, forming the nonprofit Life After Hate, in 2010.

Romantic Violence: Memoirs of an American Skinhead is Christian's testament to how frighteningly easy it can be to find yourself down the wrong rabbit hole with no way out. It is his tale of redemption, his Hero's Journey, his descent into hell and his return, ultimately, to the land of the living. I admire him greatly, not because he once hated, but because he once hated and he fought hard against his own mired determination and discovered that his prejudice and hatred were paper-thin lies. We all have to discover life on our own path, find our truth. Christian writes his book to expose his truth, and we can be grateful in at least some small part for his sacrifice, of running for a while on the dark side and then breathlessly sprinting for the light at the end of the tunnel. The result is a cautionary tale that furthers and educates us all.

In the end, we all need guidance, direction, and help along the road of life. We all need a mentor. For many, music is a major influence, and that can be used for good or bad. I was able to find myself through music, and, in a way, so did Christian. That night after the gig, throwing my arm around his shoulder was my way of showing empathy, compassion. Telling him that whatever he was feeling, like so many others, I'd been there too. Taking his band on tour was my handing of trust over to him. Like Kenny with me, I hope I was able to lead him, if only for a moment, out of the deep fog hovering around him. Christian pursued music in other capacities after that tour, and he maintained contact with Kenny and me through the years. I am so incredibly proud of his life's work since he left the movement in 1995, and I can see the real change and transformation he has made.

So, if you want to practice empathy—or if you just want to experience one hell of a redemption tale—come along for the ride and find out how it all started, where it went, and why it ended. Take the journey with Christian, and let yourself fall down alongside him. Feel the anger, violence, and rage as he climbs the rungs of the American white power movement. Feel his fear and depression as he finally exits. Feel his sadness and hollowness after the battering waves have at last ceased. And, beautifully, watch him change and grow, evolving into a fine human being who accepts all people, including himself.

Watch him turn into the man he always, deep down inside, wanted to be. Watch him make you proud to be a part of his experience, a part of this diverse global community, a part of this world.

Watch yourself change along with him.

—Joan Jett

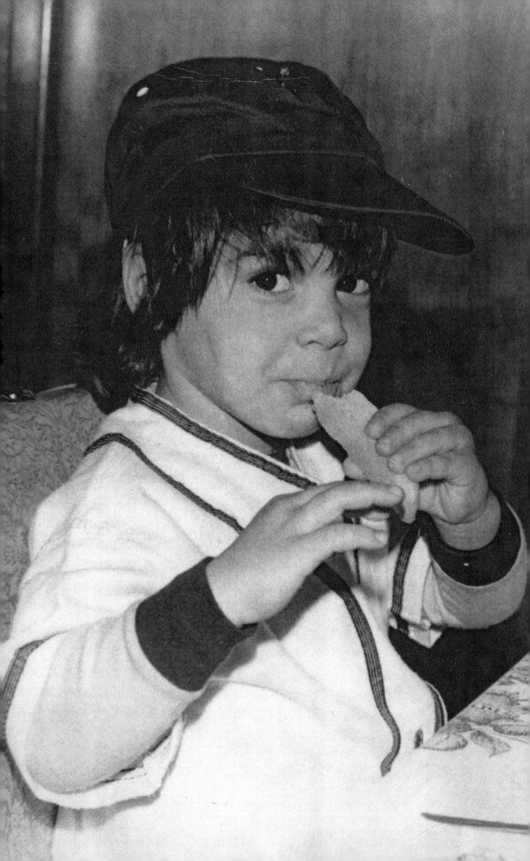

INTRODUCTION

I AM NOT MY FATHER.

Nor my mother.

Not my grandparents.

I am neither my brother nor my friends.

My life is my own.

The actions and decisions of my youth and early adulthood were not determined by anyone who came before me.

I am my own invention, shaped both by my imagination and ambition, and it wasn't until my two sons were born that I began to understand my responsibilities and connection to others.

But I'm getting ahead of myself.

And you deserve an explanation, a glimpse into the lives of those people I claim not to be—a claim that does not imply any lack of love on anyone's part.

One thing that distinguishes me from my immediate family is that I am the first born in the United States. When my mother tells the story of my birth, her warm Mediterranean eyes light up and her voice, normally steady and sure, quickens. She laces the story with Italian phrases when she recounts it to someone in Blue Island, the

Christian Picciolini, 1976 (Photo by Maddalena Spinelli)

working-class neighborhood on the South Side of Chicago that her Italian family immigrated to when she was sixteen. When she chronicles the tale of my birth to family and friends, she peppers her story with frequent references to the notion that everybody, Italians and Americans alike, loved me.

If I could recall my entry into the world and tell the story myself, I suspect it would be a bit different than hers. While she was pushing and straining for nearly twenty-four hours to get me out, I was impatiently wriggling my way down the birth canal ready to take charge, or so I imagine, in a rush to see what was ahead of me. I may have been annoyed that I hadn't been given ample warning, but as I felt the first blast of air fill my lungs, I would have already been calculating the best way to handle the situation.

To the attending doctor I was yet another little miracle, a slippery, mucus-covered newborn like all the rest of his deliveries. He was so intent on making sure I took my first breath and verifying that all parts were there that he missed the clear signs I had been born alert, brave, and ready to take on the new reality into which I had arrived.

Blinking rapidly, my eyes impatient to adjust to the cruel bright lights, I was eager to take in everything that was going on. Had I been able to talk, I would have asked the nurse to step back, pleaded with my mother to calm down, and warned the doctor to think twice before slapping me again. I would have objected to their tests, and insisted that I didn't want to be compared, labeled, charted, or measured in any way.

I was swaddled in a soft, warm blanket. The unmistakably warm love my mother bestowed on me when the nurse put me in her arms set me up for life with the patent knowledge that love and attention were clearly well worth pursuing.

I came equipped with a desire to live life fully, to explore the unknown, and to have my existence count for something. For many years, I thought this meant being an instrumental member of a group undertaking a significant mission. Considering how vitally having a place in the world defined my actions throughout my childhood, youth, and early adulthood, I have to believe that I came hardwired with those desires.

From as early as I can recall, I wanted to be the game-winning athlete who was carried off the field on my team's shoulders after hitting an upper deck grand slam to win the championship series in the bottom of the ninth inning; to be the hero who tackled the gun-toting hijacker; to have a national holiday named after me for my contributions to the human race. I didn't always care how I achieved greatness, but that hunger for glory was what made me tick.

I went to great lengths to try to fulfill that dream, and some of the actions I took still fill me with dread and regret. For more than two decades I have searched my soul, wondering how I could have strayed so far off-track, committed such vile acts of hatred, and advocated for the annihilation of people based solely on the color of their skin, who they loved, or the god to whom they prayed.

In trying to reconcile my actions, I have come to believe that at the root of my motivations lies a basic human necessity. Far stronger than my overwhelming desire to achieve prominence was the profound, essential human need to belong—a force I could not have articulated at the time, but one which propelled me to actions both good and bad, harmless and treacherous, self-fulfilling and self-destructive. This need, coupled with my tendency toward ambition, defined my actions and led me down a troubled and dark path to prejudice, racism, and violence.

What follows is my story. Because I cannot recall conversations verbatim, I have taken some liberties in recreating scenes to capture events and portray the people in them as closely as I can remember. Memory colors things, and I fully admit that others may have perceived events differently. However, I have been careful to report as truthfully as my memory serves me, with the intention of accurately revealing what took place. I have also deliberately changed many of the names to protect the privacy of the individuals involved.

Though I wish I could rewrite a significant part of my life, I have been honest. I have not sugarcoated my past, even though the bitterness of my convictions during my troubled years was brutal and immense. My reservations about my hateful actions were also true at the time, and I haven't changed them to fit a retrospective view. If anything, I hope the reader despises my duplicity as much as he or she abhors my deeds. It is worse to have acted as I did when I knew better, and I include my doubts to emphasize, not relieve, my guilt.

My hope in writing this book is that others will read it and heed how disturbingly easy it is for someone without prior inclination toward prejudice or violence to enter a world laden with unadulterated hate; that others may see the desire to belong—if taken to the extreme and not addressed early enough—can have repugnant results, and that the promise of power is sometimes so seductive, an impressionable mind can be persuaded to commit atrocious acts in its pursuit.

I write this book with optimism that others will search for identity, belonging, and acceptance in healthy, inclusive communities and will have the strength to walk away from empty promises, and that people will listen to those who encourage them to be compassionate human beings instead of finding a place among those who prey on the insecure and exploit their loneliness, fear, confusion, and feelings of worthlessness.

I hope that by exposing racism, hate will have fewer places to hide.

1
RIGHTS OF THE ABUSED

JAKE REILLY PICKED ME RANDOMLY that soggy April afternoon to be the target of his malicious playground taunts, insulting me for anything he could think of. He was the quintessential class bully—"Goliath" as we had secretly referred to him since the first grade—and he took great pleasure in routinely tormenting his less fortunate eighth grade classmates at St. Damian Elementary School.

Today, for what seemed the millionth time, he chose me.

"Fuck you!" I fired off. I instantly wished I could take back my words as I spun around straight into the puffed-out chest of the grinning Goliath, who I realized had just rifled the handful of frozen grapes at the back of my head.

Fuck me.

The whispering chatterboxes in plaid smocks and pigtails and the skinned-knee jungle gym rats who were gathered around various puddle clusters on the playground wasted no time sensing the fresh blood in the water. Like hungry sharks smelling chum, they closed in around us in a flash.

"Oh look, isn't *Pick-my-weenie* tough?" Jake snickered while jabbing me hard in the chest with his chubby index finger. He loved to mangle

Christian Picciolini, St. Damian eighth grade yearbook photo, 1987

my foreign last name and never ran out of creative ways to do so. How I longed for a normal name like Eddie Peterson or Dan Cook or Jimmy Mayfair. Anything but the impossible-to-say Christian Picciolini— pronounced *"Peach-o-lee-nee"*—which made for all kinds of god-awful rhyming nicknames. *Pick-my-weenie. Suck-my-weenie. Lick-my-weenie.* Basically, anything-*weenie.* "You gonna sic your greasy Blue Island *dago* friends on me?" he mocked, making fun of the largely Italian neighborhood just outside of Chicago where my parents had moved us from before landing in this suburban hellhole of Oak Forest, Illinois. "After school, cheese dick, I'm kicking your slimy *Eye*-talian ass back to the ghetto where you belong."

Jake didn't flinch at calling another student an "ass face" or a "dick with ears" whenever he felt like it. And he never lied about delivering a beating. But no one had ever dared challenge him with a "fuck you" before. Even if it had escaped my mouth by regrettable accident. I was a dead man, and everyone knew it. Certainly was nice of him to suggest I had friends, though.

"And if you don't show up again this time, pussy," he sneered, reeling me in close by my hood strings, "I'll fucking *kill* you."

Throughout eight years of elementary school I'd managed to invent enough excuses to avoid getting physically rearranged by Jake. But before I could muster a lie good enough for me to skip out on this particular jam, word spread faster than Nutella on warm toast. And by the time the final recess bell rang, everybody knew about the fight. Except for the adults, of course. They were never there when you needed them.

I prayed one of the teachers—or the principal herself—would catch wind of the fight and put an end to it, but my prayers went unanswered. Doom loomed over me. Jake Reilly was much bigger—thick and tall and strong—and he'd surely have his cronies behind him. I'd be in it alone. I didn't have any friends in Oak Forest, or even Blue Island for that matter, to back me up. Other than the few moves I picked up when

I watched Rocky beat up Mr. T in the movies, or how Rowdy Roddy Piper smashed Hulk Hogan over the head with a steel chair on TV wrestling, I had no clue how to fight or defend myself. But I couldn't back down now. Not this time. Not with four years of Goliath-dominated high school and an endless supply of ridicule on the horizon. Running away and being forever branded a "pussy" would be infinitely worse than getting pummeled.

Hoping that more time meant I might be able to come up with a believable last-minute excuse to not show up and get my ass kicked, I took the longer route home after the final class bell rang. No such luck. All I could think about was how to convince my parents to let me transfer schools by tomorrow so I wouldn't have to deal with the mockery that was sure to be heaped on me by my classmates the next morning. But my parents weren't home.

I changed out of my light blue school uniform and navy slacks, grabbed my Santa Cruz skateboard, and apprehensively rode the six blocks to the park where the fight was to happen. I knew the entire eighth grade class would be there to witness my slaughter. People had even placed bets, and proclaimed the loser—who everybody fully expected to be me—would have to pay the winner ten bucks.

The moment this fight was over, I'd be ruined forever. Beaten. Stigmatized and forgotten. Cast atop the growing heap of junior high nobodies who'd already been humiliated by Goliath. I couldn't care less about where I'd get the money to pay off the stupid bet, knowing I could easily swipe that from my grandmother's purse without her knowledge. But I also knew that once I was dispatched into nothingness, there was no coming back. No one ever recovered from that.

As I rode up, I spied the giant lumbering confidently among the large group that had gathered like buzzards anticipating a fresh roadkill buffet. Attempting to steady my shaking knees, trying to keep my fear under wraps, I stepped off my board and struggled to take in my final gulps of air. Wiping away the nervous sweat that was already trickling down my brow, I thought one last time about running away. Maybe being exiled from the ranks of St. Damian's lower order wouldn't be worse than getting my face pounded by this massive beast.

As I retreated backwards, planting my foot back onto my skateboard deck and turning to push off with my unsteady leg, some of the more spiteful onlookers suddenly broke into a clamor: "Pick-my-weenie! Pick-my-weenie! Pick-my-weenie!" Sensing my dread, the whole crowd turned against me.

I felt myself becoming dizzy and detaching from reality—fading into the ether—as I inhaled another series of quick, shallow breaths to try to calm my nerves. I turned toward my tormentor to accept my fate, just as a colossal wad of spit flew through the air and landed with a wet gooey thwack dead on my cheek.

Hushed silence. Except for Jake, whose loud, guttural snort only meant that another loogie was imminent.

Anxious panic flushed through me, and before I could wipe his spit from my face, another glob of thick yellow phlegm struck me in the chest like a sniper's bullet and slowly dribbled down my turquoise Ocean Pacific T-shirt.

"What's wrong, dick breath," Reilly jeered, pudgy arms crossed over his chest, "are ya chicken? *Bawk, bawk.*" The crowd formed a wall around us. "Suck-my-weenie ain't got no balls," he proclaimed. A shock of laughter broke out from the enclosing group of spectators.

Jesus Christ. This kid was *big*. Goliath was growing twice as big as he stood before me, while I shrunk smaller and smaller. This is suicide, I thought. He took a step towards me and spat a third time at the ground near my feet as if to mark the spot of my execution.

As the grip of the taunting mob tightened around us, we circled each other, the requisite trash talk spewing from the ogre's crooked smile. Jake was name-calling. I was stalling. My swollen, purple eye from last week—the one I'd gotten when three black kids from Blue Island jumped me and stole my bike—was finally beginning to heal, and I didn't want to have to explain a fresh one to my parents. Terror overtook me and I could barely hear the crowd's increasingly muffled chants over my own fearful thoughts and the dull, echoing crackle of crisp leaves under my feet. "Quit being a faggot, like your pussy hairdresser dad, and stand still so I can friggin' kill you!" Jake made a beeline towards me.

The tendons in my arms tightened. Pulsed. My mind spun with fear, becoming further detached from my surroundings. My heart thumped out of my chest. Out of sheer despair, I summoned the nerve to step in with him and throw the first punch. Kill or be killed. What more could I lose? At least I'd go to my death valiantly. My baby brother, Buddy, would be proud that I wasn't a complete coward. I shut my eyes and tensed my sweaty right hand, pulled it back and swung wildly, landing squarely.

Jake went down.

Holy shit.

My first instinct was to bolt, but my legs weren't cooperating.

From the sudden jumble of gasps and groans behind me, I made out the frenzied voice of Jake's goon Kyle McKinney yelling, "Hit him! Hit him!" But Jake stayed put on the ground, confused, whimpering, covering his bleeding nose.

"Hit him again!" his pal shouted. Shocked, I realized he actually wanted *me* to beat up his best friend. Could it be? Was everyone as sick of Goliath's bullying as I was? Or was it that the rush of fighting was so intoxicating even his most loyal subjects savored the blood and violence over their friendship?

I shook the thought out of my head and fell hard on that bastard Jake Reilly with eight solid years of Catholic school retribution on my mind. Adrenaline pumping, I pinned him down with my knees, pulled back my fists, and slammed them into his face again. And again. And again.

Sobbing, he cried, "Stop! Stop! I quit! Just stop! You win." Streams of tears turned into crimson rivers flowing down his bruised cheeks.

I rose to my feet and wiped my bloodied, swollen knuckles across my T-shirt. "You owe me ten bucks" was all I could mutter through a mouth that was absent of any saliva. I turned to leave, though my wobbly legs were barely able to carry me, and I thought I might pass out right there in front of the whole stunned eighth grade class. Just then, my oxygen-deprived lungs remembered to breathe. I inhaled deeply as the faint sounds of hooting and hollering slowly became audible and then filled my ears.

The giant lay defeated before me.

The next morning, my classmates swarmed around me the moment I got to school. My once non-existent stature had grown to epic proportions overnight: I'd become a Bully Slayer. Even the cool kids who'd ignored me for the last eight years looked up to me because I'd taken down one of their own. Not to mention I was ten bucks richer.

I was drunk with my newfound significance. Suddenly, I wasn't the weird Italian kid who spent all his afterschool free time with his elderly grandparents in their Blue Island "ghetto" instead of the stale upper-middle-class confines of this Oak Forest suburbia. For a brief moment, I wasn't the little boy with the peculiar mom and dad who couldn't speak proper English. Who owned a beauty shop and brought their kid sloppy lunches in oil-stained paper sacks.

No, I was the tough kid. The most dangerous kid in school, in fact. In all of Oak Forest even. And if Oak Forest had been any closer than the twenty miles away it was from downtown Chicago, then perhaps the mayor would have even thrown a parade down State Street in my honor.

During my first period math class, I flexed my fists, silently studying them, trying to take in the reality that these two balled-up, bruised hands were my ticket to respect and power. My baby brother wouldn't be the only kid who looked up to me anymore.

I took this lesson to heart, absorbing it in every fiber of every muscle and organ in my body. It would end up serving me well in the years to come when I'd help build one of America's most violent homegrown terror organizations.

2

COLD

Perhaps who we truly become begins with our parents' emotional state at conception, multiplied at least tenfold by our pregnant mothers' dreams for us. It may well begin with DNA combining randomly, taking some from Dad here and Mom there, but that's only the bones—the hair and eye color, nose shape, height, and other physical characteristics by which the outside world recognizes us.

Maybe the real person, the inner being, is determined not by the arbitrary mixing of genes, but by some mystery science has yet to unravel—a metaphysical occurrence of two souls inviting another soul to come to life.

In my case, the two souls were Enzo Picciolini and Anna Spinelli.

My father, the youngest of six children, had been fatherless since his early childhood growing up in a tiny southwestern valley town near Salerno, Italy, called Montesano Scalo.

After my father's dad passed, my grandmother moved the family from Italy to Chicago to be near a sister who had already emigrated to the United States. So, in 1962, when my father was sixteen, he boarded an overcrowded passenger ship and a month later settled down with his family on the South Side of Chicago, near Midway Airport.

Christian, Blue Island, 1978 (Photo by Maddalena Spinelli)

Enzo later enrolled in beauty school and learned enough English from his older brothers to pass his licensing exams. When he was twenty-five, he met my mother who, like himself, was also an Italian immigrant and a hairdresser.

Within six months, they were married. I know little of their courtship. I've seen wedding photographs and old films, but I can't say whether they were in love or just at the age when they both knew the time for marriage had come. I imagine they were both relieved to wed someone with a similar background—someone who understood the trials of being an outsider, of struggling with a language to which they had not been born, adjusting to odd and unfamiliar customs, all the while trying to build a new life on foreign soil.

And so, in Chicago on a cold and frosty St. Valentine's Day in 1973, I was conceived by two young Italian immigrants torn between two lands. Awkward and ill at ease in one country, and far away from the other, they were determined that their offspring would know none of their struggles. Anna and Enzo's child would not suffer language barriers, would get a fine American education, and would have options beyond blue-collar jobs in the great land of opportunity in which they had planted their roots.

To prepare for my birth, my parents made a drastic and culturally uncharacteristic decision. They stretched themselves well beyond their financial means and bought a house in suburban Oak Forest, ten miles away from Blue Island, the working-class Italian neighborhood on the southwest edge of Chicago where my mother's family lived.

Nonna Nancy, my mother's mother—the matriarch of our family— and Nonno Michele, my grandfather, had left Ripacandida, their close-knit and quaint farming community near the ankle of the Italian boot seven years earlier, in the mid-1960s, to join the ranks of other Europeans who believed the United States was the "Promised Land." After trying to emigrate for many years—the process complicated because my grandfather had also lived and worked in South America upon completing service as a master corporal in Mussolini's Italian Air Force during World War II—they finally settled into Blue Island, an urban enclave populated with people much like them—hardworking *Ripacandidese* families who believed in family, old-world traditions, and daily consumption of olive oil and pasta.

My grandparents advised my mother against her decision to move out of the neighborhood. Nonna and Nonno lived in adequate comfort in a friendly community made up of old three-story apartment houses made of cinder blocks and bricks, small gardens overgrowing with bell peppers, herbs, and tomatoes, and basement *cantinas* crammed with aging Mason jars of homemade tomato ragù, cured sausage, and bottles of vino. They may have moved to a country full of people with strange customs, rude behavior, and no respect for the old ways, but they had the good sense to live amongst those who adhered to the right way of life—the Italian way.

Outsiders may have considered Blue Island to be a lower-middle-class town, but it had everything my mother could want. Family, friends, sustenance growing in the backyard. Fresh eggs and milk delivered right to her front door every Saturday morning. Early Italian settlers had even built the St. Donatus parish, named after San Donato, their patron saint back home in Ripacandida. And every year, the congregation threw a huge festival in honor of the saint, a feast that matched the one in Italy for devotion, wine, song, and celebration.

My grandmother couldn't understand why her daughter would want to move out of Blue Island to hoity-toity Oak Forest. "Forest?" she'd mock in her fractured English. It was nothing but fancy split-level houses and manicured lawns. Trees wouldn't dare congregate on all that tidiness, even if there was room left over after all those two-car garages were built. Why would families need two cars to begin with? And why did they want all their houses to be made of wood and aluminum siding and look the same? The whole notion didn't make sense to her. In Nonna's eyes, my mother would be paying more for substantially less. Besides, where would they get the money? It wasn't like Anna and Enzo were going to be able to afford it on the money they made from giving perms to old ladies.

My mother consoled Nonna with the promise that she would bring me back to Blue Island every day. "Now that the baby is a few months old, I'm going back to work doing hair with Enzo and you will care for him while we're away. Not a day will go by that we won't see you, and Christian will know you as well as he knows us."

I was barely a couple of months old when a routine that lasted for the first five years of my life began. Every morning my mother strapped me into a car seat, raced over to Blue Island, dropped me into Nonna's waiting arms, and hurried off to work at the modest hair salon she and my father had opened after I was born. Half a day later, either she or my father, or both of them, would come back to swoop me up, eat dinner with my grandparents, put me back into my car seat, and rush back to Oak Forest. As an infant, I was usually asleep by the time we reached the house, and I imagine it must have been confusing for me to wake up in one place and spend the rest of the day in another, only to wake up again in the place I had begun the previous day with no memory of how I got back there.

I never considered who played what role in my life and whether or not the various adults in it were going about things the right way. Nonna provided the nurturing and guidance a mother normally would, and it never struck me as odd that she was actually my grandmother. And just as Nonna played the role of mother while my parents were busy working, the fatherly responsibilities fell to my grandfather, Nonno. I spent hours at his side, watching him saw wood and pound nails. A master carpenter, he showed me how to hold a nail just right. I trusted him so completely it never once occurred to me that the hammer he swung could hit my finger instead of the nail I held in place for him.

My grandparents practically raised me, and it was the sturdy, three-story brown brick building they owned in Blue Island, not my parents' cookie-cutter tract house in Oak Forest, that I considered home.

But, despite having grandparents who gladly took me in and kept their watchful gaze over me, as a young child I longed for my mom and dad while they were away at work. I wanted to be with them, unsure of why they were always absent. I became the good kid, working hard to give them every reason to want me around. I picked up my Matchbox cars without being asked. I kept my clothes off the floor to keep my room tidy. I didn't leave my soccer ball where my mother or father could trip over it. And I made sure to say "thank you" and "please" and tried to eat everything on my plate.

Still, it wasn't enough. I simply couldn't compete with their steadfast pursuit of the American Dream. They had their growing business to tend to, and they were satisfied I was well cared for by people they trusted while they were away. But as full as my life was, as much as my grandparents and I loved each other, I yearned to be more a part of my parents' lives.

When the time came, convinced I was naturally brilliant, my mother made sure to find a school equal to the fine mind she was certain I possessed. Early on, she decided I would become a doctor—both wealthy and respected—and searched diligently for proof she had judged correctly.

But my future as a doctor was not the only factor that made her resolute in her desire to ensure I was well educated. Her own schooling experience had been less than stellar. She had come to America with her family in 1966, during what would have been her high school years, not knowing a word of English. Blue Island's public high school, Dwight D. Eisenhower, had been a disaster for her. Totally indifferent to the traumas a foreign student might face, the school had no classes, tutors, translators, or resources to help a non-English speaker—or her family—assimilate.

Anna, a simple sixteen-year-old girl from a tiny hamlet in Italy who could neither read, write, nor speak English, was on her own.

Instead of helping her adapt, the other students called her names, threw snowballs at her at the bus stop, made fun of her hand-me-down clothes, and mimicked her parents and their backward ways.

My mother lasted less than a year in high school before she dropped out and never went back.

She vowed to herself that her child would grow up knowing all about fitting in and belonging. People would respect him, even look up to him. They would all recognize his studies would lead him to his rightful profession as a doctor.

Of course, it all depended on where he got his education, so he would go to a nice private school, not one of those public schools where kids acted like animals.

St. Damian Elementary School and its attached namesake church spanned the length of a football field. The long, low, blond brick building that encompassed the parish was huge in my five-year-old mind. Inside, the heavy wooden doors to each of the classrooms were closed, making the narrow, desolate hallways dim and dreary. The heels of my mother's Italian shoes click-clacked like my grandfather's tack hammer as we found our way to the principal's office. The chairs the ancient head nun offered us seemed unnaturally tall and my feet dangled high above the floor. My mother perched on the edge of her chair, her leather purse clutched tightly in her hands. Her hair was stylishly swept to one side, her makeup appropriately minimal for meeting nuns.

The principal, Sister Lucinia, smiled at me, leaning over her formidable metal desk. "I hear you'll be starting school this year, young man," she said peering down at me through large round spectacles that magnified her eyeballs like giant glass marbles.

"Yes, Sister," I replied, looking her in the eye like my mother had taught me.

"And is this the school you'd like to go to?"

"Yes, Sister," my mother answered for me.

Sister Lucinia continued to ask questions and we continued to say "Yes, Sister," for what seemed to me an hour or more, but which was probably less than ten minutes at most.

Finally, the principal turned to my mother. "We are happy to have your son join us, my dear," she said with a wide wrinkled grin. "He is clearly a bright child. He will be president someday."

I waited for my mother to correct her, to tell her no, I would be a doctor, but instead she clutched her purse so tightly that even the hair dye that had permanently stained her fingertips turned white. "The president? Of America?"

"Yes," the old nun said, winking at me. "The president."

After we left the nun's office, my mother stopped midway across the parking lot and pointed back at the building. "Look at it, Christian. Your first school. In your own neighborhood. In a nice place with nice children from nice parents who have money and doctors in their families. And one day they will be able to say the president of the United States of America went to school right here at St. Damian in Oak Forest. Imagine that."

Off to the far side of the parking lot, I spied a baseball game in progress. "Mamma, can I play baseball when I go here? On a real team? With uniforms?"

"You will be able to do whatever you want. They know who you will be when you grow up. You can do anything."

I liked the sound of that. A ray of hope broke through the despair that had filled me since finding out I would not be going to school in Blue Island—the place I considered my real home.

But my mother had lied. Inside a week of stepping into the long dark halls of St. Damian, I knew the kids there weren't anywhere near the same as the ones in Blue Island.

They didn't eat spaghetti with clams for dinner. They ate noodles and fish sticks. They drank Pepsi with their meals, not homemade wine like families in Blue Island did. They lived in single-family homes, one family per house. When you grew up, you went to college and got a degree in accounting and then moved away and got married and had your own house and kids and noodles and fish sticks. The priest at the church said mass in English, not Italian. And they had no idea the annual St. Donatus festival was the highlight of the summer.

I learned pretty quickly to keep to myself, that school meant boring books and too much praying and itchy uniforms and stupid rules about tucking in your shirt. And like all the other kids who were unfortunate enough to be judged as "different," I was picked on by Jake Reilly—who I understood was the kid loudly calling all the shots, the moment I stepped into the first grade. But I kept my thoughts to myself, rationalizing that this school didn't matter. These kids didn't count. Blue Island and anyone connected with my life there were the real world and nobody in this school was any part of that. School was nothing more than a place I had to endure until my mother or father took a break from work to pick me up and drive me to Blue Island where I belonged.

Throughout the early years of grade school, my life followed a predictable, well-traveled path. During the week I attended classes at St. Damian and spent evenings and weekends with my maternal grandparents in Blue Island, usually drawing or playing detective by myself in their enormous, dusty coat closet that offered me the perfect space to create a fantasy world of my own.

Through a small rectangular window built inside the large closet, I admired the Blue Island neighborhood kids as they careened by on bikes with magnificent steel handlebars and long, glittery banana seats. I'd watch them ride without using their hands as they made their way to friends' houses, drop their bikes carelessly on the sidewalk, hop up the stoop two steps at a time, and bang on the door to summon their pals. Within heartbeats, the screen door would fly open, the friend would appear, they would jump on bikes together and off they'd go, disappearing down an alley, slowly swallowed by the horizon.

Ultimately, I suspected, they'd pedal to the St. Donatus church parking lot which even I, a refugee from a faraway land, knew held the life force of every kid who called the East Side of Blue Island home— the unofficial playground, softball diamond, Wiffle ball stadium, and rendezvous spot for every youngster around.

Sometimes I'd practice making friends with the other kids on the block while I sat alone in the closet drawing Snoopy and the other Peanuts characters in my sketchpad. Nestled beneath the moth-riddled parkas and coats of seasons past, I'd imagine myself knocking on someone's door, or that my grandmother would send me to a neighbor's house for some sugar, and one of the kids would answer my knock and invite me in to play. While I sat pensive and alone in the closet, I'd find myself unexpectedly pausing, Crayola marker held midair while I pictured someone dropping their bike by the back door and asking Nonna if I was around and if I could come out and play.

But I knew it wouldn't happen. The kids in Blue Island had each other. They went to school together, probably copied each other's homework, maybe even passed love notes in class to girls with names like Gina and Maria, who dotted the "i's" in their names with little hearts and smiley faces. Sleepovers, goofing around, and eating over at each other's houses filled their every moment. Why would they spend time with me, someone who didn't even live or go to school in Blue Island? Someone who was different than them?

They were all such good friends, a tight-knit group of pals. Wild, even, throwing tomatoes and snowballs at passing cars, hopping fences. Laughing. Having fun together.

I'd been entertaining myself, sitting solitary in that closet for years, but now I desperately wanted to be a part of something. And I wasn't. It was me alone, dangling between two totally dissimilar worlds ten miles apart. I knew I was an outsider—at school in suburban Oak Forest because I was culturally different and spent all my free time in Blue Island with my grandparents, and in urban Blue Island because I didn't live there or go to school with the rest of the Italian kids in the neighborhood. Even with adults constantly hovering over me, I felt so alone.

All that changed when I was ten years old and received something as ordinary and innocent as a shiny little red bike for Christmas.

As we did every Christmas, my parents and I went to Blue Island to celebrate with family and to await Santa Claus, although I stopped believing in him the moment I noticed him wearing my dad's gold pinky ring and Italian loafers. My mother and father didn't quite understand the whole American Santa-came-down-the-chimney routine, but they did know American kids got presents from him, so they made sure we had a decorated tree and that there were plenty of gifts for their wonderful son who everybody adored.

We opened presents on Christmas Eve after eating a traditional Italian holiday dinner. Loads of pasta, of course, and various seafood dishes including a salted codfish called *baccalà*. Wine that had fermented in the basement and was stored in any glass bottle my grandmother had saved—recycled wine jugs, old glass pop bottles, spent whiskey handles—flowed like water from a hose.

After dinner, we'd all head into the family room, sit on the plastic-covered sofas, and open gifts.

On this particular Christmas Eve, the adults talked far too long, wine and espresso making them more chatty than usual, which in an Italian family where tongues are never still and opinions rarely held back, was really saying something. I vividly recall thinking dinner would literally never end, but finally my mother leaned close and said in her teasing tone, "What do you have to say for yourself, Christian?"

I stared glumly at my plate. Would all the talking never end?

My mother tousled my hair, becoming aware, as all the adults suddenly were, that I had only one thing on my mind—opening presents. "Shall we see if Santa Claus brought you something this year?" she asked. "Have you been a good boy? I bet Santa brought you something very, very special."

The suspense was too great for good behavior. I pushed my chair back and jumped down to the floor, shouting greedily, "I want to see!"

Their laughter and the sound of chairs scraping against the ceramic tiles filled the stuffy kitchen as I dashed to the archway that led into the living room. They were hot on my heels as I crossed the threshold and snapped on the lights.

And there it was.

A beautiful, shiny, red bicycle with the biggest bow I'd ever seen. Ignoring all the other gifts, I sprinted to it and yanked off the bow.

There had to be a Santa Claus after all. My parents would never have thought to buy me anything so perfect. So cool. So amazing.

I hugged it, kissed it, and jumped onto the seat, my feet reaching for the pedals.

"No, Christian, no!" my grandmother cried. "Not in the house! Bicycles are not for inside! You'll ruin the carpet. You'll scratch the tiles."

I jumped back off the bike and, holding the handlebars tightly in both hands, plowed through the stacks of gifts to the back door.

"Stop!" Nonna called after me. "It's freezing out there. It's too dark. You'll fall and hurt yourself. Or you'll catch a cold and die!" She crossed herself and added, "God forgive me."

Ignoring her pleas, I wrenched open the door and made my escape. I darted down the steps, holding tight to my new prized possession, and at the foot of the stairs, I scrambled onto the seat and wobbled down the sidewalk that ran along the house. Strings of sparkling Christmas lights on bushes and fences lit my path like a runway as I made my debut ride on the coolest bike on the planet. If it was cold, I didn't notice. If Nonna and my parents called out warnings or prayed to God for my safety, I didn't hear. Only one thing mattered.

Freedom. I was no longer a helpless little boy in the perpetual care of old people, a child transported from one place to another without a word to say about it. Oh no, I was all grown up. I had my own wheels. I had come to life! I could join the other kids in the neighborhood now. Ride with them, tearing down alleys, up side streets, on my way to visit even more friends. But first, I had to make some.

When that summer following fifth grade came, following the cheers and the crack of the bat, I rode my new bike across several Blue Island blocks and discovered Schrei Field. I watched Little League baseball games from behind the left field fence. I knew who was a threat at the plate, which pitcher had a wicked fastball, who cried when his team lost. If I'd snuck change out of Nonna's purse, I bought a hot dog and a cold pop.

I studied the parents at the games—mothers talking to each other in the stands, warning their babies not to climb too high on the bleachers, fathers grumbling under their beer breath at the ump, telling their kids to shake off a bad call. I'd get an empty feeling in my stomach, wishing I was part of the team, wondering what it'd be like to hit a home run, to make a great catch, to high-five the other guys, to crow, "Hey, batter, batter…swing batter." To have my parents there watching me play, cheering my name, being proud of me, was unimaginable, but still, I let the image rise and fall in my mind.

And so I watched from behind the left field fence, sitting on my little red bike, the fingers of my right hand curled through the chain-link diamonds, tiny plastic mitt on my left hand ready to catch any home run ball that soared over the wall, imagining it smacking right into my glove. I'd roll as I caught it, hold my hand up triumphantly, showing I had the ball, and with barely any effort I'd pull my arm back and rifle it like a laser beam all the way to home plate.

The coach's jaw would drop at the sight of my magnificent arm. "Who's that kid?" he'd ask, spitting onto the first base line.

He'd find out. Call my parents. Insist they let me play. "Hell," he'd say, "I'll drive him the ten miles back to Oak Forest myself after games. Pick him up from school, even. We gotta have him."

How could my parents say no?

I'd punch the palm of my little plastic glove with my right hand. "C'mon, baby," I'd whisper, "Right here. Put that ball right here."

But the ball never made it over the fence and day after day, weekend after weekend, I'd climb back on my little red bike and ride home, wishing with all my heart that somebody—anybody—would pedal up next to me and say, "Wanna race?"

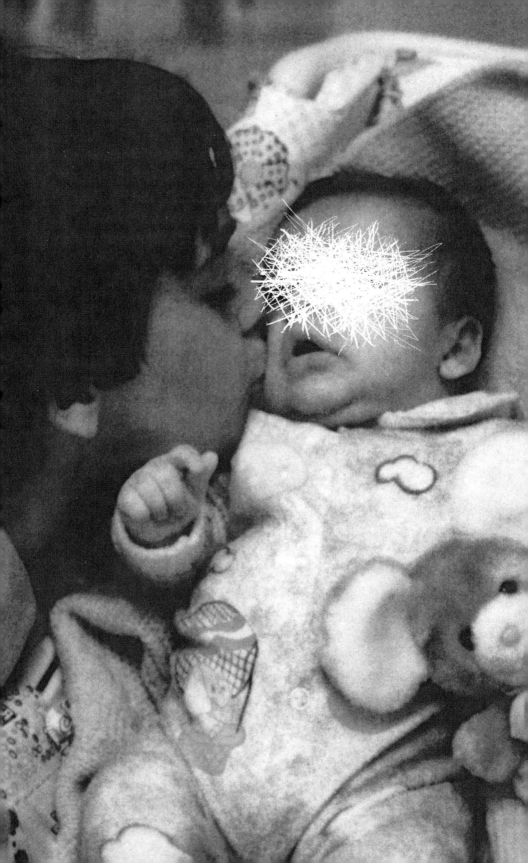

3
HAIL VICTORY

By the time I was in sixth grade, I could no longer bear the stigma of being an outcast at St. Damian. I loathed it so much I actually stooped to praying every day around lunchtime. The other kids bought hot meals from the school lunch lady or had colorful tin lunch boxes full of homemade cookies and ham and cheese sandwiches prepared by their moms. My mother was often rushed to get to work in the mornings, so she'd show up during lunch period with something she sped to buy through a fast food window between doing a hairstyle and rolling a perm.

Shortly before the bell rang for lunch every day, I'd close my eyes and pray—turning to the false hope the nuns gave us that God watched out for us if we humbled ourselves to ask for help.

"Dear God, if you're really out there, just this once please pay attention. I know there are probably a whole lot of other sinners down here, but I'd appreciate it if you'd ignore all of them but me this afternoon. Hear my prayer, oh Lord, and you can take the rest of the day off. I'm not asking for anything huge like a new Sony Walkman or world peace or that another gust of wind will fly under Miss MacGowan's dress and blow it way up to her neck again. I only want one simple thing."

I paused for a minute to give the Big Guy a chance to realize how little I was asking for. "Please, God, I beg you, don't let my mother show up with another McDonald's Happy Meal at lunchtime today."

But these words apparently never had enough time to travel from my mouth to His ears because every day, like clockwork, when the bell rang and my class streamed into the lunchroom to eat, there my mom would be, stationed at the door, hurrying toward me, her long leather jacket looking stylish to nobody but herself and her blonde hair sticking out at odd angles because she'd rushed out of the beauty shop in the middle of a self-dye job. Her high-heeled boots would hit the polished linoleum floor with sharp staccato notes, tapping out impending doom.

This particular day was no different. Jake Reilly tripped me as we lined up for the cafeteria. "What's for lunch, Lick-my-weenie?" he sneered. "Your mommy bringing you another little baby Happy Meal today?"

When the bell rang I prayed she wouldn't be in the hall, but there she was. She broke into a wide grin, her arms outstretched toward me, the grease from the fries already seeping through the box and onto her black Isotoner gloves.

"Shit," I said, loud enough for Kathleen O'Hara to hear. She'd tell on me for sure for swearing. "Goddamnit," I added, for good measure. If prayers didn't work, maybe curses would. Maybe God would strike me dead.

But no such luck. My mother was upon me, yanking my hand out of my pocket and thrusting the sad, soggy box into it.

I wished I was like Jake Reilly. I imagined his prayers were heard. He had everything he wanted the second it entered his head. He probably spoke to God in monosyllables and even got to skip the "Dear" part the nuns insisted start every prayer.

Maybe my prayers needed to be more specific. Maybe I should have said, "Dear God, Jesus, Mary and Joseph, and all the holy saints: don't let my mother or father or anybody they know who owes them any favor or who works in their beauty shop or who came from Italy or who even knows somebody from Italy or has dark hair for that matter or speaks in a funny accent come anywhere near me carrying any food for my lunch. I'm not that hungry and anyway Dickie Cooper owes me his chocolate pudding because I forged his father's name on the test he failed last week. Amen."

"*Kreestyan,*" my mother trilled, her heavily-accented voice nasal from perpetually inhaling various hair-coloring products, "Did you think I forgot your lunch today? What kind of mamma would do that? I came all this way to give it to you, but now I have to hurry back to the shop and get Mrs. Foster out from the dryer or her hair will dry and fall out and that's not good to have an unhappy customer."

Behind me I could sense Goliath snarling, strands of dangling drool beginning to form puddles at his feet. Like smelling salts, the Chicken McNugget aroma had awakened the beast.

At the same moment every day, I wished I didn't have a mother. Who needed one? Or a father, for that matter. All they did was make me a laughingstock whenever they decided to show up. I wished they'd go back to Italy and let me fend for myself. Or that they'd let me move in with my grandparents. At least then I could go to school in Blue Island instead of at St. Damian with the spoiled rich kids who lived in boring Oak Forest.

I couldn't understand why they wanted so badly to fit in with these people. We weren't like them. We didn't have money like they did. Besides, they worked such long hours every day, it wasn't like they even had the time to enjoy it if they wanted to.

Thankfully, as soon as the bell rang at three o'clock I could leave them all behind. The bratty kids and snobby parents. My own parents. The priests. The nuns. The prayers. The God who would send me to hell if I ate meat on Friday.

Come three o'clock, I'd be out the door and in a car headed to paradise.

When the final school bell rang later that afternoon, I hung back and daydreamed about what the weekend had in store. As anxious as I was to get to my grandparents' house, I had learned to bide my time. My parents were always the last ones to show up at the end of the school day, and even though other parents had stopped asking me if I needed a ride or if I was sure somebody was coming to get me, I still hated the disgrace of being the last one picked up.

"You still here, Pick-my-weenie?" Jake Reilly jeered, breaking my reverie, as his mother pulled up in their station wagon.

My body stiffened up and my blood ran cold, but there wasn't a thing I could do. I was one of the smaller boys in my class. He was bigger. Mean. The school bully. Goliath. And the most popular kid in the sixth grade. The same as he was in fifth grade and fourth grade and third and second and first and probably even kindergarten and pre-school—and the baby corral in the hospital where he was born.

As I'd been the odd, different, scrawny kid every single one of those years.

The shy foreign boy who went over to Blue Island, that poor, far-off Italian neighborhood, after school every day and every summer. The kid with the strange mother and father who both styled women's hair for a living. The dork with the fancy bowl haircut whose mom delivered him soggy fast food for lunch every day instead of sending him to school with a crustless, triangle-cut peanut butter and jelly sandwich in a bright *Dukes of Hazzard* lunch box. The outcast with the unpronounceable name.

Eventually I saw my dad's silver Corvette pull up. Another trinket we could neither afford nor sustain, but my dad had to have it. It was the cherry atop his slice of the American pie.

His arm shot out as he shoved the passenger door open from the inside. "Hurry up, let's go, I have to get back to the shop," he said, even though I was already half in the car, pulling the door shut behind me.

We didn't usually greet each other. What was the point? My father's thoughts were always somewhere else, and if I had said anything, Frankie Valli or Elvis Presley blaring on the Corvette's tape deck would have drowned my words out. Once, with me in the car, he drove through a flashing railroad crossing gate because he was so distracted. The oncoming commuter train missed us by a hundred feet. We didn't talk about that either.

When I'd told my mother about our narrow escape later that night, my parents got into an argument over it. To vent his frustration, my dad turned on me, yelling and smacking me in the back of the head, his preferred method of communication. My dad wasn't a very imposing guy physically—he was rather short in stature with a round belly and prone to wearing heavy gold jewelry—and his slaps were never hard enough to really hurt me, but having him poke away at my head like that was insulting, infuriating, humiliating.

We drove to Blue Island without speaking, my dad stout and listless in his red leather bucket seat. I occupied my time imagining myself at the helm of a fast spy car watching the earth peel away behind me. Rows of storefronts and industrial buildings, miles of oil-stained highway pavement and cracked concrete, stoplights, and road signs swinging in the breeze zipped by in a blur as my father rushed to deliver me to someone else's care. A burden unloaded.

I didn't try to prolong his agony. Before he came in for a crash landing, I'd flung the door open and one foot was already stretching for the curb.

We didn't exchange goodbyes. Didn't make plans for any definite pickup time. Didn't discuss dinner or homework or even when we'd meet again. It didn't bother me that neither he nor my mother ever asked about my day at school or what I was learning. I didn't even know that other kids' parents pestered them about their homework, their grades, whether they'd eaten their fruit at lunch, or how they'd done on a science project.

Like a silver bullet, I watched my dad's Corvette disappear. His pride and joy. Maybe some people thought it was cool, but I didn't. It was just another thing that stood between me and the Blue Island kids. Just some "rich" kid from another neighborhood where nobody rented out basement apartments in their houses and maybe even had two cars.

With a sigh of resignation, I scuttled up the sidewalk to the back door of my grandparents' house. The wind cut through me as I turned the doorknob and let myself into the kitchen.

"Is that you, Christian?" my grandmother called out in Italian.

"Yep, Nonna. I'm home," I yelled back in English.

It was still too early for dinner when I got there, so I grabbed a spoon and the Fiat-sized jar of Nutella from the cupboard and nestled myself into the coat sanctuary for a sweet snack.

Not more than a few minutes later, I overheard my grandmother say something to my grandfather so unusual that I opened the closet door a crack so I could decipher their thick Italian accent better. "Anna made a mistake moving so far away. It's hard enough with one boy, let alone with another child on the way. They don't have the money for that. What is she thinking?"

I leaned back against the wall, cushioned by a sizable collection of Alitalia carry-on bags.

Another child? My mother was having a baby?

Mixed emotions flooded through me. Would I have to babysit? I hoped not. Then I couldn't ride my bike. I thought of the other kids in the neighborhood. Every one of them had younger brothers and sisters. I thought now I would be more like them and hopefully they'd let me hang around. Maybe it wouldn't be too bad.

I heard Nonna's footsteps in the hall. Raising her voice, she shouted, "Christian, time for dinner. Wash your hands first, like a good boy."

When my brother or sister got there, I'd race them to the kitchen. If there really was going to be a baby.

My brother's birth on August 8th, 1983, changed my life, although it would be many years until that became clear to me.

Having virtually no experience with babies, I didn't have the slightest notion of how small a newborn would be. I hadn't spent a great deal of time thinking about little Alex but I certainly expected someone larger than the tiny infant my mother held out to me the day he was born. In the back of my mind, I knew newborns didn't walk, but I'd pictured more of a toddler. Diapers, yes. A bottle? Sure, babies drank from them. But a tiny, blanket-wrapped blue bundle with a sleeping baby all curled up into a ball snuggled so deep inside it I could only make out a crinkly face and the top of a dark furry head? That image hadn't even been close to the one in my mind.

But it didn't matter. When my mother came home from the hospital with Alex, and leaned down and pulled the blanket back so I could get a look, my heart swelled with pride. It was as if I'd known him my entire ten-year-old life. He was a part of me, and I was a part of him. He yawned and opened his shining brown eyes. I reached out and touched his cheek, soft as the puffy ski vests I'd floated under during my frequent daydreams in the coat closet. Our eyes met in an admiration so pure that nothing existed for a few endless moments but the two of us.

I accepted this person with all my heart, but I was still a kid, and knowing I wasn't going to be able to have fun with my brother for a while, I asked, "When can I go out and ride my bike?"

"Tomorrow," my mother said. "Tonight we'll all go home to Oak Forest to be together."

I did want to poke at him and look him over.

Having a brother, I discovered, had many benefits. For one thing, my mother had taken time off from the beauty shop, so things were pretty calm in Oak Forest the remainder of the summer. When school started again, I still spent weekends with my grandparents in Blue Island and had time to ride my bike, but it was easy to get accustomed to staying in one place all week long.

When Alex heard me coming up the steps, he'd scamper to the front door and throw his pudgy little arms around my knees. His crooked little bucktooth grin was contagious. We'd wrestle and roughhouse, my mother telling me to take it easy, feisty Alex begging for more. He wanted to do everything I did, so I tried to teach him how to play catch and hit baseballs before he was out of diapers. I sang him songs and drew funny pictures and made up stories about the characters, narrating in playful voices. When he was two, I gave him a My Buddy doll for Christmas. It looked like him, with his straight brown hair, faint freckles on his nose, and a chubby little body that could be twisted any direction without complaint. Always with a smile on his face. And so from that day forward we exclusively called each other "Buddy."

My parents were more attentive to him than they had been with me, perhaps because they were older or because they weren't so preoccupied about making good in a new country. But as they became more aware of his needs, it's fair to say they did the same for mine, to some degree.

And so I never resented having a little brother. We were pals, comfortable with each other, safe together. We shared a bond neither of us ever doubted would last until the end of time. Buddy filled a huge void in my life. I felt I actually had a family member who wanted to spend time with me.

No matter how comfortable I became in Oak Forest, my heart, and therefore my real home, was still in Blue Island.

Since Blue Island had been my second home from the time before I could crawl, I already knew a lot about the kids in the neighborhood. Most of the families had come from the same region in Italy, which meant our families talked about each other all the time.

I'd been watching the older kids for a while. I'd seen them playing Wiffle ball in the St. Donatus parking lot, Nerf football up and down High Street, and strikeout baseball across the way against the brick wall at Sanders School.

They were known around the neighborhood as the High Street Boys because they all lived on the same block. And it was high time I became one of them, no matter that I lived a street over and was a full grade younger.

The hardest one to win over, I figured, would be Dane Scully. Mr. Popular. He was athletic and cool and the first person I'd ever seen do tricks on a skateboard. All the girls loved him. But he didn't pay all that much attention to them, even though they showed up to his Little League games just to watch him play. I thought he might see we were alike because neither of us had brothers or sisters close to our age, although in his case, he was the much younger sibling instead of the much older one like me.

There were two cousins on High Street who acted like big shots—Little Tony Gianelli and Big Tony Gianelli. Little Tony was good at sports and was the unofficial leader of the High Street crew. Unlike Little Tony, Big Tony was tall and lanky and usually one of the last ones picked for a team because he had about as much athletic ability as a lawn chair. Not only were they related, sharing the same first and last names, they were born the same year and lived right across the street from each other. Neither had a reputation of being particularly agreeable, so I wasn't sure they'd want me around.

There was Jimmy Callahan. He was Scully's best friend since birth. As skinny as a piece of licorice, he had fiery red hair and a face covered with freckles to match. He lived with his single mother and older sister. Everybody was intrigued by tales of his estranged older brother, a cowboy living someplace out West with his dad. I hoped that I'd find out more about the cowboy stuff if we got to be friends.

Chuck Zanecki was tall and skinny like Callahan. He lived across the street from Little Tony and I felt sad for him when I learned his father had died in a horrible work accident at the local oil refinery. A constant jokester, Chuck was quick to play tricks on people—switch gloves in the dugout, put shaving cream in people's hats, that type of thing—but had a good heart. Of all the kids on the block, he was the only one I thought might possibly—maybe—want to be my best friend.

I didn't exactly have a plan about how I was going to make friends with these guys. I guess I figured if I hung around nearby and talked to them more, it had to happen eventually. So that's what I did.

After watching a baseball game at Schrei Field, I'd ride up to High Street on my little red bike and fall in with them, not saying much, but I listened to them talk and once in a while I'd say a few words. When I saw them playing softball in the St. Donatus parking lot, I'd jog out to the outfield to shag a few balls and would join the game by default. I played alongside them more than with them, but to me that was the same as being friends.

Almost.

Little Tony liked to ridicule me. He'd put me in my place when I tagged him out by making fun of my little bike. In fact, everyone made fun of my bike. They also mocked me for my small size, pointing out I was short for my age, for not living in the same neighborhood, or for going to a "rich kid" school.

I had to prove myself if they were going to take me seriously.

I reached my limit the day I rode up to a serious game of Wiffle ball already in progress.

"Well, if it isn't little baby Christian," Little Tony mocked, punctuating his comment by hocking a loogie on the asphalt. The spit wasn't personal. We all did that as much as we possibly could. In fact, we had a spitting fascination—saliva, sunflower seeds, gum, anything we could get in and out of our mouths was fair game.

"Nice bike there," Callahan chided. "For a baby." The guys cracked up laughing.

I swung my leg over the bike and let it drop to the ground. "Can I play?" I asked, ignoring their jabs.

I'd posed this question a dozen times before, as had everybody else who showed up once a game was in progress, but this time my question brought laughter.

"Game's locked," taunted Little Tony.

"Locked tight," Big Tony reiterated, spitting.

"Nice little toy bike," Chuck Zanecki cut in.

That did it. I was sick to death of them making fun of my bike and pointing out it was pretty small for a twelve-year-old.

Without another word, I picked up my bike in one hand and took the steps of the adjacent church building two at a time. When I reached beyond the uppermost stair, I spun around on my heel, mounted the offending bicycle, pedaled as hard and fast as I could, and when I hit the landing at the top of the steps, I released my grip and leapt off. The little red bike soared through the air as I watched, transfixed, feeling both thrilled and pained that I was destroying some intrinsic part of me. Before I could blink, my once-beloved red bicycle crashed against the pavement, bouncing on every third stair on its way down to the parking lot below. A small part of my heart broke as what had once been my passage to freedom somersaulted down the steps, hitting the asphalt hard enough to snap the chain.

I bolted to pick it up again, my cold eyes meeting the stunned silence of the High Street crew.

Again I climbed the steps and tore towards them with the little red bike at my side, running even harder, more furiously this time, letting it coast from the top of the landing.

When the bike tumbled down the steps and smashed to a stop the second time, the hushed silence erupted into howls, and Little Tony, Big Tony, Chuck Zanecki, Callahan, and Scully ran up after me.

In a wild frenzy, we took turns throwing what was left of the bicycle down those stairs over and over and over until the crimson paint stained the church steps like blood and the pedals and handlebars fragmented away from the frame.

The shattered pieces of my childhood lay scattered across the St. Donatus parking lot.

I was one of them now. One of the High Street Boys.

A month later when I was riding back from a pickup baseball game, a group of three black kids from the other side of Blue Island stopped me and beat me up. They stole the brand new black and red Schwinn with mag wheels I'd just bought a month before with my thirteenth birthday money. I don't remember much from that day, except I was angry and disappointed in myself for not doing more to protect my new bike from them. Rage swept through me that someone could come into my neighborhood and take what belonged to me.

I got a black eye over it, but my pride was hurt more than anything. My mother was incensed anyone would do that to me, my father berated me and punctuated his words with slaps to the back of my head saying I was stupid for getting my new bike stolen, and my baby brother cried because somebody had punched me. I had to keep reassuring Buddy my eye didn't hurt, it only looked bad.

A couple of days later some stoner kid from the West Side of Blue Island told me he'd seen the bike in a shady apartment complex on the outskirts of town, so I went over to check it out. Sure enough, I saw my bike on a third floor balcony in a row of apartment houses we considered the "Blue Island Projects."

Without thinking of the potential consequences of my actions, I flew up the stairs and pounded on the door. A black man more than twice my size and at least ten times stronger opened up.

"Damn. Why you bangin' like you's da muhfuggin' cops, white boy?"

"That's my bike on your balcony, sir," I told him. "I'd like it back."

He looked puzzled for about three seconds, before bellowing out a boy's name.

The boy, who I took to be his son, appeared faster than I could come up with a plan if he denied the allegation. This giant of a man lunged for his son, grabbing him by the collar.

"This boy say dat's his bike out there. Dat true?"

The kid must have known there was no point in lying because he immediately nodded and recoiled. Whack! His dad backhanded him so hard he fell down. Without missing a beat, he yanked the kid back to his feet and smacked him again. I stood there watching, my mouth open, torn between feelings of vindication and regret. I didn't think it was right to hit a child that way, but then again, the kid and his friends had beat me up. I had one nasty black eye to prove it. Even more so, he'd stolen the new bike I'd bought with my own money to replace the little red one we'd trashed a few weeks before.

Once this towering man had reduced his kid to a crumpled, wailing heap on the floor, he stepped over him, walked out to the balcony, and came back with my bike.

"Be more careful wit' it next time," he told me. I didn't dare point out the injustice of blaming me for something his kid did. I'd seen the power of his fist and sure didn't want to be on the other end of it.

The real impact didn't sink in until I showed up to school on Monday. I'd expected everybody in my eighth grade class to make my puffy black eye the butt of their jokes, but instead they studied me like some artifact. They weren't particularly interested in knowing who won; the mere fact I'd been involved in a fight serious enough to end up with a gnarly-looking black eye elevated me out of obscurity and placed me on a momentary pedestal.

And it seriously angered Goliath.

My fist throbbed the moment it slammed into his face the first time. A sudden unexpected crack, an explosion of red, then no sound at all. My vision fish-eyed and I paused to think of how the fresh smattering of blood felt oddly comforting on my stinging knuckles. In an instant, my hearing flooded back and I found myself straddling the fetal heap of Goliath. Recoiling on pure adrenaline and the swelling auditory encouragement from the spectators, I pounded him four or five more times until he surrendered, his face covered in streaks of blood.

On spent legs I stood over Jake Reilly. And while he wept, my heart pounded out of my chest. My dehydrated mouth murmured something before my trembling limbs led me back to my skateboard and I hastily sped away.

I stopped after struggling to ride a few blocks and collapsed on some grass alongside the road. I pulled off my T-shirt and wiped my bloody knuckles on it before ditching it in a trashcan. As I sat on the curb inspecting my tender fists, I was overcome with a sudden rush of emotion. Relief streamed down my face.

I knew at that moment something inside of me had begun to change. My innocence and insecurity had cracked and were giving way to entitlement and a sense of duty. I had brought down a giant. I could do anything.

When I got back to the house, rather than asking me why I wasn't wearing a shirt, my parents sat me down and gave me the best news I could ever have imagined.

Moving to Blue Island was no big deal.

Moving to Blue Island was a *huge* deal.

It was no big deal because I had considered it my real home for most of my life.

It was a huge deal because now I got to hang out with my new High Street pals every day. No way could I ever again be considered an outsider.

I belonged.

I graduated in 1987 from St. Damian, bloodied its proverbial nose and flipped Oak Forest off on my way out of town, ready, at last, to be where I belonged, with people like me. Both Italian and American, almost each and every one of us. And, as far as I was concerned, the best people on earth.

Oi   Oi   Oi   Oi

THE FINAL SOLUTION
THIS IS WHITE NOISE

The music of the Skinhead is a
most powerfull, hard driving style
of Rock N Roll we call "Oi".
Oi is nothing like Punk Rock,
Hardcore or Heavy Metal. Oi stands
alone in classification with its
crisp beat and melodic tune variat-
ion. Oi is for warriors

Stronger
than
Before

FOR RACE AND NATION

SKIN

HEADS

ROMANTIC VIOLENCE
P.O.Box 431
Blue Island, IL
60406

DEAD
REDS

Send Names & Addresses
Of Commies To:

COMMUNISM
IS JEWISH!
ADOLF HITLER

Romantic Violence
P.O. Box 431
Blue Island, Illinois 60406

MARCHING MUSIC
ROCK AND ROLL MUSIC
BAND IN THE WEST
ALL OVER EUROPE,
RISINGS IN GERM
RANKED ALL THE
ARTIES AND PERS
BY THE FAT CATS A
QUANTITY. ORDER
TODAY FOR ONLY $7
BOX 50317

BACK
WITH A
BANG

Chicagoland

Oi   The word means "hey" in London cockney slang. It refers to a
British social and sound movement that has been characterized as
"music to riot by."

WHITE POWER
ROCKERS UNITE
AGAINST COMMUNISM
IN CHICAGO

A NEW BREED OF HEROES HAVE SPRUNG
FROM THE MIDWESTERN SOIL, BRAVE
SKINHEAD PATRIOTS READY TO FIGHT
FOR RACE AND NATION.

THESE TALENTED MUSICIANS AND
COURAGEOUS WARRIORS HAVE PUT
TOGETHER WHITE POWER LYRICS
WITH AN ENERGETIC BEAT TO PRODUCE
THE BEST AMERICAN SKINHEAD ANTHEMS.

THE
FINAL SOLUTION

TO HELP THE CHICAGO AREA
SKINHEADS SPONSOR WHITE
POWER ROCK BANDS SEND
DONATIONS OR PURCHASE HIGH
QUALITY CASSETTE TAPES OF
U.S AND ENGLISH WHITE POWER
ROCK BANDS THROUGH:

ROMANTIC VIOLENCE
P.O. BOX 90317
CICERO, IL. 60650

1. SKREWDRIVER 26 SONG TAPE
2. WHITE PRIDE- U.S CHA

THE WHITE BACKLASH!

4

WHITE POWER

CARMINE PATERNO HAD BEEN ONE OF MY IDOLS since I was old enough to have one. His father was Nonno's best friend, so Carmine had been at least a small part of my life in Blue Island for as long as I could remember. He was brash and boisterous and stood proud at not much more than five-and-a-half feet. Stocky. Built like an American bulldog, his demeanor was no less fierce. He played the drums and drove a muscle car. He was six years older than me, and if I could have had a big brother, I would have picked Carmine.

Carmine always thought to pay attention to me when he and his father visited with my grandfather over beers in the garage that served as Nonno's workshop. He never treated me like I was beneath him simply because I was younger. He swore when I thought swearing was a sin, and smoked and drank openly in front of adults when I was still buying candy cigarettes and root beer from the corner store on High Street.

"Is that a tattoo, Carmine?" I asked when I saw the fresh ink on his arm.

The new design was a burning torch wrapped with a banner and some words I couldn't make out. "Yeah, I just got it last week," he replied after draining his Old Style can of its last drops of beer.

"What does it say?" I asked wide-eyed, trying to get a closer look.

He lifted his sleeve to show me the full design. "It says, 'The Power and the Glory.' It's the name of a song by a band from England called Cockney Rejects."

I thought the band's name was funny but I didn't dare laugh at Carmine. "That's sweet!" For the rest of the afternoon I hung out behind the garage singing to myself what I thought the chorus might be for a song with that name.

By the time I was thirteen, Carmine had firmly established himself as one of the coolest guys on the whole East Side of Blue Island.

My pal Scully lived directly across the alley from Carmine, and was mentored by him into ever-deepening levels of defiance. With his finger firmly on the pulse of underground music, Carmine would make Scully bootleg cassette copies of albums from the best punk bands the moment they hit the Chicago scene—The Effigies, Naked Raygun, Bhopal Stiffs, Big Black, Articles of Faith.

Those dubbed mixtapes got Scully and me hooked on punk rock music, and we began to collect vinyl albums of any punk bands we could get our hands on, local or otherwise, competing to buy every new release and imported record we were lucky enough to come across.

Scully seemed to find out about those bands first, thanks primarily to Carmine. Anybody he thought was worth listening to won our immediate respect. Cockney Rejects. The Clash. Ramones. The Pogues. Stray Cats. Joan Jett and the Blackhearts. Angelic Upstarts. X. Sham 69. Combat 84. The 4-Skins. The Business. Cock Sparrer. Bad Religion. Social Distortion.

Scully and I drew the bands' names and their logos all over our ripped jeans, white tees, and Chuck Taylor high-tops. When my mom found my marked-up clothes she threw them out, sure they would turn me into a delinquent. So I hid them. Before I left the house, I tossed them out my bedroom window and changed in the alley before going anywhere.

Punk rock became a part of our lives in a way that outsiders, especially adults, never understood. It spoke to us and allowed us to speak when we didn't feel we had a voice. It was uncensored and raw and proved it was okay to be lonely or angry or confused about being a teenager in the world. Music was the common link allowing us all to see we were not lost and alone. In it we found each other, and through it we collectively directed our teen angst at a grown-up society we saw as intolerant of us.

The punk scene provided us with an alternative to lame, manufactured, popular culture and it promoted individual creativity and personal action, albeit through rebellion. Through punk lyrics we found release from the pressures of growing up. Watching our parents, we caught depressing glimpses of who we were sentenced to become someday. Slamdancing—moshing—to the driving rhythms was an outlet for our pent-up energy, anger, frustration, and insecurities. We were just kids looking to belong. To something. To be accepted, despite the bitter promise of the boring world our parents had built for us.

It was exciting to be a part of something in the mid-1980s that wasn't characterized by mass conformity, Top-Siders, neon popped collars, and endless brown corduroy everything. Punk rebellion felt natural—right—important. It was alluring.

Naked Raygun concerts were our go-to reprieve from the ordinary. Hailing from Chicago, the band performed in clubs and rented halls and Scully and I attended every concert we could. It hardly mattered where they were playing, we'd hop on a train to the North Side of the city and go to a five-dollar all-ages show at Cabaret Metro or sneak our way past the bouncers into an adults-only gig at Club Dreamerz or Cubby Bear.

The concerts were exhilarating. Colorful mohawks, combat boots, and ratty clothes riddled with safety pins were the fashion mainstay for the hundreds of embittered punks that crammed the venues they played. The energy in the band's songs was electric and the crowd swayed as if the surge of power lit a fuse and ignited our collective aggression. Our sweaty bodies, driven into each other by razor sharp guitars and wild drumbeats, pulsed and swirled in unison, packed like sardines in front of the stage. A never-ending stream of willful youths clad in bullet belts and studded denim jackets dove from the edge of the stage into our eager arms in the pit where we awaited their tumbling, sweat-slippery frames. The electric energy in the room was profound and we felt alive with every distorted power chord.

Along with Naked Raygun, Carmine also blasted music from a group called Skrewdriver all over the neighborhood, and I fell hard for the edgy British punk band the moment I heard them—their tunes and beats, the slick way they dressed, and the raspy voice of Ian Stuart, their gruff lead singer. His songs were different than those of other punk bands, unlike anything I'd ever heard. They brought life to a different and wildly more exciting level. They had something to say, and Ian Stuart voiced it with unmatched intensity. But that was inconsequential. I became too engrossed in the energy of the music itself, and I barely registered their lyrics.

I stand and watch my country
Going down the drain
We are all at fault
We are all to blame
We're letting them take over
We just let 'em come
Once we had an empire
And now we've got a slum

Are we going to sit and let them come?
Have they got the white man on the run?

My benign appreciation of Skrewdriver's music screeched to an abrupt halt the night I met Clark Martell.

Early one evening, Scully and I stood zoning out, high on weed, staring at a squawking ebony crow perched atop one of the twisted light posts that lined the alley behind his house. We passed a joint back and forth, giggling like little girls.

The garages on either side of the narrow dead-end alley were crammed with a myriad of old furniture, stacked boxes of orphaned Mason jar lids, piles of plastic nativity sets, and unraveling lawn chairs. With no space left inside for even half a Yugo to squeeze in, we weren't worried about anybody pulling up on us. As far as we were concerned, these deserted backstreets existed solely as a gathering place for us kids—and chatty, odd blackbirds.

"Hey, Scully," I said, face pointed to the sky as I studied the winged intruder looking down on us from atop the flickering streetlight. "Do you think that old crow knows what we're doing?"

He laughed. "I don't know, man. But that's a seriously dumb question."

As Scully craned his neck to look up at the watchful bird, the shotgun roar of a car bursting up the alley broke the calm.

"Shit!" He tossed the joint.

I retrieved it. "Chill out, man. It's only Carmine."

But as it turned out, I was wrong.

Carmine's primer-black 1969 Pontiac Firebird screeched to a skidding halt in the gravel beside us. I gawked at the stark contrast of the white death's-head skull freshly spray-painted on the corner of the matte hood. *Damn.* Could anyone be cooler than Carmine?

With the intermittent amber glow of the streetlamp lighting the car from above, the passenger door snapped open, and this older dude with a shaved head and black combat boots headed straight toward us. He wasn't unnaturally tall or imposing physically, but his closely cropped hair and shiny boots smacked of authority. Over a crisp white T-shirt, thin scarlet suspenders held up his bleach-spotted jeans.

He stepped across the beam of headlights and swiftly closed the distance between us. You'd have thought he'd turned in that alley specifically to hunt us down. I pulled back, wondering what the hell we'd done to piss this guy off.

Inches from me, he stopped and leaned in close, his beady, ashen eyes holding mine. The whites surrounding his granite pupils looked old, timeworn. Intense. Barely opening his mouth, he spoke softly, with a listen-closely-now attitude. "Don't you know that's *exactly* what the capitalists and Jews want you to do, so they can keep you docile?"

Not knowing exactly what the hell a capitalist was, or what "docile" meant, my nervous instinct was to take a swift draw from the joint and involuntarily cough smoke straight into his face.

With stunning, ninja-like speed, this guy with the penetrating gray eyes smacked the back of my head with one hand and simultaneously snatched the joint from my lips with the other, crushing it with his shiny black boot.

I was speechless. Frozen. I turned to Scully, but he'd vanished.

Blood retreated like flowing ice water through my veins and pooled in my heavy, tingling extremities. Shaking my head to regain my composure, I mustered enough confidence and tried to save face in front of Carmine. "What…what do you know…and who the hell are you, anyway? You're not my father," I sputtered. My voice sounded weak in my ears.

The stubbly, sharp-jawed man straightened up and gripped my shoulder firmly, drawing me in toward him. "What's your name, son?" His voice was steady and earnest.

I stammered nervously into lukewarm, broken pieces. "Christian…
Chris…Picciolini."

"That's a fine Italian name," he said, his voice suddenly sounding
kind. I braced myself for the inevitable knockout punchline. Sensing my
nervousness, he leaned in and said, "Your ancestors were quite exquisite
warriors. Leaders of men. You should be proud of your name." From my
experience in Oak Forest, I wasn't, though. "Did you know the Roman
army, the Centurion commanders specifically, are considered among the
greatest white European warriors in the history of mankind?" I didn't.
He took out a folded piece of paper and a pen from his jeans pocket and
scribbled the word "Centurion" on it. "And Roman women are divine
goddesses," he added with a sly smile. That much I knew. I cracked a
slight grin as he thrust the paper into my hand. "Go to the library and
look it up. Then come find me and tell me what you've learned about
yourself and your glorious people."

In the background, Carmine was leaning against his rumbling
Firebird, glossed boots with white straight-laces covering his crossed
ankles. He looked different. Focused. Pinching his cigarette and exhaling
a thick, steely plume of smoke, he could have been James Dean. "The
kid's cool, Clark. They're waiting for us. We should go."

"Well, Christian Picciolini," he said, grasping my clammy hand,
"I'm Clark Martell, and I'm going to save your fucking life."

With that, he nodded to Carmine, who jumped into his car and pulled
it up alongside us. As quickly as he'd arrived, this guy climbed back inside
the roaring beast, and he and Carmine tore off down the alley like a burning
phoenix, leaving me surrounded by a cloud of exhaust and confusion.

Clark Martell. I'd heard his name around the neighborhood before—
most likely from Carmine—but I hadn't paid much attention. Now

I made it my business to find out everything I could.

I started with the piece of paper he'd handed me. Scrawled on the back was the word "Centurion," but the front side revealed a photocopied flyer for a mail-order service called "Romantic Violence" that sold Skrewdriver tapes and other music for "white people with guts" through a post office box in Blue Island. The typed handbill described Skrewdriver's tunes as "marching music, fighting music, spirit-scaring white power rock and roll music from the finest white nationalist skinhead band in the West." That was the first time I ever heard the term "white power."

Martell's clothes marked him as a skinhead. Skrewdriver was a skinhead band and I'd seen what they looked like on the back of Carmine's albums; I'd even seen a couple of skinheads at Naked Raygun shows, so I knew enough to recognize one when I saw one. Carmine told me they were a spinoff from the London punk rock and hooligan subcultures and that some skinheads were about more than just music and causing a ruckus at soccer matches. But I didn't particularly care. I didn't feel called to action by the lyrics dominating their songs, words that spoke about politics, police oppression, war and history, and British unemployment. I didn't relate.

Skinheads dressed sharp. Tough. They looked intimidating and were rowdier than punk rockers. They wore British Dr. Martens work boots like their factory-worker fathers, slim denim jeans or tailored Sta-Prest work trousers, and thin suspenders they referred to as "braces." They shaved their heads and got tattoos and lived in England and a few other places in Europe, but there weren't many in the United States that I knew of. Certainly not in Blue Island.

I wanted to learn more. So I took the city bus to the mall bookstore and shoplifted a copy of the only book I could find on the topic, appropriately titled *Skinhead*, by a British photographer named Nick Knight. In it, I discovered skinheads, or "skins," first appeared in London sometime in the 1960s among working-class teenagers reacting against hippie culture. Upon further investigation, I learned skinheads were pissed off about the lack of jobs and opportunities to make a decent living, so they rebelled against what they believed were the causes of those problems. They didn't fall for the "flower power" notions of peace and love, and they blamed everyone from politicians to immigrants for their troubles. They shaved their heads, both to distinguish themselves from their hippie counterparts, and to keep their opponents from grabbing their hair during their frequent street fights.

While I learned that not all skinheads were violent—many factions just adopted the music and look, not the nationalist politics or aggressive attitudes towards immigrants—I learned those that *were* prone to violence typically attacked beatniks, gays, upper-class students, and local Pakistanis, who, they claimed, were taking their much-desired jobs. In the early '70s, Scotland Yard cracked down on skinheads in London, and more or less put an end to their riotous activities.

For a while.

Then, thanks to Ian Stuart, whose Skrewdriver lyrics I'd practically ignored as their music beats pulsed through my veins, the more radical offshoot of skinheads made a comeback in the mid-'80s. Stuart formed a political youth action group called White Noise. That, in turn, led to affiliations with the British National Front, a neo-fascist political organization, and the creation of a right-wing music coalition called Rock Against Communism. Skrewdriver shed their initial punk rock aesthetic and soon became the most well-known nationalist skinhead band in Europe.

The ideologies expressed in their music found an instant audience with many punks and skins who had become disenfranchised with the soaring levels of immigration and unemployment in 1980s England. Add to that feelings of alienation and a strong desire to disrupt a system that seemed the source of many of their problems, and many skinheads adopted more radical right-wing politics—and the pro-white nationalist skinhead subculture was born.

To parlay the sudden popularity of the band, Skrewdriver left their independent British record label Chiswick Records—where they were labelmates with more mainstream punk acts such as Motörhead and The Damned—and secured a recording contract with Rock-O-Rama Records, a West German record company specializing in edgier and more extreme Oi! music, a British brand of skinhead-styled punk rock. As a result of that partnership, Skrewdriver's racist skinhead message reached throughout Europe and Canada and their music then became available through Martell's mail-order service in the United States.

Carmine told me Martell had even arranged for Skrewdriver to come the United States to perform, the plan foiled when several members of the band couldn't acquire travel visas. Martell, with Carmine's help, settled for being the sole conduit to import Skrewdriver and other Rock-O-Rama records into the United States. And so, the Romantic Violence mail-order service became the first in the United States to distribute white power music in America.

It was 1987 and while I'd seen a handful of skinheads—some even non-racist, black and Asian ones—throwing kids around in the pit at Naked Raygun and other punk rock shows, I'd never actually met one in person. That's because this guy who'd smacked my head, having borrowed and adopted the style in 1984 from his radical British counterparts, was only one of a few dozen existing in America.

"Be glad Clark took an interest in you," Carmine told me. "He knows what's going on. He's sick of watching white people lose ground to all the affirmative action job discrimination bullshit and seeing minorities mess up clean white neighborhoods like Blue Island. He does something about it, too. Doesn't sit back and let shit happen."

"How does he feel about Italians?" I asked clumsily.

"What, you don't think Italians are white?" Carmine laughed. "Who do you think taught all those fucking pasty Krauts and Limeys to be civilized? If it weren't for the Roman Empire and its 1,500-year rule, most of Europe would still be living like savages and have black skin like the invading nigger Moors of Northern Africa. Thanks to us Italians, ethnic Europeans today are still white...Italians, Germans, Greeks, English, the fucking Spaniards and the drunk Irish, the Nordics...the whole goddamn lot of us." He pulled out a Marlboro cigarette, lit it, and offered me one.

"Thanks," I took a shallow drag, more interested in what he was saying than the smoke in my hand.

"Even those pansy French bastards," he hacked. "Though, on second thought, maybe we should've let them fuckers go. Regardless, if you're a native European, you're white. White power! And don't you forget it."

"So Clark's a...white power...skinhead?" I asked, still not exactly clear on what exactly that meant.

"Yeah, but he's more than that. He's a neo-Nazi skinhead, here to save white people from everyone who's trying to destroy us, like the Jews and niggers. After he moved to Chicago from Montana, where he's originally from, Clark worked with the American Nazi Party. But he thinks they're a bunch of kooky old white guys who just sit around and complain about how bad things are, so he's using skinhead music to get the message out to younger people. We have a band."

"We?"

"Clark, Shane Krupp, and Chase Sargent...you know them from the neighborhood, right? And me. Final Solution. You've gotta hear us. You'll love it. Ain't nobody else doin' it and we've already played a few shows around town. People are starting to listen to what Clark says about whites needing to watch their backs and fight back."

"Like who? I mean, who's hanging out with him?" I wanted Carmine to keep talking.

"Look around, man. Pay attention. Those shaved heads you see hanging out in this alley aren't some bullshit fashion statement like punk rock has become. They're about showing the world what we're about. Our message is spreading. Word is getting around. And it's starting here, in Blue Island, right before your eyes. We're going to take our country back."

I had no reason to doubt him.

Carmine further explained that Martell believed firmly in the supremacy of the white race over other ethnicities. He was sick of "muds"—as he referred to all non-white people—moving into quiet white neighborhoods, bringing crime, and taking jobs. Martell despised drugs, because he saw them as a tool that blacks and fat-cat Jews with political agendas used to enslave white people, and keep them dumb—docile. Like Adolf Hitler had done for Germany, Martell—and now Carmine, and a small, but expanding group of Chicago skinhead guys and girls— wanted to stop Jews, blacks, Mexicans, and "queers"—who Martell considered sub-human—from poisoning white culture in America. He was especially adamant about recruiting and protecting white women, so they could continue to propagate the white race.

"So…what…he's going around warning people?" I asked, trying to figure out what Martell was really all about.

"For the last two years, he's been putting together the first white power skinhead crew in the country, that's what," Carmine replied. Leaning forward and dropping his cigarette before crushing it with his boot, Carmine said in an uncharacteristically low voice, "And he's doing a shitload more than that."

I kept digging. "Really? Like what?"

He paused, considering how much I should know. "He's catching heat from the cops for some serious stuff that happened this past spring."

Again I pushed for details. But Carmine wouldn't say anything more.

I thought the skinhead look was cool, and their music pumped me up. But, aside from getting roughed up a bit when my bike got stolen, I had no real beef with blacks, or even Mexicans—let alone Jews or gay people. I'd never even met any. I was just happy to finally be living in the same neighborhood as my friends.

I didn't see much racism in our community, although, because most families had come from the same small village in Italy, there was an overwhelming amount of Italian pride and we tended to stick together.

My High Street friends and I had chased black kids out of the St. Donatus carnival before, but not as a racist or political act; we simply didn't want outsiders messing with our rituals. Some Mexican families had moved onto our block, and our parents and grandparents weren't too happy about it, so we did hear the random "there goes the neighborhood" remarks. But there was no significant racial tension that I was aware of.

So was I initially drawn to Martell's racist agenda? Not really.

But he was magnetic. Charming. I wanted to be like him, and like Carmine and the other people I saw them hanging around with. Why? Because Martell was the first adult—even though he was only twenty-six years old when I met him—who had ever disciplined me and provided a valid explanation for doing so. He hadn't asserted his authority without good reason. When he scolded me for smoking pot in the alley, it was because he thought it was bad for me and took the time to explain the consequences; it wasn't merely, "Put that joint out, because it's illegal, and I'm an adult, and I said so." This persuaded me that he wanted what was best for my future—so much so that he'd smacked my head. Just like my dad did.

And so, I changed my behavior: I swore off weed, even though I had barely been introduced to it. When Martell and Carmine and their friends were in the alley listening to music or monkeying with their cars, I made sure I was in visible proximity. I followed Martell around and observed his mannerisms. His racial rhetoric sank in, too. Some of my High Street friends had begun moving away to the suburbs. Was that because Blue Island was less safe now, with other races moving in? My new bike had been stolen by black kids, after all.

I looked at my neighborhood, family, and friends with wary eyes questioning all of the things I'd once taken for granted. I'd never liked school, which made it easy to accept that teachers lied to us about history—presented it the way that suited them. Maybe Martell knew something about Jews they weren't teaching us in school. Maybe he was right when he claimed the people who wrote the history books were all Jews—and fed us a bunch of altered historical bullshit. Blacks were certainly tied to the increase in crime. I knew that firsthand.

Aside from seeing him with Carmine, Martell kept cropping up more and more in neighborhood discussions. His intensity scared people, cops included. Conversations stopped when he walked into a room. That was something I admired. Intentionally or not, Clark Martell had made me a whole new person. I wanted to carry his weight.

By the end of the summer, when Carmine was busy working his job at a local muffler repair shop, Clark would regularly task me with going to the post office or running off copies of flyers and literature for him. He had begun publishing a newsletter called *Skrewdriver News* that he handed out in front of concert venues when trying to recruit punk rock kids. I'd over-deliver by cheating the copy counts when it came time to pay the cashier. That typically meant we got at least two times what we'd paid for.

Clark would reward me when I did particularly well. He'd give me a pair of his secondhand boots, or a faded Skrewdriver T-shirt, or more music cassettes, which he seemed to have an abundance of. I ate it all up and would squirrel these gifts away so my mom couldn't find them. Then, one day, Clark handed me a tattered red paperback titled

The Turner Diaries. Until then, I hadn't read even one of the books my teachers assigned in school, and I'd faked my way through every book report. But I couldn't wait to read the gift from Clark.

I had been comfortable as a High Street Boy, but now, I had awoken to the larger world, and wanted more than to just fit into it. I wanted to matter. Ever since I was a lonely little kid, playing make-believe in my grandparents' coat closet, I'd felt called to do something truly big. Now I wanted people to look up to me, the way I looked up to Clark, and for as noble a reason: saving the white race. The more I thought about him and his mission, the more it appealed to me. This was important.

Like most people who are caught up in someone's charisma, I looked for evidence that Clark was right, not wrong. I visited bookstores and sat and read books from the shelves, and took an interest in history and current events. Sure enough, I concluded that giving college scholarships to minorities meant passing over more deserving white kids. I noticed lots of muds, blacks and Mexicans mostly, working labor jobs and in restaurants—which seemed to prove whites were being shoved aside in favor of lesser-paid illegal immigrants. In place of trustworthy families from Italy, strangers with different ways of living had moved in. I soon began perceiving life through Clark's shrewd lens, and started to believe Blue Island, my beloved home, was in danger.

My family and friends didn't listen to my new ideas. My parents weren't concerned. They shrugged me off and changed the subject. That made it clear they needed to be protected.

A seed began to germinate inside of me. The racist skinhead movement had only just begun in the United States, born right here in my own Blue Island backyard. I could become part of the new movement, spread the word, win Clark's full acceptance and the respect that came from being on the cutting edge of something significant.

Rapidly, living for innocent fun faded, playing Wiffle ball and riding bikes with the High Street Boys didn't seem exciting anymore, and the need to live for a greater purpose came sharply into focus.

I was about to turn fourteen years old and start high school. Sitting in class all day would only slow me down.

I was already learning about things that mattered. Things most people took for granted.

And I didn't need a classroom or some double-talking teacher to try and change my mind.

5

SKINHEAD PRIDE

WHEN MY FRESHMAN YEAR OF HIGH SCHOOL STARTED in August of 1987, despite my vehement protests, my parents enrolled me in Marist High School, a private, all-boys Catholic school on the South Side of Chicago. I'd scored high on my entrance exam and was given a full load of honors classes. Those I could handle, but the last thing I wanted was more God and saints and prayers pounded into my head. It had no relevance to my life. Eight years of Catholic elementary school had been enough.

Misery loves company, so on the first day when I bumped into Sid and Craig Sargent—the two younger skinhead brothers of Chase Sargent, a close cohort of Clark and Carmine—I was ecstatic. I recalled seeing them drinking beer in the alley on occasion and recognized them right away by their cropped hair and the white laces in their boots. Even if the school did require them to wear a necktie and slacks to cover up their skinhead appearance, they remained identifiable.

The three of us became fast friends and a few days later, Craig gave me my first very own Skrewdriver cassette with *Hail the New Dawn* dubbed on side A and two short albums, *Boots and Braces* and *Voice of Britain*, on the flipside. While I'd heard Carmine blasting Skrewdriver's music nearly every day, and I knew enough about them from listening to Scully's tapes, I didn't own my own copy. Now I did.

"This is some sick shit! This band knows what they're talking about," Craig said, echoing Carmine's sentiment. Despite being in the same grade and only a few months older than me, Craig had been mentored for some time by two older brothers who were skins—Sid and Chase—and already knew the ins and outs of recruiting. Craig was tall and imposing and had the routine down pat. "White people are going to be in big trouble if we don't pay attention to what they're saying. Just like England, European whites built America and now we're being pushed aside by the Jews in favor of blacks," he'd say, "and we're not going to let that happen."

Skrewdriver, and more specifically Ian Stuart, had a real knack for creating music and lyrics that inspired young people to take action. The band had given birth to the white power music genre and with Ian Stuart's keen ability to identify and deliver what embittered youths wanted before they even knew they wanted it, it was only a matter of time before his politically-infused anthems stood apart from those of his contemporaries in the London punk rock scene and made it to the United States.

Skrewdriver wrote anthems with relatable directives built in, unlike the whiny punk protest songs I'd become used to. The lyrics gave us the truthful education our schools refused to deliver, for fear we'd see through their manipulated account of history. "White Power." "Blood & Honour." "Tomorrow Belongs to Me." "Free My Land." Songs that filled me with purpose and pride instead of childish, nihilistic impulses like punk music did.

Armed with my new cassette and a Walkman, I played this Skrewdriver tape over and over and over until I heard the songs in my head even when my player's batteries had run down. I moved beyond the pounding beats into the heart of the lyrics.

Walk around the city and you hold your head up high
The sheep they'll try and drag you down with their aggression and their lies
Your life is just a struggle 'cos you're proud of your country
But you just keep on fighting, that's the way it's got to be
People try and put you down and stamp you to the ground
They don't seem to realize there's no way you'll back down
There is nothing they can do to step on you and me
'Cos we'll just keep on fighting, that's the way it's got to be

The cadence and conviction of this music spoke to me as nothing else ever had, brought me under a spell that sent me craving more information about its message, the culture behind it, skinhead lifestyle, and attitude. I wanted to be part of this. Body, heart, mind, and soul.

Again, I turned to my immediate surroundings, half hoping to find evidence that hordes of minorities were messing up Blue Island and nearby neighborhoods. Determined to find evidence to support the claims in the music I was listening to, I began seeing strangers who couldn't even keep their yards clean. Junk cars cluttering up the street. Black men hollering at white women, trashing up our town. Dealing drugs. Mexicans, and their dozens of children, creeping out of their dirty little section of Blue Island over to our side. Bringing their smelly rice and beans along with them. Greasy food not fit for pigs.

Scully waded into the skinhead mindset with me. We dubbed and swapped more tapes, listening to more Skrewdriver and expanding our collection to other like-minded English skinhead bands. Brutal Attack. Skullhead. Sudden Impact. No Remorse. I took their lyrics to heart. The music was no longer a solitary beat bringing me to a new level of alive—it was both knowledge and prophecy.

We pooled together our holiday and birthday money, purchased bank money orders and stamps, and sent away for Ben Sherman and Fred Perry shirts from Shelly's, a store on London's Carnaby Street specializing in skinhead couture. By now my body had begun to fill out and grow and I was no longer shorter and smaller than everyone else my age, which meant that Scully and I could swap clothes and essentially double our skinhead wardrobe.

We set out to find shiny, steel-toed Dr. Martens boots—"Docs"— in obscure Chicago Goth boutiques like Wax Trax and 99th Floor. We wore braces, the thin suspenders Clark wore. I rolled the cuffs of my Levi's like I'd seen the others do in the alley behind Carmine's, and I sported a military surplus black nylon bomber jacket purchased from the local flea market, which I adorned with symbolic patches like American and Confederate flags. Standard issue for any skinhead worth his salt. I looked sharp. Tough. Turned heads when I walked down the street. Adults were nervous when I was too close. I liked a look that intimidated without my needing to do a damn thing. And people made assumptions about my willingness to fight rather than take shit from anybody.

Scully and I shaved each other's heads in his dingy basement. Concrete floors, exposed pipes, and dangling lightbulbs were the ideal ambiance for us barely-teenage boys taking a stand for white working-class adults everywhere.

I shaved his head first. Adjusted the guard on the clippers, not meaning to shave him completely bald. But it was my first time using the shears and before I knew it, Scully's hair was cut down to his scalp.

He cried. I'm not putting him down for that. I didn't blame him. A pasty, bald head was not a great look on him, and he'd have to go to school looking like that on Monday. Maybe the girls would avoid him. Laugh at him even. Shit.

I pulled him to his feet and put the clippers in his hand. Plopping down on the metal folding chair myself, I said, "Go ahead, I messed up your head. Now it's my turn. Take it off. All of it."

So he did.

When my mom saw my fresh buzz cut later that night, she cried. "Oh my God, Christian, what did you do? Why did you cut off your beautiful hair?" She attempted to caress my head as if the tears welling in her eyes and her pleas to God could magically make it grow back faster. "You look like you're sick and have cancer," she said, sobbing, and she pulled me close. "It's this punk garbage, isn't it? I knew it. I want my little boy back!"

I let her grieve, silently reckoning that while I wasn't the one who was sick, my shaved head meant I was working on the cure to the multiracial cancer that was eating away at our society.

Gone were the days of my pageboy hairstyle. And my youth.

Only four months had passed since I'd met Martell, but we were skinheads now. Literally. Officially.

Politics meant little to Scully. He only liked the look and the music.

So, apparently, did other people.

With our tough new look and shaved heads, our popularity soared. Girls liked being around us. I met Jessica, a cute Blue Island cheerleader who took to wearing a bomber jacket and Docs, and we both soon proudly shed the "virgin" label.

I was all of fourteen. Life was good.

If it hadn't been for school and my mother—who spied on me and pestered me with constant questions and suspicions—and other signs the white race was about to be annihilated, I would have had no complaints.

But I lost no sleep over the annihilation part. Clark was building a resistance army. He'd already founded the Chicago Area

Skinheads—CASH—in 1985. The first organized white power skinhead crew in the United States. Between CASH and Romantic Violence—CASH's small-time white power music mail-order operation—Martell now had a regular following of a couple dozen skinheads in Blue Island and around the city. A handful of the original female recruits, like Mandy Krupp—Shane Krupp's sister—and Kat Armstrong, had been Charles Manson worshippers before becoming skinheads. Now they were Martell devotees.

This wasn't some fluke. Clark would have had more followers, but opposing skinhead crews began popping up around Chicago to counter his racist advances, like the Medusa Skins and Bomber Boys, who just liked to party and fight mostly, but didn't claim a side, and the more outspoken anti-racist factions of skinheads, the Pitbulls and SHOC—Skinheads of Chicago. The "Antis" as I began to call them all—short for anti-racists—somehow managed to lure some wannabe skinheads to their side.

Skinheads scared people. When a bunch of them were together, fights broke out. Bad shit happened. On the eve of November 9th, 1987, the week of my fourteenth birthday and the 49th anniversary of Nazi Germany's *Kristallnacht*, the infamous "Night of Broken Glass," when SS stormtroopers had raided Jewish stores in 1938, white power skinheads stormed the North Side of Chicago, smashing in windows of shops they suspected to be owned by Jews and painting blood-red swastikas on synagogue walls.

I hadn't had anything against Jews before, in fact, I didn't even know any, but from the lyrics I'd been studying and Martell's hatred of them, I had come to the conclusion that Jews were indeed evil masterminds trying to undermine unsuspecting American whites into extinction.

Clark was whispering to two older, long-haired American Nazi Party twin brothers in the alley when I mentioned that it was my birthday. Carmine, who was changing the engine oil on his muscle car, pulled a frosted Old Style can from a Styrofoam cooler in the garage and tossed it to me. "Happy birthday!"

Clark paused his conversation with the mustached twins to approach me and shake my hand. "I have something important for you," he said, smiling. "Might be going out of town for a bit to take care of some business. Can I rely on you to check the Romantic Violence post office box and hold the mail for me until I get back?"

"Yeah, of course! You can count on me, Clark," I responded, before the question had even fully escaped his lips. With that he handed me a small brass key and returned to hushed conversation with the two jackbooted men.

I was unaware that Clark didn't know if he'd be coming back. What was inescapable, though, was the utmost importance of what the three men were discussing. I felt the tiny ridges of the key with my fingers and squeezed it tight in my palm, knowing fully this key would unlock more than a mailbox. I had no idea this would be the last time I'd see Clark Martell.

Rumor got around that Clark was behind the Kristallnacht rampage and he was arrested, along with a few members of the CASH crew and one of the long-haired American Nazi Party fellows from the alley. It wasn't the first time the police had been after him, either. It proved what Carmine had told me—the cops, the feds, maybe even the CIA, were watching Clark's every move.

It wasn't only Clark who was being watched. Carmine was, too, and so were Chase Sargent and his brothers Sid and Craig, the Manson-loving skinhead chicks, Shane Krupp, and the other people I'd seen hanging around in the alley. FBI raids of their houses were becoming pretty standard. Their home phones were wiretapped, and they were routinely tailed and photographed by less-than-subtle law enforcement officers. The Romantic Violence mailbox got monitored. Letters were opened and resealed.

My desire to be part of their group escalated until it consumed me. It was inspiring. Made me feel proud to be a skinhead. This was the stuff of gangster and spy movies. Serious good guys and bad guys in action. And while we good guys were being deceptively portrayed as violent thugs by the Jewish-run media, this was for the good of a cause. An honorable cause. Protecting the white race. Clark had even prophesized it in some lyrics he wrote before going to jail.

> *We're Chicago gangsters in braces and boots*
> *Bloodthirsty Vikings sticking to our roots*
> *We're the Waffen SS going off to war*
> *White warriors here to even the score.*

"Can you believe it?" I asked Scully when the Chicago Kristallnacht story came out in the news. "Martell's not just saying he's going to save the white race. He's actually doing something about it, like Carmine said."

Adolf Hitler hated Jews because he felt they were destroying his beloved Germany and were the cause of his country's intense economic struggle after World War I. He saw Jews as parasites that leeched onto healthy nations and destroyed them like a cancer. Now Clark was going after them the same way Hitler did, because he saw the same things happening in America at the hands of Jews who ran the media and banking systems.

I was awed to imagine Clark doing this level of damage. He and his followers shook people up, had minorities and Jews locking their doors and putting up For Sale signs. I wanted to stand beside him. People were too meek; they needed a leader like Clark Martell.

I had the same fury running through me, waiting to be unleashed.

After the news hit that Chicago neo-Nazi skinheads were behind the violence and destruction of Jewish property, the terms "skinhead" and "fear" became synonymous. Some people considered skinheads racial terrorists. *Terrorists.* I liked the sound of that. The power behind it. But people had it wrong. Skinheads were brave patriots, not terrorists. They were fighting battles other whites talked about but were too complacent to take up.

Honest, hardworking white people like my parents were being forced to work day and night just to make ends meet to support their families, while the minorities sat back collecting unemployment and pumping out more crack babies to boost their monthly welfare checks. My mom often worked three jobs—in the salon, as a caterer, and in the evenings during election season as a vote tabulator. My dad ran the beauty shop all day and looked after Buddy while my mom was away working at night. And when Buddy grew up he'd have to do the same just to survive. That didn't sit right with me.

All the while, Clark said the Jews enjoyed the turmoil they secretly created as they sat in their ivory towers rubbing their greedy hands together, watching whites and minorities finger-pointing at each other while it all unfolded to their benefit. If scaring white people into submission meant that they'd ultimately see the truth behind the Jewish lies, then Clark was well on his way to opening their eyes. It was for their own good.

Over the last fourteen years when my parents were absent, busy at work trying to make ends meet, I'd been angry with them for not being there for me. Now it had begun to make sense. The Jews were to blame, not my mom and dad.

In January of my freshman year I found out more of what Carmine's hushed innuendos concerning Clark's activities had been about. He and five other CASH skinheads had broken into the apartment of a twenty-year-old woman the previous April.

Angie Streckler had been a CASH skinhead at one point, but quit the crew abruptly. Clark and the others heard she had a black friend—a totally intolerable behavior for a white power skin. To discipline her, Clark and some of the CASH crew stormed into her place, pistol-whipped her, sprayed mace in her eyes, and used her own blood to paint a swastika and the words "race traitor" on the walls of her bedroom. She'd never reported it, until the cops somehow caught wind of the attack when the group was arrested for the Kristallnacht episode and pursued additional charges.

Some other things Clark had done around Chicago before setting up shop in Blue Island in late 1984 came out, too, including physical assaults on six Mexican women, the fire-bombing of a minority's home, spray-painting swastikas on three other synagogues, and perpetrating numerous incidents of vandalism on various Jewish-owned businesses.

A fucking legend. That's what he was to me. He had a clear purpose and put action behind his words. The violence didn't scare me. It excited me, made my blood lust to participate.

I hungered to talk to Clark again and schemed ways to meet up with him when he got out, but he failed to make bail. He was sentenced to prison for eleven years.

About a month later on a cold February afternoon, less than a year after the Angie Streckler incident, I settled in with a six-pack of Old Style to watch black talk-show host Oprah Winfrey, who was having some white power skinheads from California on her show. Dave Mazzella. Marty Cox.

Tom and John Metzger, the leaders of WAR—White Aryan Resistance.

The show's producers were even able to get Clark on the phone to make some comments from prison. While on the line, not only did Clark put the poser Anti skinheads in their place by calling them out for their cowardly unwillingness to stand behind their race, he was clearly able to communicate that power-hungry rich people—or capitalists as he called them—were the real enemy, plotting every race against each other in the name of the almighty dollar and ultimate global control. Now that was something that made sense. Those of us without any real money or power were all being sold out. It was every race for itself. The only way to fight back was to stick with your own kind or die with the rest.

And then, right there on national television, for all the country to witness, Cox stood up from his seat in the audience and said it was a proven fact that blacks came from monkeys. Oprah went crazy, pushing Cox's arm down when he shoved it forward in a Nazi salute. I couldn't believe my ears. It happened in a split second, but he'd called her a monkey to her face in front of millions. The segment aired repeatedly on news stations across the United States. And I knew beyond a doubt, from that moment on, the white power skinhead movement was going to be staggering. Oprah, the capitalist media lackey that she is, had done our work for us. These older guys were ready to take on a celebrity like Oprah. And they knew how to get under her skin for the entire world to see.

The American public knotted up with fear. Skinheads weren't a passing curiosity anymore. Antis and black skinheads began to fear that white power "boneheads," as they called us, would ruin the music scene in their cities with their violence, and made it their mission to eliminate racist skinheads. What the fuck? White power skinheads were the real deal, Antis nothing more than posers. Into fashion and partying, nothing more.

I stepped up my efforts to be noticed. I dressed the part, talked the talk, and brought up my new ideologies whenever I found the chance.

The High Street Boys weren't into it, and we started to drift apart, but I knew something big was coming down.

I checked the post office box religiously and delivered the mail to Carmine. In return, Carmine began supplying me with stacks of photocopied pamphlets blasting everything non-white. I would use these to recruit new skins like I'd seen Clark do. White power music was now the only thing I listened to. I let the messages within the lyrics and leaflets root deep into my soul. They spoke to me. I listened.

6

FOURTEEN WORDS

SKINHEAD RALLIES, get-togethers in shabby, moldy basements, were better than hanging out in the St. Donatus parking lot with the High Street Boys, as far as I was concerned. Swastikas and racist slogans crudely painted on crumbling cement walls. Driving music. Skrewdriver. Talk of blood and honor and loyalty. Skinhead girls in plaid miniskirts and fishnet stockings. Beer. Lots of beer, flowing from cans, bottles, and kegs when we could scrape enough money together.

But there were always brawls. Rowdy, drunken scraps. Shoves over a crooked glance quickly advancing to fists punching anyone within range. Blood flowing. Stomping and kicking. With heavy steel-toed Doc Martens, the results could be brutal.

This part puzzled me. What kind of camaraderie was this? Weren't we all on the same side? We were all on the same team, fighting against massive odds that needed us to operate as a single focused unit.

Even the High Street Boys and I weren't perfect, though, and sometimes our propensity to mock authority and break rules got us in trouble, but underlying all of our actions was the sheer joy of discovering life together—not battling against each other with every liquor-fueled impulse.

When the High Street Boys were together, most of the games we played involved working together as a team—baseball, Wiffle ball, strikeout, Nerf football. Most sprung up spontaneously, teams changing according to who was around at any given moment. Neighborhood dogs barked, strained to join us, chasing us up and down behind chain-link fences as we streaked past them. Some dogs would love to sink their teeth into us when balls fell into their yards, but we had a steadfast rule that whoever hit the ball had to go in after it. Nobody liked the job, but we all took our turn as both retriever and dog decoy. And we all survived because we had each other's backs.

As I'd experienced playing sports on High Street, a team can't beat its opponent if they aren't operating as a single force under the same directive. But the skinheads didn't seem to operate this way. It was as if, without a single voice to guide us, everyone was out for himself. We needed Clark Martell. I kept these observations to myself, though. Too early for me to weigh in, but I knew my realization of the situation proved I could be leading this group. Someday.

I attended every local gathering I heard about. Observing, and being seen. Passing around copies of literature I'd collected from Carmine and Clark. Promoting CASH. The remaining older skinheads, many of whom had begun growing their hair out to avoid attention from the police, showed up now and again, and I felt their eyes on me. They knew I was more than just a kid, even if I was only fourteen. I yearned for an opportunity to show them I was their equal and I wanted to demonstrate it in a big way.

One Sunday morning, Chase Sargent pulled his rusty Cadillac Seville up alongside me and Scully while we were riding skateboards in the St. Donatus parking lot, and asked if we wanted to go to a meeting with him that afternoon. A rally.

Fuck yeah! Besides Clark and Carmine, Chase was one of the original CASH skins. He was tall and gangly, but his reputation as a fighter was second to none and he also played guitar, two skills I hoped to acquire myself someday. The cool factor was off the charts. We didn't hesitate to say yes when he asked.

Scully and I attended the meeting, held in Mandy Krupp's ramshackle apartment in Naperville, Illinois, a turn-of-the-century settler's village turned manufacturing ghost town about an hour's drive west of Blue Island. We drove up with muscle, Scully behind the wheel of the patchy blue and gray 1971 Camaro he'd recently bought on his sixteenth birthday.

We were dressed to kill.

Scully wore his dad's old army boots. I polished the pair of boots Clark had given me a few months before going to prison, for a job well done. I had flyered three hundred windshields of the cars parked for a demolition derby at Raceway Park. The racetrack was only three blocks from my parents' apartment and I knew the patrons who flocked to the Sunday derbies were the types of low-hanging marks Clark could easily convert. It had been my idea to target the event and Clark rewarded my initiative with a pair of his old, worn-out Docs. They were a little big, but I'd grow into them. In the meantime, I stuffed some newspaper into the toe area. I tore the white laces out of my gym shoes and straight-laced my new boots with them. Ready to kick ass. Big boots to fill.

Neither Scully nor I spoke much during the drive up. Instead we cranked the car stereo and sang along loudly to a poorly dubbed copy of Skrewdriver's *White Rider* album. Maybe it was nerves that kept us avoiding the obvious conversation. More likely it was because we both knew the road ahead of us was about to swallow us up—and I was thrilled for it to happen.

Close to thirty skinheads, most of whom were in their early twenties, had packed the cramped apartment by the time we arrived. Newly minted skins from Michigan, Wisconsin, Texas, and Illinois. Carmine. Chase Sargent. Sid and Craig. I was the youngest; Scully and Craig the next youngest at barely sixteen. There was hardly room to stand. Clark had been busier gathering people than I'd thought. It was a shame he couldn't be there to see the fruits of his labor.

Somebody handed me a cold can of Miller High Life. I was already high on the thrill of being there, but I wasn't about to say no to this display of acceptance. Besides, to tell the truth, the whole thing was a little overwhelming, and some alcohol could calm my nerves. Everywhere I looked were shaved heads, tattoos, boots, braces. People had this down. Nazi battle flags doubled as window curtains. Armbands with swastika insignias were plentiful. Some tough-looking skinhead girls hung on to the arms of some of the bigger guys, making it easy to see who the key players were.

Before I finished my first beer, a large skinhead with a pockmarked face and a thick swastika tattooed on his throat brought the meeting to order. Rising, standing in the corner of the living room, he spoke a simple statement, one I would know by heart by the end of the night. A creed I would live by for the next seven years of my life.

"Fourteen words!" his voice thundered.

Immediately, everyone in the room turned to him, stopping mid-conversation to yell in one voice, "We must secure the existence of our people and a future for white children."

"Do you believe in the fourteen words?" he demanded.

All around the room, arms shot out in Nazi salutes.

"Heil Hitler!" everyone around me cried in unison.

I threw my arm out, too, looking sideways at Scully, who appeared unnerved. Not me. This was fantastic.

For over an hour my heart pounded with purpose, as I stood mesmerized, listening to fiery words I would soon be able to recite in my sleep.

An upside-down and partially charred American flag hung on the wall beside the speaker as he gripped his beer can firmly and spoke loudly to those gathered. "Our traitorous government would have you believe racial equality is advanced thinking, brothers and sisters. That all races should live in peace and harmony. Bullshit! Take a look around. Open your eyes and refuse to be fooled. What do you see when niggers move into your neighborhoods? You see drugs and crime pour into your streets, not equality. Your gutters fill with trash. The air starts smelling foul because these porch monkeys don't do anything but sit around and smoke crack and knock up their junkie whores all day. Can't bother to clean up.

"Only thing they're cleaning up on is all that hard-earned money you and I pay in taxes. Living off welfare. Unemployment. First in line for every handout the government can offer. Section 8 housing. Free lunch programs at school. The only reason those little nigger babies go to school is to get those free lunches and welfare checks. All paid for by us white people. By hardworking white Americans who'd never dream of having our kids eat free meals because we take care of ourselves.

"And while you and me work our fingers to the bone, these niggers are out selling drugs to your little brothers to make them stupid. Selling them junk so their teeth will rot and they'll look sixty by the time they're sixteen. Getting caught in gang crossfire and dying at the hands of these criminals.

"Making them dependent on drugs so our innocent Aryan women will fuck them for a taste of whatever vile substance they've hooked them on. You think they're selling this garbage just to get rich and buy their Cadillacs and gold chains? Get your heads out of your asses, brothers and sisters. They're selling this poison to make white kids as stupid as their mud kids. They want our people to become so dead inside they'll smoke and snort everything in sight. Shoot drugs into their arms and between their toes. They want to see our people destroy their brain cells and end up in jails where they'll get violated by nigger gangbangers who are locked up for murdering and raping innocent young white women.

"And who is leading these degenerate nigger animals in the destruction of our race? The Jews and their Zionist Occupation Government. That's who!" The speaker launched into a tirade against Jews and Israel that I'd hear at every rally I attended from that moment on, but never with such fervor. The cords on his neck looked ready to tear, spit foamed in the corners of his mouth. His eyes were ablaze with anger. Self-righteousness. Indignation. Truth.

Nobody spoke as he reminded us that Jews and their shadowy Zionist Occupation Government—ZOG as the movement referred to it—controlled the media and were lying through their gold-crowned teeth trying to pit whites against blacks, Christians against Muslims, so they would kill each other off, leaving nobody but the Jews, who had the ignorant, pretentious belief they were God's "Chosen People." They, of all people, who nailed the goddamn Son of God, Jesus fucking Christ, to the cross. Catholic school had even taught me that.

He ended as he began. "Fourteen words, my family! Fourteen sacred words."

On our feet, we shouted those fourteen words over and over and over.

"We must secure the existence of our people and a future for white children! We must secure the existence of our people and a future for white children! We must secure the existence of our people and a future for white children!"

We closed with stiff-armed salutes and ear-splitting chants of "Sieg heil! Sieg heil! Sieg heil!"

Adrenaline burned through me like fire, nervous sweat extinguishing it, spreading from head to foot as the caustic smoke of racist rhetoric filled the room. I was ready to save my brother, parents, grandparents, friends, and every decent white person on the planet. How could white people not see what absolute and utter despair they were facing? It was going to be up to me and those like me. It was a huge mission, but I had no doubt where my loyalty would be.

Conviction ran so high that if it could have been channeled into electricity, it would have powered a small country for a month. The dank air was thick with personal stories about losing jobs to illegal aliens willing to work for less than minimum wage so they could send the cash back to Mexico to their families of dozens of little "wetbacks" who would, in turn, use the money to smuggle more illegals into the U.S. to take away more white jobs. There was a graphic firsthand account of a virginal white sister being raped in a school bathroom by ruthless blacks for a gang initiation. These hardened skinheads ripped apart the media, exposing the lies that money-hungry powerbrokers heaped upon the ignorant masses to keep them in line while they plotted our demise.

I learned "innocent" Jews hadn't been mass-exterminated during World War II. There had been no Holocaust. Simply necessary casualties of war in a fight against the enemy. Hitler had realized the truth that the Jews were trying to undermine European culture by manipulating its financial systems and polluting its beautiful legacy of fine art. He had tried to save his people by identifying the cancer and cutting it out. Instead, he'd been vilified by the Jewish press and historian spin-doctors for decades, a hero turned monster under a barrage of outrageous lies and distortions.

Scully stood beside me, tense, scared, and barely breathing when they broke into another round of ear-splitting "Sieg heil" chants, one person after another thrusting out his—or her—arm in solidarity. I joined along with the others, their faith contagious.

This was what education was all about. Not being handcuffed to our school desks and forced to learn about the Emancipation Proclamation or the Gettysburg Address. *This* was the American Revolution. The truth. Right here. Right now. We were losing our rights to minorities and Jews, and as a society we were so clueless and self-satisfied, we were letting it happen right under our goddamn noses.

This meeting was about action. About combining forces and bringing the various scattered skinheads throughout the United States under one unified banner. A drunk from the Confederate Hammer Skinheads crew from Dallas suggested a shortened version of their group's name as a name for the new collective. Someone else chimed in that proposing a simple logo with two crossed hammers, similar to those used by Pink Floyd in their movie *The Wall*, could signify strength and the idea of a working-class ethic. The group, eager to move on to the partying, quickly approved the suggestions and the Hammerskin Nation was officially born. Even so, CASH voted to remain separate and operate independently for the time being.

When the meeting cooled off a little, somebody suggested a beer run. Food and booze were running low. There was a grocery store next door, apparently an easy place to steal from. For the next hour or so, people ventured out in shifts, shoplifting food and liquor and bringing it back to the apartment. Somebody stole a disposable camera and took pictures of people giving Nazi salutes, arms around each other, beers in hand. When it came my turn for the obligatory theft, I bought a bag of chips that was on sale. I couldn't risk getting caught stealing and have to explain to my parents what the hell I was doing way out in this neck of the woods, but I didn't want to come back empty-handed and look like a pussy either.

While that night was the most alien and intense thing I'd ever experienced, I was instantly hooked. The white power skinhead culture appealed to me, even though I knew I wasn't exactly like the others in the room. I didn't come from a family down on its luck. I hadn't been brought up to hate people different than me or with any us-against-them mentality. But my heart beat hard in my chest. More than ever, I wanted to be part of this. It was overwhelming.

Grown up.

Real.

And it was black and white; no middle ground. I couldn't sit on my hands any longer. I had made my decision and it was this side of the fence where I landed firmly with both feet.

While I felt I was likely smarter than most of the people I'd met, despite the fact I was the youngest, the others in the room seemed to have the inside truth about what was going on in the world. They understood the imminent danger the white race faced, and took it upon themselves to stand up strong against that threat. They were willing to lay down their lives for their convictions, even though most white people would scorn and reject them, writing them off as little more than racist white trash.

The politics of race began to pump me up. I was involved in something far more significant than what any other kids my age cared about. I'd become part of a secret brotherhood, an exclusive society so new it scared people to death because they didn't know much about it. And here I was—all of fourteen years old, in at the ground level of something significant, with a real chance to make an impact, to demonstrate my courage. My dedication. This was my family now.

Were blacks and Mexicans—excuse me, niggers and spics—all that bad? Well, not by my previous limited accounts, but the skinheads saying this were older, wiser. They'd paid attention longer and understood the problems. They were the ones whose jobs were being taken over. And I wasn't all that down with minorities moving into my neighborhood. I could help keep Blue Island white. Italian. These skinheads knew their shit. They were here to save the rest of us, and I knew with my eagerness and talent, I would be able to help.

Looking at Scully's lily-white face, feeling his anxious urge to leave, I knew he was out. He wasn't a racist. I'd have to save the world without the help of my friends. Or make new friends. Either way. I was in.

7

ALLEGIANCE

By the end of my freshman year of high school, I came and went as I damn well pleased. I snatched the keys and took my mom's car out for joyrides as if I owned it, unhindered by the fact that I was still legally too young to drive. Showed no respect in my speech or demeanor toward my parents, swearing at my father, walking out of the room whenever my mother tried confronting me about it.

They had stopped making any real efforts to interfere in my life after the last time my father had tried to smack the back of my head.

I'd come home drunk, well after midnight one school night. My parents were perched at the front door waiting for me as I stumbled in.

My dad pounced on me before I was able to fully cross the threshold. "Where the hell have you been?"

I chuckled and retorted, "Where the hell have *you* been?"

My father's irritation quickly intensified to anger as my reaction to his scolding manifested as an apathetic fit of laughter. I brushed him off and made my way to my bedroom. As I entered the kitchen, my father caught up to me and drew his hand back to slap my head. I may have been impaired at the time, slower in my reflexes, but I'd become conditioned to never let him fully out of my periphery when he was

Christian in his Nazi frat-boy dorm room, 1989

incensed. Before he could fully commit his swing, I turned and grabbed his arm mid-recoil and pinned the rest of his body hard against the refrigerator with my forearm. A ceramic vase with some acrylic flowers that rested atop the fridge came toppling down and crashed into pieces on the floor next to my hysterical mother.

"Don't you ever fucking raise your hand to me again or I'll hit you back ten times harder than you've ever hit me. And it won't be a little love tap on the back of the head. Do you understand me?"

I pushed him away and continued stammering down the narrow hallway until I reached my bedroom, slamming the door hard. Immediately, I heard my mother wail in a way I'd never heard before. Now, what the hell is she screaming about, I thought.

"My God! Christian, open the door!" My father stood outside my room, crying for me to unlock the door, pounding, trying frantically to turn the knob. My mom had unfortunately been just a step behind me as she laid her hand on the doorframe to stop me from slamming it. I'd crushed her middle finger in the doorjamb and she was bleeding profusely, dripping on the ceramic floor.

"I'm sorry. But next time leave me the fuck alone," was all I said when I opened the door and realized what had happened. Needless to say, my words did not match how I felt. I was torn up over it, but couldn't come up with anything sincere to say to express how remorseful I really was. I was angry with my father and my unfortunate mother had borne the brunt of my attack.

My father wrapped my mom's bloody hand in a towel and drove her to the emergency room to get stitches.

The loud ruckus woke four-year-old Buddy. He started to cry as he wiped the sleep from his eyes and emerged from his room to see the anguish on my mom's face and the blood running down her arm.

I quickly let him into my bedroom, pulling him up into my arms to avoid the small pool of blood on the floor, and consoled him as we sat on my bed in the dark room. "Why is Mamma crying, Buddy?" he sniffled.

"Because I made a mistake, Buddy." I couldn't lie to him. "She'll be okay. They'll be back soon."

"Okay." He rubbed his tired eyes. "Can I sleep in here with you tonight? I'm scared."

"Yeah, of course. Why are you scared, Buddy?" I wiped his tears with my thumb and held him close.

He was starting to doze off. "Because you smell like beer and you're fighting with Dad."

I kissed him on his forehead as his heavy eyelids shut.

I spent the rest of the night lying next to Buddy with a clenched chest and a lump in my throat, crying quietly inside and feeling deep regret for the pain I'd caused my mother. She never mentioned anything about the incident to me afterwards, though I could sense how hurt she was by my actions. I never found the right words to apologize to her.

My father didn't stop giving me grief about it, but he never laid a hand on me again after that night.

Right before Marist let out for the summer, I let my parents know they'd better enroll me in a different school for my sophomore year. "I'm not going back to that mental prison."

"Christian," my mother whined. "Don't call such a nice Catholic school a prison. You did just fine there and of course you'll go back."

"No way. They're sheep. And you shouldn't even want me to go back. They wasted your precious work time calling you because I skipped school one day. Bullshit."

"It was silly for you to do that," my mother said. "But your father and I straightened it out for you, didn't we?"

"Straightened it out?" I said contemptuously. "What you did was lie."

"We protected you. What did you want us to do? Let them suspend our son?" my father said.

"The point is, you lied. Exactly like they do. You didn't straighten anything out and I don't need you to protect me. It's a prison, and I'm not going back. You should be glad. You won't have to lie for me anymore."

"Wait and see," my mother said, trying to gently embrace me. I snapped my body back, letting her know to keep her hands off me. She backed off, adding, "By the time summer is over, you will see it's the best school. A fine Catholic school. That's what you deserve."

No way was I going to waste another year in a school with teachers trying to shove their liberal propaganda and tedious religious dogma down my throat.

By now my parents knew I was becoming something else, no longer their innocent little boy, but they assumed it was a teenage phase and didn't push back hard enough to realize it wasn't. Had they stopped to look more carefully, they might have seen I'd substituted the attention I once longed for from them with something far more sinister.

My parents' two-flat building had a good-sized private garden apartment that sat unrented, just accumulating boxes of clothing and old furniture. With some elbow grease and paint it would make a great little place to live. Without asking for permission, I commandeered the space. I gathered some free scrap material from the lumberyard and framed out a bedroom and living area.

Neither of my parents liked this idea, of course. My mother hated the notion I could now come and go as I pleased through a separate entrance. She wouldn't even be able to hear the door open or close, and I could have anybody I wanted down there. But neither of my parents stood up to me. They didn't have the courage anymore to go beyond trying to guilt me with a few forceful words.

First thing I did was have Jessica over. Tall, voluptuous Jessica with her long legs, dark eyes, and apple-red cheeks. Her full mouth and soft lips. My Nazi cheerleader girlfriend.

The first time I snuck her into my basement apartment, the two of us laughed so hard we nearly wet our pants. The place wasn't finished yet, but we couldn't keep our hands off each other. Nearly every night and some days during school, we took advantage of the freedom that came with my having my own place.

Late one night while we were having sex, we heard my mother snooping by the front entrance. We must have been louder than we thought. I tried to pull my jeans on with one hand and shoved Jessica, as she was getting dressed, out the window with the other, while my mom banged on the door like she was the damn FBI serving a felony warrant.

"Christian! Christian, open the door. What are you doing that takes you so long to answer me?"

The second Jessica's foot was outside, I shut the window and zipping my pants, went to unlock the door. "What's your problem?" I snapped. "Can't you let me sleep?"

Suspecting something was amiss, my mother barged in and took her sweet time checking out my place. What the hell was she going to do if Jessica was in there, anyway? When was the last time I listened to her about anything? But shit, who needed the aggravation? At most, my parents would try to force me to move back in with them. An unbearable thought that I'd never agree to anyway.

By the time my mother was satisfied that her suspicions were unfounded and I had finished laying a guilt trip on her for waking me up and always being on my back, I went out to find Jessica. She was nowhere in sight. Obviously, she'd decided to walk the three miles home in the dark by herself.

Real chivalrous of me. Especially knowing that niggers were out there everywhere just looking for a beautiful white girl like her to rape. No fucking way. I'd kill someone if they so much as looked at her. They couldn't treat my girlfriend that way. Who did those nigger assholes think they were, anyway? Luckily nothing happened.

Jessica and I didn't last long after that night.

I worked quickly, motivated and driven by plans beyond what any other kid, even the High Street Boys, dared to concern themselves with.

Buddy, still a stout little guy full of wonder, would come down to look around. Just like I used to follow my grandfather around when he was building something in his workshop, my chunky little five-year-old brother watched me put up the walls in my new domain. He tried to help me paint. I let him hang out, like Nonno had let me when he was working. Buddy made a mess, but so what? It's how he'd learn. Watching his fifteen-year-old big brother would teach him all he needed to know.

Within two weeks, the place was ready. I used some of the old furniture my parents kept in storage, and decorated my walls with neon beer signs and Nazi and Confederate flags for which I'd traded my old baseball card collection at the flea market.

"Can I live here with you, Buddy?" my little brother would ask. Of course he'd want to. I was his cool older brother. He'd want to do everything I did.

"I would love that, Buddy," I said, patting his little head, "But I'm sure Mom and Dad would really miss you if you didn't live with them."

"But I miss *you*," he said, his voice quivering. "Why did you have to move out?"

I was hit with a bitter wave of sadness brought about by the genuine innocence in his round brown eyes. Trying to respond without letting the lump forming in my throat get the best of me, I got on one knee and hugged him tightly. "Well, there are some things that I need to do and sometimes it's best if I do them alone."

His bottom lip trembled. He fought back tears, wanting to be tough like me. But he wasn't a tough kid. Even at his tender age, I'd been much tougher than him. More independent.

The lump in my throat was making it hard to talk. "Why don't you go and see what Mamma made you for dinner?" Holding back my emotions, I tried to comfort him.

He was still a mama's boy in many ways. Closer to her than I'd been. And why the hell wouldn't he be? She'd actually made time for him. I shouldn't be so mad at her, though, I thought. Maybe at my dad, either. Because of my beliefs, I'd begun to reconcile that my parents needed to work long hours when I was a little kid. Providing for the family and all that. That's what respectable white people were supposed to do. I understood that now. And even if we didn't get along, I was going to see they could hold on to all they'd worked so hard for.

"Hey, you'll be right upstairs," I told him. "You can come down any time."

His round brown eyes lit up. "Really, Buddy?"

"Sure, Buddy." I patted his head. "We can even come up with a secret knock."

"Really?"

"You bet." I held my hand up for a high five. "Now get outta here," I said. "Go eat some dinner."

I shut the door behind him and leaned my back up against it as I wiped a tear from my eye. Then, taking a look around, I cleared my throat and grinned. I had my Nazi frat-boy dorm room.

I turned my attention fully to skinhead activities. Marched into the Blue Island post office, filled out an application, laid down twenty bucks, and took over a vacant slot next to the now-abandoned Romantic Violence post office box. I immediately began communicating through mail with other skinheads across the country. There was no World Wide Web then, but the opportunity to build a network was there if you played it right and were willing to put in the work.

To be a leader, I knew I needed to show initiative, establish myself as an entrepreneur. Be innovative. I sorted the leaflets I'd been collecting from the older skinheads, and began photocopying them at the local convenience store, mailing them off to other skinheads with post office boxes halfway across the world. In the envelope I'd always include a handwritten note asking the recipient to pass along the literature to someone new after they'd read it, hoping to continue the chain indefinitely.

The first correspondence I sent out contained a copy of one of Clark's earliest writings about skinheads. I clipped the article from one of WAR leader Tom Metzger's White Aryan Resistance newsletters:

How we gnashed our teeth in misery before. Helpless with broken limbs as the beast did its dance of death upon our children and piled their bodies high. How we cried out for help, for vengeance, for life. And yet our plea went unanswered for years, until it came—the plan of salvation, the hope of redemption; we became warrior skinheads!

The literature that came in provided the addresses of other pro-white organizations, which I added to my mailing list. Ku Klux Klan. American Nazi Party. Aryan Nations. American Front. Church of the Creator. National Alliance.

As soon as I received a new flyer or newsletter, I reprinted copies and mailed them to other groups on my list, delivered them in bulk to other skinheads, or handed them out to local kids—skaters, punks, stoners—anyone who I thought might be interested in getting off their lame asses and doing some good fighting for their future. I missed no opportunity to market the ideology of white supremacy. Now that Clark was doing hard time in prison and Carmine, Chase, and the rest of the original crew were avoiding the spotlight, I added my own words and contact information to anything I copied, personalizing the message about defending ourselves against inferior races as I spread information about rallies and meetings. I made sure my name and post office box address were on every piece of literature I sent out.

The summer of 1988 had proven to be a watershed moment, not only for me personally, but also for the burgeoning American neo-Nazi skinhead movement at large. I had established myself as an integral cog in the machine moments before the storm clouds gathered. White power groups began sprouting up like weeds in metropolitan areas across the country and, with the rapidly increasing numbers and the hottest summer temperatures recorded in over a century, utter pandemonium erupted.

American Front skins in Portland beat an Ethiopian immigrant student to death with a baseball bat. At least one Los Angeles skinhead was being tried for murder in another case involving a minority. The arid weather incited the brand new Tulsa, Oklahoma, Hammerskin crew who were particularly intent on causing as much violent mayhem as they could. They took great pleasure in targeting minorities and homeless people for random beatings, or "boot parties," as they called them. The detailed letters they'd sent me seemed to describe an endless supply of fodder for their vicious recreational activities. And, closer to home, six original CASH members, including Clark Martell, had been formally sentenced to lengthy terms in penitentiaries across the Midwest for charges including aggravated assault, criminal damage to property, and home invasion—a Class X felony in Illinois.

Truth be told, while we may have publicly tried to wrap our politics in flowery catchphrases like "white pride" and "pro-white" for the sake of positive marketing to the unwitting masses, internally we fucking hated anyone that wasn't white and willing to fight vehemently against those who weren't.

Those few months in 1988 became known in skinhead circles as the "Summer of Hate."

Indeed it was.

Since the widely-publicized Angie Streckler and Kristallnacht trials had resulted in a significant chunk of the CASH skins being imprisoned, the time was as good as any for me to make my mark. By now I'd become the only remaining active associate from the original CASH crew and I began inheriting pieces of what Clark and Carmine and Chase had left behind. Still too young to be on the cops' radar, it wasn't long before any new recruits began to look to me for leadership and direction.

Becoming the de facto leader of the second wave of Chicago white power skinheads took little serious effort. Blue Island was an easy place to recruit. Most kids and their families were barely making ends meet from one paycheck to the next and they lived in a neighborhood that was rapidly deteriorating economically. Kids in Blue Island liked to let loose and blow off steam. Girls were plentiful and willing to hang out. The guys were into music and could easily be made to relate to the message I was peddling.

What we were doing was magnetic. Like attracting moths to a flame. We partied, made sure we were seen, bowed to no authority. I pushed the skinhead lifestyle to the limits. Eager to sharpen my street fighting skills at every opportunity, I picked fights with anyone I thought I could intimidate or outpunch. We were gentlemen thugs intent on having a good time while on duty protecting our race. And our numbers grew rapidly.

One of my best recruiting scores was Al Kubiak.

Kubiak was a natural-born bruiser who loved to fight. He was solid and muscular, with a baby-faced grin that seemed to smile even wider when he was throwing punches. We hadn't liked each other much during my High Street days, when we'd been given to cursing at each other rather than sharing a beer or a kind word. He was a spoiled kid from the West Side of Blue Island, which made him an enemy of us East Siders.

We couldn't stand him and his group of friends, so if we caught them on our side of Western Avenue we'd try and chase them out.

Not keen on running away from confrontation himself, Kubiak always stood and fought while his friends ran, coming to blows or backing down only if one of us happened to be carrying a baseball bat or a hockey stick. Every time we saw each other we called each other every foul name we could think of, but somehow we never threw fists. Now we were on the same team. He'd come to me after a party asking if he could become a skinhead. I think he just wanted more people to terrorize. But I knew I could use his muscle, so we put our past differences aside and became fast pals.

If not for Kubiak's unwavering racist attitude and eagerness to punch people without provocation, I'd never have given him a second thought. But his skills could come in handy as I was growing our crew. He would be my extra muscle when I needed it. Our commitment to each other grew exponentially over the summer, cemented by our unspoken mutual desire to throw down with every wannabe gangbanger and Anti invading our territory. Kubiak thought nothing of walking up to non-whites and shoving them to provoke a fight. And when he did, I never hesitated to join in the fray.

Since the Jake Reilly romp in eighth grade, I'd taken to fighting with relative ease and comfort. My training came in the form of almost daily fistfights with anyone I felt threatened the safety of my neighborhood. Violence became pleasurable and I enjoyed dominating the mind game that led to me throwing the first punch and knocking someone flat on his back. It was like a drug. Sometimes Kubiak and I took on three, four, even five guys at once. The bigger, the better. They never saw it coming from such young guys. Our undying allegiance to each other and the element of surprise were definitely on our side. That's what best friends did together.

One such testosterone-filled weekend, me and Kubiak and couple of neighborhood guys jumped in a car and headed to the University of Illinois in Champaign-Urbana, a two-and-a-half-hour drive south of Blue Island, in Central Illinois. An older brother of one of the other guys attended school there and invited us to come hang out and party for the night. The moment we arrived, aided by the fact that we'd been pounding beers the entire drive down, all hell broke loose.

The four of us arrived at the apartment complex where we were supposed to meet the brother and knocked on the door of the unit number we'd been given. It was loud and clear that a party was underway as the cacophony of music and conversations, even as we approached from down the hall, was deafening. No one answered when we knocked, so we let ourselves in.

As the four of us entered the overloaded apartment, the largest white human being I'd ever stood next to intercepted us immediately. This enormous, thick-necked, semitruck of a frat guy put his meat-hook hand on my shoulder and lurched me backward to align my face with his.

"If you jagoffs wanna come in, it's ten bucks apiece." His breath stung my eyes like rubbing alcohol and I pulled back.

"We're just looking for my brother. He told us to meet him here," one of our guys said. "His name is…"

"Hey, punk! Did you hear what I said?" the incredible white hulk cut in. "Twenty bucks."

"Twenty bucks?" Kubiak swiped the monster's hand off my shoulder. "You just said ten, King Kong."

He got in Kubiak's face. "Yeah, but I don't like you, so now it's thirty, sunshine."

"Yo, Gator, we got a problem here?" Another colossus from the party intervened and blocked our entry. This time it was a tall, lean, muscular black guy in a tank top who was flanked by an equally large, muscled beast of a Samoan guy.

"No fellas, we're all good here. I got this," I acquiesced as I reached toward my back pocket and threw a sideways look at Kubiak who was thinking the same thing I was. Mayhem.

"Well, I don't have a twenty. I only have five," I said, and I cracked Gator square in the jaw with a fistful of brass knuckles from my back pocket.

Kubiak grabbed the nigger and kicked him in the balls. He went down as Kubiak turned to slug another giant. He grabbed a beer bottle to smash across the other guy's face.

The other two skinheads with us started slugging anyone within arm's length. The stream of people coming at us seemed infinite.

Before we knew it, the four of us were punching, kicking, and smashing bottles over the heads of half of the University of Illinois football team's offensive line. These guys were big and strong, but none of them had any fighting experience like we did. The place looked like a tornado had spun through it, with banged-up bodies and furniture strewn everywhere.

When the apartment and the frat guys were sufficiently destroyed, and the remainder of the party guests had scrambled for the exit, we bolted for the car.

On our way out of the complex, several of the neutral partygoers and a pizza delivery guy on a bicycle who had witnessed the intense action came up to pat us on the back and revel with us on our intense brawl. Without any remorse, being the testosterone-filled attack dogs we'd trained ourselves to be, we started fighting with them and laid them out on the street as well. Ruthless.

We were banged up sufficiently, but we were the ones who could still walk out of that place on our own two feet.

Within minutes, the streets were swarming with dozens of police officers and a legion of campus security vehicles putting up roadblock checkpoints to try and track down the gruesome mob of thugs who were capable of inflicting that much damage and injury to their star football athletes. Lucky for us, they were searching for a large mob, not four dudes in a Honda Accord. We barely made it out of town, re-enacting the brawl and laughing uncontrollably the whole drive home.

The following Monday, a Blue Island police detective asked me to come down to the station to answer some questions about the incident. Apparently, the Illinois State Police had put out an APB for a dozen or more skinheads who'd brazenly assaulted and sent several University of Illinois football players to the hospital. Immediately all eyes fell on us, since we were the only skinhead crew in the state who were capable of such damage. Barely able to control myself from bellowing at the hilarity of the situation, I told the cops I had no idea who could have done such a thing. "After all, officer, I'm not even sixteen years old and I don't have a driver's license or a car. How would I get down there?"

They couldn't prove it was us and dropped the investigation, but me and the guys laughed about it for weeks after that.

It didn't take many bruised and banged-up bodies for Kubiak and me to establish our notoriety as the two toughest motherfuckers around Blue Island. Every teenager in our neighborhood either looked up to us or feared us. Sometimes both. For the first time I felt completely in control of my own life. I'd yearned for so long to fit in with my peers and now they'd begun to vie for my attention. The ones that had once ignored me now revered me.

But beyond my own age group, I still wanted the respect of the older skinheads. I wrote to those doing time in prison. They'd eventually get out, and I counted on them standing at my side as an equal when that day came.

The main person to get to was Clark, though. I still wanted his official blessing. Nothing could top communication with him. Carmine gave me his address without hesitation, and I immediately began a regular correspondence with him in prison. I didn't expect him to answer, but I thought at least he'd start to appreciate the effort.

I added the numbers "14" and "88" right above my signature at the end of every letter I mailed out. "14" represented the fourteen words and "H" was the eighth letter of the alphabet, which, translated as "88," was secret code for "HH" or "Heil Hitler." Within a few weeks I was communicating not only directly with Clark, but also with dozens of other pro-white activists and prisoners across the country.

My parents eventually gave up their battle to send me back to Marist for my sophomore year. They still wouldn't let me go to Eisenhower, the public high school I could find myself tolerating, because it had scarred my mother as a teen. Instead, they enrolled me in an experimental high school called Project Individual Education, colloquially referred to as PIE, a small magnet school that took a sampling of kids from all three Blue Island-area public high schools. PIE was experimental in the sense that they tried to give students more educational freedom. Since it wasn't one of the primary public high schools in the area, my parents accepted that it was the next best thing to a private school. Buddy laughed at the funny name.

A few things put PIE above Marist in my book. Teachers seemed more relaxed, at least in theory. No more religion. And if you got good grades, you could "opt out" of going to certain classes. Some kids thought it was cool, but it didn't make any difference to me. I'd opt out of anything I damn well wanted, good grades or not. The state still gave my parents the authority to decide if or where I attended school, but they sure couldn't make me do anything I didn't want to once I was there.

The one truly great thing about PIE was its connection to Eisenhower. Since both schools belonged to the same district, it meant I would be allowed to play for Eisenhower's football team with Kubiak. Playing football on a real team was something I'd wanted to do since my High Street days. I loved being a gladiator out on that field, and every game brought the promise of being a hero carried off the field on my teammates' shoulders. Moreover, Kubiak and I would now be connected through school, as well as Blue Island, our fists, and our beliefs.

But, despite our impassioned philosophies, none of our white power activity occurred on the football field. In fact, my teammates—an equal mix of white, Mexican, and black players—nominated me as their team captain. A true testament to my unrelenting commitment to whichever mission I chose to undertake. My fierce determination to lead. Perhaps it was my charisma or maybe it was driven in part by fear, but either way their faith in me to provide results on the field was unmistakable.

Intense competitors, Kubiak and I were determined to win above all else. To win took the strength of a team and, even though most of our teammates were not white, we were able to stay focused for the good of the squad. I learned to work with the black and Mexican kids on the team because I reasoned that these particular minorities weren't the same ones who were out there destroying our culture. These guys were okay. They were athletes that I learned to trust and football had given me a singular reason to see beyond our differences. When we put those helmets on we all became the color red—Eisenhower Cardinal red. We weren't black or white or brown. The dichotomy of the situation was never able to eclipse the thrill of combat that I experienced with these brothers-in-arms. Despite our differences, we were out there as a collective unit working together to beat our opponents into submission and we all learned to temporarily put our conflicting ideologies aside. I may have been an extreme racist outside of the locker room, preaching the need to get muds out of our neighborhoods and schools, away from our innocent women, blaming them for polluting our people with drugs, but when the school bell rang and the coach's whistle signaled the start of football practice, the cognitive dissonance of the situation became a non-issue. We were a team.

Soon as the games were over, though, Kubiak and I traded our football cleats for Doc Martens boots and were ready to ruthlessly stomp anybody we considered an enemy of our race.

8

WHITE REVOLUTION

I wrote Clark about our frequent fights with the Antis and non-whites and updated him on recruiting progress, knowing he'd be excited to hear I was carrying on his proud tradition. By this time, he was sending me three or four letters a week. I made sure the other skins knew I was in touch with him, to keep their spirits high, but I kept the content of his letters to myself.

To my dismay, as time passed, his packages arrived full of explicit pencil drawings of naked skinhead women attached to stories he had written that read like a Third Reich *Penthouse Forum*. Didn't seem right he'd send me that weird shit. I tried to ignore it. Then whole notebooks full of erotic stories he'd written and illustrated started showing up. He became obsessed with a Chicago skinhead girl named Reina, who he claimed to have knocked up before going to prison, and titled his pornographic love story *Right As Reina* in tribute. I'm not sure she knew about it or if she was really even pregnant with his child, but he epitomized her as the ultimate skinhead woman and wrote that she was the "goddess of all white women."

Clark also shared stories about how the prison guards treated him poorly and ranted about how he thought he was going mad.

The guards wouldn't let me out into the yard again today. The coons and queers get all the special privileges like extra juice and clean socks. I want clean socks too. I am not an animal. I am a warrior. God wants me to have clean socks and I'll have them if I want. I took a shit into my hands this morning and smeared my whole body with it so that I could look like a nigger and get an extra juice or package of bologna and some clean socks. But they didn't buy my ruse. The goons made it into my cell and bashed me before I was able to castrate myself with a sharpened salad tong I stole from the chow hall yesterday. I'm writing you this letter from the psych ward. For God and Hitler and Reina! Hail Warrior Skinheads—C.M. 14/88.

Clark's letters embarrassed me, and I began to believe that he wasn't quite right in the head. For the short period that I'd known him he never struck me as a jokester, so it was hard to distinguish if Clark was serious about what he claimed in his letters or if he actually did try to castrate himself with salad tongs. I never really wanted to ask. It made me uncomfortable, so I avoided thinking about it altogether.

I kept my thoughts private, though, to protect his reputation—CASH's reputation. And what the hell, I rationalized, maybe it wasn't true insanity I was seeing. Maybe it was just desperation from being locked up. He was the first person—the Aryan Johnny Appleseed—to bring the white power skinhead lifestyle to America, and people still trembled when they heard his name. Media bulletins always reported he was a top neo-Nazi sociopath, "one of the most terrifying men in America," and that was tough. The stuff of heroes and revolutionaries. Being crazy was pathetic, so I kept those suspicions to myself and burned his notebooks and most of his letters after I read them.

In November of my sophomore year, television talk show host Geraldo Rivera invited three skinheads, as well as John Metzger—the leader of the White Aryan Resistance's Aryan Youth Movement—to appear on his show. Media lackey that Geraldo is, he named the episode *Young Hate Mongers*. To up his ratings, he also invited Roy Innis, a full-of-himself nigger troublemaker who chaired the Congress of Racial Equality—CORE—and some "we are God's chosen people" kike rabbi.

Not long into the show Metzger called Innis an "Uncle Tom" for helping push the U.S. government's multiracial agenda and also criticized him for not admitting that blacks were a detriment to civilized white culture. But rather than own up to it, Innis went crazy, jumped out of his chair, and began choking Metzger on stage. Naturally, Metzger defended himself—his goddamn constitutional right to do so. Geraldo got back on stage as all hell broke loose and a skinhead in the crowd threw a chair in his general direction catching him square in the face, busting his spic nose wide open. The braver people in the audience streamed up on stage and joined in the melee; others in the audience acted like lunatics, scared to death, not knowing what to do as they huddled in a back corner of the studio.

This made national news on every television network, every newspaper, magazine, and radio station. Pundits and shock jocks rehashed the clip over and over again. And did this event prove we were barbarians like the media had hoped? Absolutely not. The three neo-Nazi skinheads and Metzger were well dressed. Clean-cut. Intelligent. Clearly stating our purpose, defending our ideals. The nigger proved himself to be the instigator. The rabbi an afterthought.

We didn't do drugs. We believed in supporting our families through honest hard work. Our sense of pride was relentless. Our hearts genuinely wanted what was best for the white race, but nobody got that.

The newspapers—all owned by a bunch of Jews—focused only on the racist violence. Soon after, media reports began cropping up accusing white power skinheads of attacking people in malls, pulling race-mixing couples out of their cars, and of course they dragged up every old irrelevant crime they could find. The press called us animals, portrayed us as vicious monsters attacking innocent people indiscriminately, for no reason. Headlines contained words like: "Amoral thugs." "Outlaws." "Hatemongers." "Cockroaches." What we stood for was vilified as an ideology of hate. A philosophy of fear.

Soon after, another talk show host, some puppet named Richard Bey with a show called *People Are Talking*, tried to piggyback on Geraldo's ratings and invited some Antis onto his show to spout off about their racist skinhead counterparts. He kicked off the show with a guest claiming neo-Nazi skinheads accosted him on a New York subway and when he refused to join them, they beat him and threatened to throw his two-month-old baby down the steps. Only a moron would think they'd actually throw an innocent white baby down a flight of subway stairs, but idiots prevailed and again the media sensationalized stories about what a bunch of violent, bloodthirsty, hateful monsters we were. Of course we were violent. We had to be. Revolution has a price. But hateful monsters? They were only partly right. We weren't monsters. But we did hate the enemies that were working to destroy us. Hate wasn't the impetus, however; it was the manifestation of our desperate struggle to defend what we held dear—our ardent pride in the white race. We were heroes trying to save people. Patriots. Why the hell couldn't anybody understand that?

My frustration with the sensationalist media inspired me even further, proved that I was on the right track and part of something special. Bigger than Blue Island where it began. Bigger than Chicago. Even Illinois. Our skinhead numbers were growing rapidly and we were making ourselves known nationwide.

Kubiak thought it was time to be armed. Nothing fancy. He handed me a rusty semiautomatic .25 caliber pistol that he stole from his uncle.

The gun didn't weigh much, but it was heavy in my hand. It made my heart beat faster. Power surged through my fingertips, tightening around the cold steel. Life or death sealed within my grip. I straightened my arm, held it out, felt the beat of the weapon join with my own.

"Holy shit," I said.

Kubiak shrugged. "I'm not sure it works, but what the hell, you pull it on anyone, they won't know. They'll back down, I guarantee it."

I tucked it in my waistband where nobody could see it and walked home, conscious of the metal against my skin with every step.

I let myself into my basement flat and sat down on my bed. Took the gun out. Stuck it back in my waistband and drew it over and over, practicing so I could draw quickly when the time came. I aimed it. Watched myself in the mirror. Hard. That's how I looked. Hard. That's what I was.

I heard my mother shuffling outside the door, calling for me. Spying on me again. Always there when it was convenient for her. My dad, too. But when I needed them most—the times when I adopted the applause from the other parents as they cheered on their own children—they were markedly absent. I was over it, even though they never copped to their failures. I pointed my gun at the door, imagining what my mother would do if she opened it and met the barrel of my gun. "I'm sleeping. Leave me alone," I answered.

With everything that was happening on a national level, I knew I had to stay well informed. So I turned to *The Turner Diaries* that Clark had given me for an education on survival. Clark called it "the Bible of white revolutionaries." William Pierce, a visionary, the leader of the white nationalist group National Alliance, wrote it under the pen name Andrew MacDonald in 1978. The novel was written in journal form and chronicles Turner's part in the violent overthrow of the U.S. government and the societal cleansing of all Jews and non-whites. It was nothing less than an ingenious prophecy about what would happen in the not-too-distant future if white people didn't wake up now and take action.

I read the captivating account of our chilling future in less than six hours. To say it inspired me would be an understatement. It incited me to the point that I wanted to mimic the heroic protagonist in every action he took.

I would be Earl Turner, ready to take on my own government through violent means if that's what it took to set the world straight and protect what I loved.

First, though, I had a minor annoyance to deal with at PIE. A spook named Damarcus—typical nigger name—with a bad attitude. Real gangbanger thug looking for trouble, always running his mouth. Walking down the hallway one day he had the balls to deliberately step in my way and bump me. He held his ground as if it was his right and I should step aside. I struck first. Landed a blow splitting the bridge of his nose and grappled him into a headlock, ramming his nappy-haired head into the lockers before he knew what hit him. Dragging him bleeding from one side of the hallway to the other, I smashed his head against the steel doors. The goddamn lesbian gym teacher and the janitor got between us and broke it up. Some other teachers held me back and marched me to the principal's office. Oh, boy, I was shaking. Yeah, right.

It was the end of my time at PIE. I'd chewed it up and spit it out.

A week after I got expelled, I returned and spray-painted "Niggers Go Home" in two-foot white letters across the school's front doors in case they hadn't gotten the point when Damarcus' head got banged up until he had more bumps and lumps than pearly white teeth.

The cops knew it was me. Of course it was. Everybody knew it. But they were unnerved by me at this point and were certain that targeting me would cause a backlash from my crew, since I'd managed to recruit more than a half dozen students during my brief time at PIE. Uneasy about the influence I'd amassed and certain there wasn't a thing they could do without hard evidence, they let it die. Couldn't prove it. And even if they could, what could they do about it? A few nights in jail wouldn't stop me.

No school left for me at this point but the Blue Island public school system. Broke my mother's heart. She wanted me to be a doctor. Only the best private schools for her precious son. And now I'd be in a public school. Eisenhower. The horrible school she'd attended as a young sixteen-year-old immigrant. Hardly a place for someone special like me.

I never forgot the stories she told me about her youth and not fitting in, getting picked on for being different. But she needn't have worried, because I felt her pain. And I wouldn't ever let that happen to me—or her—again. It wasn't like I had any intention of spending much time there anyway.

I had more critical priorities on my mind. Periodic tables and verb conjugation and calculating the sum of the angles in a triangle held exactly zero interest.

White revolution was my primary course of study.

9
HEAR THE CALL

ONE PIVOTAL THING HAPPENED during my time at Eisenhower. I met Tracy, who became the portal to an entirely new level of violence. But this time the perceived enemy was white like me. This turned out to be ideal for building my status in and around Blue Island.

Tracy was a year older than me. Pretty and unabashedly outspoken. Long brown hair and a petite, tight body. She smoked and drank and her innocence had vanished like aerosol hair spray long before we'd met. Abrasive as they come, she lived with her single mom, who she tormented more than I did my parents. Quite a feat.

She didn't go to Eisenhower, and she lived in Beverly, a predominantly Irish South Side neighborhood in the southwest corner of Chicago next to Blue Island. Kids from both neighborhoods lived only blocks apart, but were more likely to spit or throw beer bottles at each other than trade pleasantries when our paths crossed. Few friendships existed between the two groups, and while it wasn't exactly a Romeo and Juliet situation if people from the different neighborhoods dated, there was an unspoken rule against it that few ignored.

What did I care? There sure as hell was no way anybody would tell me who I could and could not mess around with. Same with Tracy.

She was a hell-raiser through and through. Fact that I came from Blue Island, had a reputation as a brawler, and was an outspoken racist made me irresistible. She even overlooked the fact I had been the captain of Eisenhower's football team, which was far too mainstream for a certified, self-proclaimed rebel bitch like her.

Not long after Tracy and I began dating, her mother had her picked up and committed to an alcoholism treatment facility for a week for being wasted and hurling a cordless phone at her head. Tracy gave her mother all sorts of stress. Not to mention stitches.

When Tracy got out of rehab, I made off with my parents' car and drove over to her house to make up for lost time. I'd gotten to be a decent driver over the last few months, despite still not being old enough to have my driver's license.

The first time I "borrowed" my mom's Ford Taurus at thirteen, I nearly wrecked it when I drove full speed the wrong direction on a major one-way thoroughfare. Little Tony, who'd taught me the basics of how to drive up and down High Street, quickly yanked the steering wheel to avoid an oncoming car that would surely have crushed us in a head-on collision. After that, the only careless driving I did were the occasional donuts in the St. Donatus parking lot.

Taking the car after my parents went to sleep had become easier after the first few times. I'd swiped the keys from my dad's coat and made copies at the hardware store. Buddy had even seen me pulling into the driveway very early one morning while he was watching Saturday morning cartoons, but only smiled at me from the window and never squealed. My parents never questioned me about taking the car. I'm sure they suspected it but were too afraid to confront me, knowing that I'd take the argument far beyond just taking the car and do something really reckless to piss them off even more. Especially my dad. I'd threatened him with physical violence the last time he tried to punish me over something trivial; since then, he hardly spoke to me anymore.

There me and Tracy were, sitting on her front steps making out the night she got out of alcohol rehab, not doing a damn thing to piss anybody off, when six drunken Irish Beverly Boys—a bunch of guys not unlike the High Street Boys, but violent and with more balls—settled themselves across the street in an open field. "The Prairie," as it was locally known, was the home base of the Beverly group. It was a large open stretch of flat land that belonged to the adjacent St. Walter parish. It was their St. Donatus parking lot. Beverly kids gathered in the field nightly. Surrounded by stone Irish bungalows, it was infamously known for the drinking and parties that took place more or less in plain sight of everyone's parents, which consisted primarily of Chicago's Irish cops and firefighters, union tradesmen, and their weary wives.

So this same night, right after Tracy gets home, these fools are out getting hammered in the Prairie. Acting tough and calling out to her.

"Hey, Tracy, got a phone handy? Your mom called, said she wants it back." Howls.

"Why didn't you pick up the telephone when I called, Tracy? Guess you couldn't hear it since it's all busted up."

Not exactly fighting words, but this was my girl, and I wasn't about to listen to this crap from a pack of drunken micks.

I rose. Tracy took my hand, trying to pull me back down. "There's six of them," she cautioned. "And they're trashed."

I pulled my hand away. "So what? They're getting on my goddamn nerves."

The Beverly Boys had a reputation for being tough, hot-tempered Irish lads, but that didn't deter me.

Fists clenched, I walked off into the black night, determined to shut them up. The second I reached them, without saying a word, I pulled my arm back and swung at the first human shadow I saw. They were on me faster than skate punks on speed. Coming at me from all sides. One tried to throw me to the ground, but the others were too close and broke my fall. I swung with a roundhouse punch, quickly calculating the odds were good that with this many people on me, my blow would land on someone. My fist collided with someone's face, and I was rewarded by the familiar warmth of fresh blood. I took a sharp blow to the gut. Pissed at the gall, I drove my head hard up into someone's chin, knocking him down. He grabbed at the darkness as he fell, taking someone with him. I took a barrage of quick, steady blows to my head, shoulders, kidney. One punch landed squarely in my abdomen and knocked the wind out of me. I doubled over.

"Had enough?" someone huffed.

Tracy was watching. I'd fight until I was unconscious. I sucked in my breath, sprung back up and landed a punch solidly on someone's jaw. Watched him reel back. I kept throwing rapid punches and connecting. My fists were throbbing. Seconds seemed like hours.

"Fellas. Give it up," someone from the Beverly group yelled. "He's fucking nuts. He ain't worth our time."

They retreated into the blackness. Tracy, beside me now, grabbed my arm and held her body against mine. I was out of breath.

"Let them go," she said. "They quit. Not you."

"Tell her you're sorry," I bellowed after them.

"Over your mother's dead dago body," someone echoed from the ether.

Fighting words. "Come back and say that to my face, you fucking Irish faggot," I hollered.

They disappeared across the Prairie. Drama over.

For the night.

But the gauntlet had been thrown and the call to war issued. They knew it. I knew it. Tracy knew it.

By morning, the news that six Beverly Boys jumped me and couldn't take me down had spread all over Blue Island and Beverly.

My Blue Island friends were out for blood. "Six of them attacked one of us? They're fucking dead," became a rallying cry.

The Beverly crew prepared for battle.

Never mind we were all white. Race didn't matter. This was about turf. Respect. And a statement that when someone messed with one of our own, there would be a war.

A war.

I'd started a fucking war.

Once again I slotted myself perfectly into the role of protagonist—or antagonist, depending on who you were talking to. Pitting my tribe against the other. The thrill of combat was supreme. Commanding a legion of soldiers, a group intent on achieving a singular goal, felt natural to me. It didn't matter if the opposition involved another sports team, a gang of wetbacks, or a rival neighborhood. There needed to be sides. And I needed to lead the one that won.

The power was extreme.

The most intense thing I'd ever felt.

10
WHITE PRIDE

THE SKINHEADS IN BLUE ISLAND WERE A GANG. Like the Latin Kings. Gangster Disciples. The Vice Lords.

We traveled in groups. Watched each other's backs. Instigated fights when reason to didn't exist. Protected our turf. One night a bunch of us chased Rooney, an obnoxiously ballsy kid from the Beverly group, down an alley and cornered him next to a pickup truck loaded full of construction debris. As he evaded my grasp and tried to run, I grabbed a brick from the truck bed and hurled it at him, striking him square in the base of the neck from about ten yards away. From that night on, the Beverly guys referred to me as "Brickolini."

The Blue Island–Beverly war didn't directly play into my plans to save the white race, but because of it, my prominence as a leader, as someone capable of controlling the activities of a large area and everyone in it, had become certain.

The Blue Island crew—the remaining CASH skinheads, Kubiak, and the dozen or so teenagers I'd recruited in the time since Clark had gone to prison—and the Beverly Boys waged an all-out war against each other for the rest of my sophomore year in high school. For some reason, it didn't occur to us that we had more in common than not.

Christian cutting a new recruit's hair, 1989

Like my skinhead pals, the Beverly kids were racist. Their Irish families had kept Beverly fairly white and proudly proclaimed it was one of the last white bastions in the city of Chicago. Their politically connected parents had made sure of that. Most of the Beverly crowd also had short-cropped hair and had begun sporting skinhead attire—combat boots and bomber jackets.

But it didn't matter. Both of our groups needed a conduit for our aggressive agendas. And, because of that, we found it easy to hate each other's guts.

Almost as much as we both hated niggers.

From my first day at Eisenhower, teachers kept their wary eyes on me, waiting for me to screw up. Like most other brainwashed lemmings who called themselves adults, the teachers were ignorant of the danger the white race was in and instead of seeing me as their hero trying to protect their sorry asses, they trembled when they saw me coming and castigated me for my beliefs and actions behind my back. They were afraid of me, of what I might do to disrupt the peace of the school or their classrooms. This gave me yet more power. Fear and power went hand in hand.

I cut more classes than I attended. Called the teachers out on their lies when I did decide to show up. Let them know they were as worthless as the nonsensical liberal propaganda they tried in vain to shove down our throats.

"Extremist" and "neo-Nazi" were whispered in the halls when I walked by.

"Mr. Picciolini, can you please turn your T-shirt inside out?" pleaded Señor Anderson, my third period Spanish teacher.

Without looking up or interrupting my etching of a giant swastika on the back of my Spanish workbook, I replied, "No."

"White pride," he whispered. "Those words are inappropriate and offensive to the other students. *Por favor!* Can you please turn your shirt inside out or I'll have to write you up again."

"A lot of good that'll do," I laughed. "What's wrong with my shirt stating that I'm proud to be white?"

"It's upsetting the other students. Will you please just follow the rules so I don't have to report you?"

Stupid me. I hadn't realized there were rules forbidding me to respect my heritage. "Tell you what, I'll make you a deal. If you want me to cover up my shirt, even though it's my right to wear it, then tell the spooks to turn their Malcolm X or 'It's a black thing, you wouldn't understand' shirts inside out. Better yet, start teaching all these beaners in this school to speak English instead of forcing us to learn their fucking foreign language."

"*Te lo ruego.* I beg you. Please cover the shirt or turn it inside out."

"Okay, okay. I'll put my jacket on," I conceded with a smirk.

"*Gracias.* Where was I, people? Repeat after me please. *Buenos días. ¿Cuánto cuestan los pantalones rojos?*"

I grinned as I put on my black bomber jacket and zipped it up over my shirt, making sure to smooth out the breast where I had sewn a vintage World War II swastika patch the night before.

¡Viva la revolución!

Only thing I was missing at this stage was a tattoo. Clothes alone weren't satisfying enough anymore. Tattoos showing my dedication to the cause became an obsession. Trouble was, I wasn't eighteen yet. My parents would never sign a permission slip, nor would I ask them to. I was a full-fledged adult in my mind, taking on issues that even most grown people weren't qualified to handle, and I sure as hell didn't need their consent for anything. But my mother would be pissed if she spotted a tattoo. She'd taken to snooping on me more and more. Going through my dresser drawers and dirty laundry when I was out. Freaking out over my T-shirts with racist overtones. She didn't have a clue what I was about, even though she was sure I was up to something dangerous.

I liked to keep her off my back, and a tattoo would make her quadruple her spying. I'd only be able to keep it hidden for so long. But I'd show Buddy. He'd like it and think it was cool and beg me to draw one on him too.

I'd heard from several punk kids about Bob Oslon's Fine Line Tattoos on the North Side of the city. Age meant nothing to him, money everything.

"Tell him you're eighteen, and he probably won't ask any questions," Kubiak told me. I took his advice and went to Oslon's tattoo parlor—a small hole-in-the-wall on the North Side of Chicago with a buzzing neon sign and a flaking, hand-painted front window.

Bob Oslon was a bona fide dick-sucking fag, both ears pierced with heavy metal hoops, and dressed head to toe in full Village People biker leather. Clark would have bashed this queer. Didn't bother me much. It was my chance to get inked.

"What'll it be, young man?" he lisped, pulling out a ragged-edged binder full of Polaroids of work he'd done, expecting me to go through it to pick a tattoo I wanted.

I pushed his portfolio aside. "Iron Cross."

"What?"

"The tattoo. I want a German Iron Cross with an eagle holding a swastika on my arm."

His dark, fruity eyes took me in. I stared him down. "Whatever. But I'm not doing the swastika," he demurred, lowering his lashes.

I didn't like this guy. Smug fag bastard thought eye-fucking me was cool or something. But I wanted the tattoo.

"Fine." I didn't want to push my luck and have him ask for my ID or turn me away. I could always add the swastika later with a needle and some India ink.

He held out his hand. "Cash first. Sixty bucks."

I reached into my coat and dropped a wadded-up paper sack filled with quarters into the pigment-stained palm of his hand.

"Jesus, kid, fucking *quarters*? Really?" he whined. "We'll be here all goddamn night."

After a few failed attempts, I'd figured out how to regularly steal change from the coin-operated washer and dryer in my parents' apartment building. I used the proceeds mostly to buy cigarettes and beer, but I'd scored big time and had over seventy-five dollars with me. Enough for the tattoo and a forty of Miller High Life. "Fine. I'll count them out," I said. "Let's go."

Fuck, did the tattoo hurt. Took everything to hide the pain and not wince while he dug the needle extra deep into my left bicep. Though I'd never admit it to him or anyone else.

As I walked out of the tattoo parlor bandaged and bloody, I knew my body was a fresh canvas begging for more ink.

They would show who I was. Who I was proud to be.

An Italian.

A gladiator.

An American.

A skinhead.

And soon, I'd have more tattoos showing my dedication to the white race and serving as a warning to all those who sought to destroy it.

One Saturday night, in our general fuck-the-world-and-everybody-in-it frame of mind, my skinhead friends and I headed over to initiate one of our frequent sneak attacks on the Beverly Boys. Didn't need a reason. That they existed on the other side of whatever imaginary line we'd created was all the provocation we needed. We busted into the garage housing their little get-together, looking to kick ass, but one of their guys held out a beer instead. He was half-loaded already, standing in the shadow of a Confederate flag dangling from the ceiling.

"What the fuck, Brickolini," he said. "It's been a year already. Ain't you sick of fighting us yet? Have a beer and relax."

Stunned silence from both camps.

People looked at me for direction.

I shrugged.

What the hell? The battle was over.

I reached for the beer and cracked it open. "By the way, that's not my name. You can call me Chris."

Instantly, we forgot all about being enemies, and for the next several years there was an unprecedented bond between the skins in Blue Island and the racist Beverly crew. My sphere of influence doubled overnight. The war had produced a stronger and larger army.

I'd changed in the few years since I'd found my home with the High Street Boys, and while those years were mostly carefree and innocent, the time with the Beverly Boys was marked by drunken parties and constant fighting. We got together every night at the nearby Mount Hope Cemetery, drinking cheap beer the Beverly crew had stolen from their alcoholic Irish fathers. With booze in hand, we climbed through a hole in the fence next to the train tracks that ran through Beverly and Blue Island to get into the graveyard. We settled in near the mausoleums and sat back to get blitzed.

We talked racist shit and they ate it up. I handed out cassette copies of Skrewdriver records and passed along pointers on recruiting kids to join the movement. An easy thing to accomplish. It didn't even matter if they wanted to shave their heads and wear boots—though they usually did; all that mattered was if they were willing to fight alongside with us.

It took little skill to spot a teenager with a shitty home life. Somebody without many friends. Picked on. Confused. Feeling lonely. Angry. Broke. A crisis of identity. Looking like he—or she—had never had any luck to be down on. Strike up a conversation; find out what they were feeling bad about. Move in. "Man, I know exactly how that is. If your dad hadn't lost his job, it wouldn't be like that. But the minorities get all the jobs. They catch all the breaks. Move into our neighborhoods and start getting handouts. Our parents go to work every day to put food on the table while the lazy blacks and Mexicans are cashing welfare checks in their sleep."

Before you knew it, there'd be a half dozen newly-shaved heads coming to our weekly meetings and rallies, looking for something to belong to. Some way to change the world. To make a difference. We gave them a reason to belong—to *need* to be there. We made their shitty lives have purpose. They were just like me two years earlier when I'd been vying for Clark and Carmine's attention. Now these lonely kids were trying to catch *my* eye. The sudden control was intoxicating.

Soon enough, there were kids falling all over themselves helping me make copies of literature at the post office, and more cassette tapes to hand out, spreading the white power gospel. Recruiting new blood. Putting flyers under windshield wiper blades in parking lots. Putting patches on their bomber jackets and getting tattoos. More loyal soldiers joining the war against the non-white enemy. More power.

I was able to host a recruitment rally in a church once because I'd honed in on Tim Harrison, a fresh-cut skinhead wannabe whose Lutheran minister father had abused him as a child. He had a deep-seated hatred for his dad, so I convinced him to steal the keys and let us hold the meeting there without his father's knowledge.

Almost twenty new kids attended that night. I dressed like a Nazi commander in a light brown military button-up shirt I purchased at a thrift store for a dollar, and attached a homemade swastika armband. Flanked by Nazi battle flags that I'd hung on either side of the altar, I told those who came that my vision was to see filthy niggers hanging from every light pole up and down Western Avenue from Blue Island to Beverly. My words echoed in the vastness of the hall.

The more seasoned skins like Kubiak seated in the church gallery stood up and threw out their arms in glorious salute; the newcomers haphazardly joined trying to fit in, not really knowing what to do. Kubiak pushed aside the Bibles stacked at the ends of the pews to make room for more recruits. Framed renderings of Jesus Christ and the Virgin Mary hung on the chapel walls as silent witnesses to my venomous sermon. Just like the sheepish Christians had believed that Christ would lead them to paradise, I made it clear to those attending that I would lead them, marching in lockstep, to slaughter the sheep and anyone else who was trying to pull the wool over their eyes.

From the pulpit I spat words of truth that hung in the air like the pungent, waxy scent of the altar's candles. "The revolution is coming and without forcing change now, future generations of white kids will not live in a free society. The white power movement is about standing up to those who want to take our freedom away from us, before it's too late.

"Look at what's happening in your schools. Black kids are favored. They can wear racist Malcolm X T-shirts and celebrate race-baiting criminals like Martin Luther King. Teachers encourage them to embrace their black heritage and openly teach about black pride.

"What about white pride? What's wrong with that? But speak up and you're told to shut up. Wear a proud symbol of the white race and you're branded a hatemonger. Ask me. I'm living proof of that.

"I'm telling you that we can change that. We *must* change it or face extinction as a proud people. I will not stand to see our great white heritage wiped out and replaced by scum who contribute nothing to our world. There is a simple solution. A final solution. We must not let them win. We must not let them beat us into submission. We must secure the existence of our people and a future for white children!"

The crowd rose to their feet and cheered. Proper Heil Hitler salutes pierced the air.

I had them. Their hearts were mine.

Soon after the meeting, someone who'd attended—a rat, probably planted by the cops—confessed to our high school principal and told him about the gathering and what I'd said. The media caught wind of the story and published a newspaper interview with the principal and staff and students all playing down the truth of my message. But it had validity or else it never would have taken up two full pages. Cops and teachers and the principal all commented on what I had to say and talked about how troubled I must be to say it. I laughed.

The church got a prominent mention in the article and poor abusive minister daddy had to resign.

The white power skinhead ideology—of which I was an undisputed noteworthy influencer—was spreading like wildfire. By now, I'd made the call to retire the CASH moniker and agreed to adopt the Hammerskin brand, the name established by the Dallas skinhead crew at that cramped meeting in the Naperville apartment a few years earlier. We had expanded our group significantly and falling under the flag of a growing international network of skinhead cells made sense. But only the name had changed. I had no intention of answering to anyone else.

I hit the streets. No doubt anymore that Blue Island's demographics were beginning to darken. Signs of it were everywhere. Niggers sitting on their stoops. Beaners painting their tags on stores, down alleyways. The pungent smell of pot wafting through the familiar aromas of garlic and sausage, spicy tomato sauce and peppers. It wasn't right.

Restless, Kubiak and I were ever alert for a chance to clamp down and kick some ass. And now the Beverly kids and a dozen new recruits were right there beside us to help, though they had their hands full cleaning up their own neighborhood.

We beat the shit out of any trespassing outsiders whenever we got the chance. One of the nastiest fights began in a McDonald's restaurant on Western Avenue and 119th Street—the road that separated Blue Island from Beverly and Chicago city limits. A few Beverly kids and I had stopped in for something to eat late one night after drinking in the cemetery, and we ran into four belligerent black teenagers standing in line.

"Well, if it ain't a bunch of fucking monkeys. You guys escape from the zoo?" Me and my friends loudly expressed that we were the only group with a right to be there. We circled the muds, staring them down. They quickly realized they were outnumbered and scurried out.

With a roar, we charged out of the restaurant after the four black teens. Fifty yards into the chase, one of them turned mid-sprint, pointed a pistol, and opened fire on us.

Three rapid shots whizzed past our heads as the smell of spent gunpowder trails filled our nostrils. Then the pistol jammed.

We didn't break stride. Rather than scaring us off, the gunshots incited us. These worthless pieces of shit were trying to kill us in our own neighborhood?

The one who'd taken the shots at us dropped the gun. Mistake. Moving through the darkness faster than bullets, we caught up with him, threw him to the ground. Kicked him in the ribs. The back. The head. Steel toes cutting through his black skin, damaging bone. Relentless. No longer able to defend himself, the jolts to his body from our heavy boots sent spasms through the motionless bag of broken bones.

The blood that stained the pavement served as a testament to our cause. We had honored the fourteen words.

Night surrounded us, and the white teeth that were once the only visible signs from this near-lifeless body were now stained crimson with blood. These gangbangers from the South Side of Chicago may have been tough, raised by hardened parents who'd lived through the civil rights volatility of the '60s, but we were fearless. We had purpose. They may have had guns and street cred, but a greater mission fueled us. Destined to save the world by eradicating the rotting cancer they represented in our society.

As I stood over the unconscious and brutalized body, his frightened, swollen eyes showed a sliver of life and connected with mine. I realized then that he couldn't have been much older than twelve or thirteen. A child. I thought of my six-year-old brother. The bloated, bloodshot eyes that gazed up at me from the ground pleaded for his life and penetrated my soul. They could just as easily have been Buddy's. And for a brief moment I saw my sweet brother lying there curled up in a pool of his own blood. A disquieting shiver cut through me like a dull blade and I felt a sudden stabbing feeling of regret in my chest.

Sirens cut through the night and broke my daze. Wasn't until the cops were around the corner that the rest of the guys stopped kicking. We got away, but the event left me feeling somber and dejected.

The remaining months of 1989 were full of skinhead and white nationalist rallies in Indiana, Wisconsin, and Michigan. No longer a quiet observer, I spoke my mind. "Fourteen words," I'd shout from the front of the room as I greeted everyone with a stiff-armed salute. I was unafraid to voice the rhetoric I knew by heart, high on the respect I got, pumped up by knowing all eyes in the room were on me. I may not have been the oldest, being just sixteen, but I was often the most respected. Tough. Dedicated. Charismatic. And smart. Way smarter than most of the others. Many were there simply for the party following the speeches. Or for the music that was central to any rally worth going to. The skinhead girls. Or the cheap beer that flowed like Niagara Falls.

Life was a constant redline. The faster I went, the further in my rear view mirror lay comfort. From time to time, I may have felt guilty for my actions and pondered if all the white supremacist stuff I was feeding these kids was right. Logical. It didn't always go down so easily for me—the anxiety from the constant violence that existed twenty-four hours a day, the hateful ideology I programmed myself with to override the old-world values I'd been raised on and the people who raised me, the stress of leading a group and growing it against all odds. Those feelings all took their toll and created a sense of uncertainty inside of me, but I'd resolved to bury those doubts deep down where they couldn't be misinterpreted as any signs of weakness. So deep it'd take surgery to uncover them.

Although there were those few who'd come before me, I inherited the legacy and single-handedly grew the numbers and put my group at the forefront. With Clark still in prison and the other original CASH founders entirely out of the picture, I was where I'd hungered to be. In charge and in a position of respect and authority. Most of my skinhead predecessors may have gone to jail, run away from the cops' scrutiny, or defected for whatever reasons they had, but I was still here building a monument on top of the foundation they'd laid through blood and sweat. I was somebody now. I belonged. Was valued. Honored. And feared. But the voice in my head begging for reason and restraint kept getting louder. I chose to kill it before it destroyed my focus.

One night I caught my mother going through my things in my basement apartment.

"What the hell?" I yelled, grabbing the shirt she had in her hand. "This is my room. My stuff. You have no right to be in here."

She didn't correct me. Instead she trembled, looking helplessly at the swastika T-shirt I'd snatched back from her. "Why, Christian?" she cried. "We didn't raise you to be this. This Nazi nonsense. This Hitler. All the killing. He was a very bad man. Why don't you pick an Italian for a hero? Even someone like Al Capone would be better."

Her ignorance astounded me.

"Stay out of here," I ordered.

She backed out, momentarily cowering. To reassert her authority, she brought my brother into it, knowing Buddy was the only family member I felt tenderness for. "Alex misses his big brother. Maybe you can stay home more and play with Buddy."

Once she was beyond the threshold, I slammed the door in her face and leaned my back up against it. Tired, I slumped over and rested my head in my hands. The rapid knocks coming from the other side of the door infuriated me and I threw it open, shouting, "Leave me the fuck alone and get the hell out of here!"

It was little Buddy. He began to cry and backed away from me. I'd frightened him.

"No, no! I'm sorry, Buddy. I thought it was—never mind—I didn't mean that." I reached out to comfort him, but he ran away bawling.

Seeing him cry like that as a result of my words pained me deeply.

When we lived in Oak Forest and Buddy was still just a curious little boy, he'd follow me around everywhere, and cry when I'd shut the door to my room to get some peace and quiet. It pulled at my heartstrings to hear him so anguished by my actions. Now I'd hurt him with my words and it crushed me. Why couldn't my goddamn family support me? They'd never made an effort to understand what it was that I believed or taken me seriously enough to listen to what I had to say. It was their fault that this happened. Couldn't they understand that all I wanted was to save them? To save Buddy? They made me so goddamn furious.

What the fuck? I was ten years older than Buddy and had responsibilities. What was I supposed to do? Get down in the dirt and push toy cars and trucks around with him? I sure as hell wasn't going to take him with me. I never knew when a fight would break out. I'd never risk putting him in harm's way. Should I take him to a rally? No way in hell. I'd keep him as far away from the drinking and violence as I possibly could. No, for now, Buddy would have to be satisfied with me letting him come down to the basement once in a while. But I remembered what it was like to be a lonely kid. I promised myself I'd make an extra effort for his sake. Get some candy cigarettes for him and we could sit on my bed and draw together or watch cartoons for a while. He'd like that. Didn't take much to make him happy. I'd see if I could find some time. Tomorrow. Or the next day.

11

ODIN'S COURT

I STARTED MY JUNIOR YEAR back at Eisenhower in Blue Island. Known throughout the school as a hardcore racist and bruiser not to be messed with, I was left alone by most people. Teachers knew I was intelligent. When I actually went to class, I'd ace their stupid honors tests despite my lack of interest. But they didn't want me in their classrooms anymore. The football coaches who'd once clamored for me cut their losses and avoided me. I was a star athlete with fire in my eyes; I could have gone far, but my liability was a dragging anchor they could no longer tow. So, they stayed out of my way.

I lasted at Eisenhower until November of my junior year. I'd missed twenty-four school days in the first three months of school, which was almost half of my total class time. Even when I was there, I cut out during lunch period to mess around with whatever girl I was seeing at the time, or check the post office box and answer some of the dozens of pieces of correspondence I received every week. The principal called my parents and told them he couldn't let me continue there because of my truancy, and they pulled yet another bullshit move against my will and enrolled me in Brother Rice High School. Another private Catholic school in the city. I couldn't believe it.

Christian and crew, 1990

I was there for all of a week before trouble began. On my way out after classes ended one day, not bothering anybody, the dean stopped me in the hallway. Out of the hundreds of other kids he could have singled out, he chose me.

Where were my books, the self-righteous bastard wanted to know.

"What books?" I smirked.

Homework, it seems.

"How do you expect to make it in life, young man, if you just close your eyes and travel the path of least resistance? The world won't do you any favors if you aren't willing to work hard."

There was truth in that. I certainly had bigger aspirations than being some glorified, middle-aged hall monitor like this dickhead. I politely smiled and explained I didn't have any homework.

"In our school, Mr. Picciolini, we have a rule stating you must bring at least one book home every night to study."

I'd never heard of such a ridiculous fucking rule and said so.

"Ignorance of the law is no excuse to break it. We'll see you in detention tomorrow after school. Bring your Bible."

"Yeah, well, I'll have to check my calendar and see if I can fit it in." I laughed and walked away. No chance I'd get reprimanded for a rule I hadn't even known about.

"Don't forget your VIP ticket," he said, handing me the detention slip.

"Are you kidding me? Do you have any idea what I do to protect your sorry ass?" I snapped. "Path of least resistance? Work hard? You don't have a goddamn clue, do you?" I promptly crumpled the yellow slip and threw it in the nearest waste bin with no intention of accepting his judgment or his sentence.

So when I didn't show up I got another detention for not going to detention.

Right. I didn't go to that either. And so on.

For missing three detentions, I was given a half-day Saturday detention, a JUG—*Justice Under God.* Fuck this school and fuck God.

Miss two Saturdays and it's a suspension.

So I was suspended.

At that point I stopped going to school at all, except when I was recruiting other students.

Life outside of the classroom was far more interesting. Parties, fights, intimidation. Survival pack assembly. Preparing for the inevitable overthrow of the U.S. government and annihilation of the mud races. It was routine by now. Necessary. Incessant re-reads of *The Turner Diaries* had taught me that.

Today it finally began! After all these years of talking—and nothing but talking—we have finally taken our first action. We are at war with the System, and it is no longer a war of words.

Goddamn right.

One night one of the Beverly guys and I were in a local record shop trying to convince the purchasing manager to carry Skrewdriver records, when we spotted a couple of skinhead-looking kids we'd never seen before, which made it a safe bet they were Antis. One was wearing an oxblood-colored bomber jacket. "That's a cool bomber," I said to my friend. "It'd look good on me. That Anti has no right to wear it."

We left the store and got into the beater car we'd come in, so rusted that both bumpers had fallen off long ago, and pulled up beside the entrance waiting for the two Antis to emerge. When they were close to our car and I was sure no one was watching, I swung the door open and confronted the kid with the jacket, thrusting my broken .25 semi-auto into his ribs.

"Give me the jacket, motherfucker." I directed his attention to the gun to emphasize my point.

"Don't give him shit!" his wiseass partner said, not noticing the weapon that was shoved in his friend's gut. He walked around to the back of the car to look for the license plate, then dashed to the front of the car, his cocky expression turning pale when he saw there wasn't one in either spot and I was holding a pistol.

I raised the gun and pressed it under the kid's chin. "Your jacket. Now!"

He tore it off, held it out in his trembling hands.

"Do you know who I am?" He nodded his head to indicate he did. "Good. Then you also know that if you say anything to the cops, I'll find you and fucking kill you."

I backed into the car and we tore out of the parking lot.

"Jesus Christ," the Beverly kid said, cringing. "That's armed fucking robbery. And that kid knows who you are!"

"He won't say shit." I checked the side mirror for a sign of the cops. "Let's get off the main streets."

We wove in and out of side roads all the way home. Halfway across town, I took my jacket off at a stoplight and tried the new one on. Too damn small. Son of a bitch!

It struck us as a riot and we laughed so hard we had trouble driving straight the rest of the way home.

Later I gave the jacket to a new girl who'd been hanging around our parties. She was impressed that it had been ripped off at gunpoint. Good enough for a blowjob.

In January of 1990, the end of the first semester of my junior year, I got called into the dean's office for my ongoing refusal to serve my mounting detentions, and with all the authority vested in him by his Lord and Savior Jesus Christ and all the money my hardworking parents paid his godforsaken school, I was expelled from Brother Rice.

I was simultaneously pissed and overjoyed.

"Thank you very much," I said in my most condescending voice. "I'll be going home now."

"Oh no you won't, young man," this dusty old asshole told me. "You have to complete the full day to finish out the semester or you'll lose the credits you've accrued."

"Fine, if that's the way you want it," I said with a crooked smile.

I skipped all my classes the rest of the afternoon. Spent every remaining period hanging out in the library reading World War II history books, or in the lunchroom passing the time with my friends.

During the last lunch period of the day, I chain-smoked cigarettes at a long table among schoolmates. The typical cafeteria clinking and clanking sounds turned to whispers, all eyes focused on me. I rose from my seat only to strut around triumphantly, blowing mouthfuls of smoke at teachers as they walked by me in the dining hall. The ultimate game of chicken and I'd be damned if I'd be the first to flinch.

For thirty tense minutes, everyone gawked at me but nobody did a thing as I marched around victoriously with a lit cigarette dangling from my lips. Not a word. What could they do, expel me twice in one afternoon?

The next day, my parents crawled back to Eisenhower and begged them to let me in so I could stay on track to graduate. Reluctantly and with stipulations, the school agreed, my mother and father no doubt full of promises that this time would be different. Which of course it wouldn't be.

Indifferent to the whole situation, I somehow managed to complete the rest of my junior year at Eisenhower without significant incident, mainly because I was under constant surveillance by an off-duty police sergeant the principal hired specifically to monitor me during school hours. I couldn't make a move without that cop on my tail.

My parents were totally lost. Not even remotely socially involved with my life at this point. I depended on them for basic needs like food and shelter, but it never escalated past that. They'd been so busy trying to manage their business and taking on second and third jobs to support their impersonation of a middle-class life, they'd forgotten that anything outside of that pursuit existed.

When she was home, my mother continued hassling me about my friends and activities, meddling, giving me grief. My dad couldn't get it through his head I was long beyond his control. Buddy had forgiven me for yelling at him, but was becoming increasingly distant and quiet. My parents never stopped me from doing anything because they knew they damn well couldn't, but it was annoying to have them around at all. Like flies dive-bombing you, buzzing in your ear. You know the little pests can't do you any harm and you can kill them with a single swat, but they make life a bitch by hanging around, not standing still long enough for you to squash them.

Deep down I knew they cared about me. I cared about them, too. I wouldn't be risking my life every day trying to protect them and what they'd worked so hard for if I didn't. But on the surface, my resentment was bitter. While I'd finally come to terms with the reasons why they were absent during my early youth, the thick skin I developed while trying to heal from it had inadvertently hardened my feelings towards them.

They knew I was into something bad and tried to steer me down a different road any chance they could. It didn't work.

I was on fire the summer between my junior and senior year. With Kubiak as my right hand partner-in-crime and most of the Blue Island

and Beverly kids on my side, there was nothing I felt I couldn't do. All the popularity and acceptance I'd ever longed for when I was invisible as a child was now mine.

Everybody knew my name, wanted to hang out with me, or was scared shitless of me. I needed to do no more than suggest something and it happened.

Antis bugged me, so we locked horns with them every time we got a chance. Never needing provocation. That they were on the planet was reason enough to crush their bleeding hearts.

Things heated up to the point that a huge brawl with the Antis was all anyone talked about anymore. We all knew it was coming. A date finally emerged without any specific planning. Just one of those things. One person told someone to "go fuck yourself." Another said something else in return. Tempers flared. Somebody challenged somebody and a date was set.

The Beverly Boys heard what was going on. Pledged their support. To my surprise, so did every other white clique, including most of the jocks, metal heads, and stoners from Blue Island—people who knew me and what I was about, but whose names I could never remember. Word about the rumble spread fast and the Prairie was chosen as the battlefield.

Night of the fight, our group showed up first, with an endless row of cars already lined up when another twenty or so cars full of supporters pulled up. Kids came from everywhere, including neighboring towns, to back us up.

Then came the Antis. Dozens of them.

Altogether there were more than a hundred kids in the Prairie that night ready to brawl.

The Antis initiated the action and jumped out from behind buildings, pumped, thinking they were going to ambush us. But they didn't take more than a few steps before they realized just how many people had come out to support us. Our cause. Our beliefs.

The Antis backpedaled slowly, and then as they saw us moving in, broke into a retreating sprint.

We tore off after them, shouting obscenities, swinging sawn mop handles, padlocks, chains wrapped around waving knuckles, baseball bats cutting through the air.

But there weren't as many of them as there were of us, so they had an advantage in terms of mobility. The sheer number of us slowed us down as we got in each other's way, shoving to be the first to draw Anti blood.

They outran us.

A few broke away from their group and some of ours pursued them. To no avail.

Disheartened that our moment to destroy the enemy had come and gone without a single punch being thrown, we retreated back to the Prairie to celebrate and get drunk. While we proclaimed victory and laughed about their gutless ways, a few Antis snuck back to the Prairie and attacked our cars, throwing bricks, kicking in fenders, trying to smash headlights and windshields with their boots, ripping off car antennae, slashing tires, any meaningless thing that would give them bragging rights.

But we were on our feet when we heard the shattering glass and gave chase quickly.

Again, they outran us.

We settled in with our beer, proclaiming ourselves the true victors. Knowing full well none of us could claim any such thing in this bullshit non-event. "They're nothing more than nigger-loving pansies," a cute blonde cheerleader said.

"Damn right," we agreed, popping open more cans of beer and toasting our victory.

"Heil Hitler," another stranger shouted.

"Fucking A," I agreed. "Heil Hitler." Things would have gone better if blood had been shed, of that I had no doubt. But this sign of unity from people that I didn't even know was huge. And the sheer adrenaline from the evening was an enormous power boost to my ego.

All types of white youth—jocks, stoners, metal heads, book worms, cheerleaders, preps, you name it—began to look up to me, emulate me. Girls wanted to fuck me and more often than not I let them.

The recruitment pool was overflowing and we spent the rest of the summer drinking and listening to blaring white power music with fresh faces, going to rallies and battling a brand new wave of anti-racist traitors called SHARPs—Skinheads Against Racial Prejudice. Yeah, right. More like *Scum Hanged After Racists Prevail.*

For a moment, I felt like the almighty Norse god Odin alongside my loyal legions of bloodthirsty Viking warriors and Valkyries in the festive halls of Valhalla. Feasting and fighting.

One big party.

Suffice it to say it was another great summer. Violence and passion to save my race driving my every move. Amp up the fights and rallies and recruiting by about three hundred percent and that's what this particular summer was like.

We had momentum working in our favor. However, the outside perception was that our group was much bigger than we actually were. While there were always new people hanging around, the reality was that the turnover was high and most of them never stuck around very long. Kids would come around for a few weeks, shave their heads, buy some Docs, party with us, then get freaked out by our intensity or get accosted by a rival gang and fade away. The Antis and cops thought we had all these sleeper skinheads in training around Chicago. In truth, we never had more than a few dozen or so at any given time. Perception became the reality. And that made us stronger. Unstoppable.

I ruled. You fucking bet I did.

BLUE ISLAND, ILLINOIS
POLICE DEPT.
ILO161000

17799 · 12-16-90

, Chris M

12

WHITE AMERICAN YOUTH

In LATE 1990, when September and my senior year rolled around, I was impatient to start high school so I could get it over with once and for all. The last year I'd be subjected to know-nothing teachers and under the thumb of a family who refused to support my vital mission.

By this time, though, my family was rarely a thought in my head. I avoided my parents at all costs. At seven, Buddy was becoming more independent and old enough to have his own friends to play with and I hardly saw him anymore. Days and weeks would pass without speaking to any of them or even seeing them. Nonno and Nonna were getting up in age and I only found time to see them on holidays, despite them living across the street.

Freedom. I was just about to turn seventeen and I was loving it.

The new Eisenhower principal warned me shortly before classes started that even a small disruption would get me kicked out permanently, so I did try toning down my rhetoric during school at first for the sake of graduating. While I had my priorities locked in with the movement, I was also ambitious. I wanted to succeed overall and if it would help, I could keep my temper under control during my last year of school. So I dropped any remaining honors classes I'd managed to hang on to and did the least amount of work required to pass. I pushed the limits of truancy, avoiding the place altogether as much as I could.

But despite my effort to skate through my last year of high school, there was no realistic chance I would fit in. It was way too late for that. I had serious goals that I wanted to achieve and I'd outgrown school and everyone in it. Not only did I not belong there, but nobody wanted me around. Administrators feared I'd cause a race riot in an already volatile multiracial environment. Teachers distrusted me. They worried I'd disrupt their classes and make it hard for other students to learn. Not to mention making the teachers themselves look stupid when I didn't hesitate to challenge them on their bullshit. They were trying to cram their skewed, ZOG version of history down our throats and I wasn't going to sit back and let it happen.

And to make it all worse, it was obvious to me they favored blacks over whites, giving them better grades for less work, letting them get away with shit the white kids never got away with like swearing in class and showing up late after the bell. They never confronted black students for fear they'd snap back, which they often did, or bothered the Mexican students because the language barrier was too great. And to top it off, the new Eisenhower principal—a black woman I'd as soon spit on as talk to—thought she could keep me and my crew in check.

It all came to a head when a black student and I got into a fierce verbal argument in art class when he refused to move away from the door as I tried to enter the classroom. Of course, the queer art teacher assumed it was my fault and sent *me* to the office to be reprimanded, but not the other kid. I sat there waiting outside the principal's door, stewing for a few minutes, before coming to my senses.

That lowlife nigger instigator wasn't going to stay in class while I got expelled for something he'd started, which would mean I definitely would not graduate. There were no schools left for me to transfer to and even I didn't want to be a dropout like the losers I saw hanging out in front of the Blue Island liquor stores and at the St. Anthony's flophouse in the middle of the day.

Incensed, I pushed back my chair outside the office, knocking it to the floor with a loud bang. If this was going to be my last stand, I might as well go out with guns blazing. I tore up two flights of stairs and threw open the heavy door to the art room with a wall-shaking rattle. As every wide-eyed, startled face in the room turned to make sense of the sudden commotion, I flew across the classroom so fast my Docs hardly hit the floor before I tackled the arrogant fucker who was perched triumphantly on his tall art stool.

"I write the rules here, you fucking nigger," I roared, dragging him to the ground by his neck and slamming my fist into his terrified black face. "Worthless piece of welfare shit. Your day just got real shitty." I punctuated my words with vicious blasts to his cheekbone and eye socket.

Shrieking, out of their minds, the other students in the class scattered toward the walls. Drafting tables flew into bystander bodies, knocking some girls to the floor, as I held my target down and began choking him with the bottom rung of the stool he'd been sitting on seconds earlier.

In a flash, the wrestling coach and the head security guard, who'd seen me barge in as they were meeting just steps away down the hall, pounced on me to try and pull me off. I fought back against them relentlessly while my adversary lay curled in a fetal heap beneath me. A row of art supply shelves and a dozen jars full of acrylic paint came crashing down around us creating a furious Jackson Pollack-esque array of rainbow colors.

"Get the hell off me," I grunted as the two large black men struggled to lift me to my feet. While I attempted to evade their grasp, I punctuated each profanity coming from mouth with stomps to this kid's throat. Because I was younger and accustomed to grappling, they couldn't pull me away until I decided I'd caused enough damage.

When I'd had enough, they yanked me to my feet and half-shoved, half-dragged me out of the classroom and down the hall back to the principal's office. The still-hefty former wrestling champ held me partially immobilized in a full nelson headlock while the security guard kept my body from swinging. As I was hauled away kicking and screaming through the hallway and down two flights of stairs by these two sizable men, classroom doors swung open like falling dominoes. Teachers craned their necks out into the corridor, curious to make sense of the raucous turmoil that my steel-toed boots caused as they dented lockers along the way.

After they got me back to the office and waited for me to cool off, guess whose side the black principal was on?

"I understand you made some dreadful remarks," she said, trying hard to hold in her contempt for me. I could tell because her hands shook and her voice cracked and pitched higher as she tried to keep calm. "Want to tell me why you would say such unconscionable things, Mr. Picciolini?"

I erupted with a barrage of hate so venomous that if the spit that formed from my words had landed on an open wound on her body, she would have been poisoned on the spot. "I don't have to tell you shit. Fuck you, you filthy nigger bitch," I seethed, conveniently disregarding that this particular "filthy nigger bitch" had "Dr." and "Ph.D." attached to the front and back end of her name. "You can take your bleeding-heart, liberal bullshit and stick it up your fat black cunt." I inched toward her with each toxic stab of my tongue. "I run this godforsaken school whether I'm in it or not. So, fuck you! Expel me!"

The black security guard who'd dragged me into her office leapt to wedge himself between us. He tore his glasses off his gorilla face and slammed them down on the principal's desk so hard that he mangled the frame and sent one of the shattered lens fragments flying toward the ceiling. Ready to take me on. He got so close to my face that I could smell the mustard from his lunch on his breath become more acrid with every word he used.

"Who you calling nigger, son?" he barked, grabbing me by the shirt and slamming me back against the wall, knocking me on my ass. "Know who the real nigger is? You!" Angry projectiles of saliva shot out with every other word. "I stood up against ignorant people like you and beat down your racist kind in the '60s on the streets of Chicago and, with God as my witness, I'll do the same now."

I was on my feet before he finished his sentence. But as I rose up he threw me back down and immobilized me by pressing his strong body against mine, his arms locked around my elbows, keeping me pinned between the wall and a tall metal file cabinet in the corner of the room.

The frightened principal picked up the phone and dialed 911. Within minutes, a police siren was wailing outside the building. "We'll see who gets arrested," I spit. "You can't abuse a student like this. Your black asses are all going to jail and getting fired. You'll be sorry!"

But when the two Blue Island police officers rushed into the room, they didn't care that a black adult was assaulting a white teenager. These brainwashed white cops were traitors to their race, puppets of the corrupt ZOG government that controlled our lives, believing the rent-a-cop security guard over me. The cops threw me down to the ground and pressed their knees into the small of my back and neck while they wrenched my arms behind me and handcuffed my wrists together. After they jerked me to my feet, the two of them marched me down the hallway toward the main entrance of the school where their flashing squad car was parked.

Almost by divine design, the bell signaling the end of class rang and students began pouring into the hallway at the same exact moment we exited the office. Their innocent chatter stopped as they saw the cops leading me out. The dense crowd parted to clear a path and I suddenly felt like a young Bobby De Niro in the grand finale scene of a Martin Scorsese gangster flick as the needle dropped into the opening grooves of a Rolling Stones tune. Everything moved in slow motion and friendly hands reached out to pat my back, some outstretched in Nazi salute to encourage me. Others threw poisonous stares of contempt at the condemned man being led to the gallows. Smiles of admiration and sneers of disdain greeted me as I swiveled my head, breathing it all in. Smiling. Nobody would forget this day. This victorious march of fate. I'd shown everyone how little authority meant and how nothing short of handcuffs could hold me back.

Though the school or the kid I pummeled never pressed criminal charges, there weren't many options left when it came to my education. So I didn't go to school for almost a month while my parents scrambled from school board director to administrator to see what possibilities remained, if any. Absolutely nobody wanted me, even though I only had six months left to graduation.

While the other kids my age were in school being brainwashed, I worked on strengthening my empire. I needed more soldiers. I continued to get the word out through my post office box. I was hungry to expand, recruiting harder and more effectively than Clark ever had. This was my time.

In November I got arrested again. Some Anti pussy named Hector Diaz went crying to the cops and pressed charges against me, saying I'd beat him up. Lies. Not that I wouldn't, but I hadn't. No doubt I would have if the opportunity had presented itself, though. Instead, this scrawny Puerto Rican scumbag gutter punk had fabricated a story about me hurting him to make sure I couldn't.

This hardly helped my parents with their efforts to get me back into school.

I had to appear in court for my arraignment shortly after my arrest. Made sure I dressed real nice. Wore a long-sleeve shirt covering up my tattoos, treated the judge with the utmost feigned respect. He set bond. The trial was a ways off, but I knew to stay away from Diaz.

The false battery charges against me only made me more driven than ever. I'd been in court now. Put in handcuffs multiple times. Like the older guys. Couldn't get more legit than this. I needed to branch out. I pondered different ways, and had a flash of inspiration when listening to Skrewdriver one day.

Son of a bitch! Why hadn't I thought about music earlier? Music was the seed, growth hormone, and harvest of the skinhead movement all in one.

Nothing like a driving bass, crunching guitars, and calls for white revolution shouted over and over and over to bring out the beast in people. Music had been a key part of the skinhead subculture from day one. It almost single-handedly inspired it. Skrewdriver. Clark and Carmine's Final Solution. Bully Boys. Arresting Officers. No Remorse. Brutal Attack. Haken Kreuz. The Midtown Bootboys. Bound For Glory. All pioneering white power bands, some even American, though most were now defunct. No reason I couldn't get in on the action. It was a wide open market. I jotted down lyrics, making up choruses in my head. Tried them out in front of the mirror.

I could do it. No—not could—I *would* do it. All I needed were a few guys with instruments and some balls. The thought of having my own white power band was intoxicating. I could taste the glory, hear the deafening roar of the crowd. With my ambition and growing network, notoriety would surely follow.

Never mind that I had little musical background.

"A band?" my mother asked when I announced I'd be practicing in the basement and we'd be making some noise. "But you aren't a musician. You quit piano lessons when you were ten."

"This is different. This is real music. Music people will listen to. Something that matters."

"I'll listen to your band, Buddy," my little brother chimed in.

"What instrument will you play? You don't even have a harmonica. Or are you going to bang on pans like when you were a little boy?" My mom thought she was a riot.

Buddy pulled two long wooden spoons from the utensil drawer and started to bang them on the counter like drumsticks.

I ignored her amusement. "I'll find other people to play the instruments. I'll sing and write the lyrics. I'm the one who makes things happen."

Her ears perked up. She liked the sound of that. Relieved. Proved she'd been right about me after all. Those posters, those Nazi flags, those ugly T-shirts and big boots were a passing phase and would be a thing of the past now that I'd settle down to be a musician. This pleased her and kept her off my back, while she continued waiting to hear if the alternative school for fuck-ups was going to let me enroll in January when the final semester began.

I traded my old punk rock record collection for some microphones, cables, and a beat-up PA system from a bingo hall, easily talked a few of the local guys I knew who played instruments into forming a band, and our group was born. Modeled us after Skrewdriver with more of an American hardcore vibe than traditional British Oi! music.

I was the vocalist and songwriter. The rest of the band was made up of former Eisenhower classmates. Rick, a long-haired heavy metal kid who'd taken years of lessons, agreed to play guitar. Larry—Rick's best friend—brought over his drum set. Davey, a promising skateboarder in the neighborhood and the only one I knew with an electric bass guitar, rounded out the group.

None of the other three were remotely skinheads or neo-Nazis, but they were white power sympathizers that hung around and partied with us on the weekends. They had no objection to racist lyrics since they hung around with some of the same people I knew from Blue

Island and shared the same views about minorities as I did. They were all psyched to be in a band, and I convinced them the fastest way to get noticed was through playing skinhead music. "There's only one or two other white power bands in the U.S. right now. We'll make history. The British skinhead bands are folk heroes. We'll be better than them."

I pointed out that not all Skrewdriver songs were about hate. "They're about social justice, man. They don't only do 'fuck-you-nigger' songs. They sing about white pride and patriotism, fighting against communism, breaking the capitalist system. That kind of knowledge can change the world. And we can be part of that."

Without much debate, I named us White American Youth—WAY for short. Perfect name considering I was going to use our music to show white kids the way out of their sleepwalk.

We took up residence for the remainder of the winter in my basement pad, practicing, learning how to play together, imitating bands we liked by rehearsing their tunes, drinking, getting original songs down. We'd stay up all hours, Buddy slipping in as often as he could to be part of this exciting new world.

"Hey, Buddy, can I sing into the microphone?" he'd ask.

"I'm working right now. Maybe later." The look on his dejected face clearly displayed his hurt feelings. Sometimes I'd see him peeking through the window when we practiced. Once I caught him in the garage jumping around singing some of my lyrics into a flashlight.

My father would come down when we got really loud, tell us to shut up, it was too late for all the noise.

"Leave us the fuck alone. Go back upstairs," I'd order, and the rest of the guys in the band would watch with their mouths wide open as my father obeyed, cursing me under his breath. I was relentless in my perseverance to piss off my dad. I resented him for not being there for me when I was a kid more than I did my mother. While he was always in the background, I didn't really get to know him and he never made an effort to know me. Asserting his authority—although it didn't carry any weight due to his lackluster parenting track record—was a prime cue for me to lash out. He'd failed me as a father and I'd pounce on any opportunity to punish him for it. I was in control.

My time for music was curtailed in February when Ombudsman Alternative School agreed to let me enroll and finish out the year. But I knew I was onto something big and school hadn't ever held me back before. WAY, I was certain, would continue.

Ombudsman was a privately run remedial alternative education school with all of fifty kids in the whole student body. A mix of degenerates. Dumb kids who couldn't read. Gangbangers. Drug dealers. Underage pregnant girls. The hopeless cases everyone had given up on. Who'd given up on themselves.

What the hell was I doing here?

I didn't have many credits left to complete before graduation, so I knew it'd be a breeze. But it was downright insulting to have been lumped in with such a bunch of derelict losers.

Ombudsman had two sessions a day, each lasting four hours. I was in the second session and spent the whole wasted afternoon sitting in front of a green-screen computer terminal clicking through reading comprehension questions about stories not even as deep and difficult as those I'd read to my baby brother when he was growing up.

The teachers figured out pretty fast that I was an asset to them. Smart kid like me with all those advanced high school classes under his belt made a handy tutor for the brain-dead zombies they had trouble reaching, thereby reducing the load the instructors carried. All I had to do was show up and help them administer spelling tests from time to time to graduate.

This was as close to acceptable as high school was ever likely to get. I wrote songs and even applied to a few colleges during classroom downtime. I was smart enough. Why not? I'd find hundreds more students to recruit on a university campus. Everyone is looking for something to believe in. They just needed a gentle nudge in the right direction.

In the meantime, I kept WAY focused on making music, which wasn't all that easy. The other guys weren't into it as much as I was and with them in school all day, time to practice was hard to come by.

And I had serious commitments. To the white race and my crew.

13

VANGUARD

NOW THAT I WAS SEVENTEEN YEARS OLD and had my driver's license, I found opportunities to travel out of state to meet other skinheads from around the country who I'd corresponded with. My new part-time job working at a pizza parlor in Beverly gave me the financial means to get around, and some friends and I drove down to Georgia to hang out and network. One of the guys in my crew who'd recently been discharged from the army was dating a skinhead girl who lived there, and we stayed at a house in Marietta, Georgia, owned by a veteran neo-Nazi skin named Teddy Dalrymple.

Marietta was one of the hottest places in the country for recruiting skinheads. It was almost child's play. White supremacy had been part of Marietta history ever since the Reconstruction era Ku Klux Klan began immediately after the Civil War ended. It grew in popularity and remained ingrained as part of the culture.

Dalrymple lived in a dilapidated wood-framed shanty at the end of Blanche Drive in Marietta that served as a bustling hub for neo-Nazi youth activity throughout the Atlanta area. At any given time you'd find dozens of kids hanging around for meetings, parties, rallies, and any number of other activities. White power skinheads passing through

Georgia were always welcome to crash there, and Dalrymple made us feel right at home. He treated me as an equal and gave me tips on scaling our recruiting efforts outside of Chicago. He was a down-home Southern good ol' boy through and through. Great guy with a round potbelly and giant muttonchops covering his cheeks. Totally inspiring. A redneck maverick, he had the line on every pro-white group in the country and was involved in organizing large-scale marches and protests in support of our cause.

It was at Dalrymple's house where I met Clay Wallaby, drummer for the legendary English skinhead band Condemned 84—one of my favorite Oi! bands, next to Skrewdriver. Another great guy. An old-school British skin who had fled his home country and was building a new life with an American girl in Marietta. We hung out together some. Drank lots of beer. I admired his musical talent and long-standing dedication to the skinhead movement. He was about more than getting into brawls and kicking ass.

"In order for the white race to prosper for the next one hundred years, mate, we need to find ways to stick together and fight in a unified way to keep other races from pulling us apart or taking what is rightfully ours," he'd say in his warbled Cockney accent. "Blacks and third-world immigrants come to England and America in droves to leech from the resources, leaving little to nothing for us native blokes."

Clay was right. It was hard enough for the average American white family to keep their head above water without other races punching holes in our buckets and drawing from the same limited water well. Sipping from his Carling lager, he went on to say, "Hard work and ethnic purity are the single most important tenets of National Socialism." Clark had taught me that early on.

"Without those two things, a society becomes weak and diseased and impossible to cure," I agreed.

Over the last few years, I'd learned to believe that American multiculturalism meant we had no solid foundation to build a healthy civilization on top of. We were a sick society. If we didn't start taking care of our own kind in this country, instead of the foreigners who milked our infrastructure and resources, we were doomed. There simply wasn't enough to go around for everyone who had their hand out.

I enjoyed talking Nazi politics with Clay. He genuinely cared about National Socialism and music, and put them together well for over a decade.

By the time we'd left, I'd made connections through Clay and Teddy that would seriously help put WAY on the national radar. My goal—my dream—was to play a concert outside of Chicago with Minnesota white power heavyweights Bound For Glory. Clay promised to make an introduction, as he had become friendly with the guys in the band. With this new contact, I was damn sure I'd find a way to get us together. And soon. Patience wasn't my forte.

It felt good to be interacting with people in higher places, people who were about more than getting wasted on beer and losing their minds once they got drunk. These Georgia guys were the real deal. They wanted to save America. Like I did. They had guns and were ready to fight for our lives.

Teddy Dalrymple and I sat drinking cold beers on his front porch, the Georgia air dense with heat and humidity. "This here is an AR-15 semiautomatic assault rifle that I nigger-rigged to fire full auto when you flip this dang switch," Dalrymple said, tossing me the weapon.

"Whoa...what the hell, Teddy?" I barely caught the flying rifle, spilling beer all over my blue jeans. "Is it loaded?" I was unsure of exactly how to hold it, nervous with its surprising weight.

"What good would it damn be if it ain't?" he said winking at me. He stuffed tobacco into his carved corncob smoking pipe.

I felt the slick blue steel in my hands and studied it, running my fingers along the thick, ridged barrel. Solid. Heavy. Spent gunpowder residue from the weapon's cartridge chamber collected on my fingertips.

The familiar burnt charcoal and earth smell sent me back to the Fourth of July fireworks displays I'd attended with the High Street Boys in my youth, on the hill next to the football field behind Eisenhower.

Dalrymple reached over and snapped back the slide on the rifle and released it with a loud metallic clank. "There, it's loaded. Now point it at something that ain't white and squeeze the dang trigger," he chuckled.

"What?" I wasn't sure if I'd heard him correctly. I let out a nervous laugh.

"I said find something you want to kill and squeeze the fucking trigger! Is you motherfuckin' deaf, Yankee?" He grabbed me by the shoulder and forced me down into a kneeling position and pressed the stock against my cheek.

"Careful...it's loaded," I stammered.

"You see that nasty white whore over yonder with that half-nigger baby?" He pointed to the middle of the block at a young white woman strapping her mulatto child into a stroller. "Shoot her in the face! Right between her nigger-lovin' eyes. Then shoot the lil' nigglet while you're at it."

My sweat glands hit overdrive and I could feel my armpits instantly becoming cool and damp. My blood ran cold. Sweat streaked down my forehead and stung my eyes. "You're joking, right? That's pretty funny." I laughed it off and attempted to hand him back the rifle.

"Does it look like I'm joking, boy?" He pulled out a shiny pistol from his waistband and pressed it firmly against my temple. "Now aim."

Frozen in place, my stomach churning, I was ready to expel the loads of smothered, chunked, and chili-topped Waffle House hash browns I'd scarfed down for lunch. The cold steel he placed against the side of my face assured me he was dead serious. "Okay, okay, Teddy. Just relax." I slowly turned my head, lowered my cheek to meet the weapon's stock, zeroing the sights in on the unsuspecting woman's forehead as best as I could. I saw her smiling and teasing the young infant. Laughing.

"Now pull the fucking trigger, cowboy."

I tried hard to keep my hands from trembling.

"Squeeze the fucking trigger or I will! Is you a cop, motherfucker?"

I took in a shallow breath, intentionally jerking my arm to the right to assure I'd miss her, and pulled the trigger.

Click!

Dalrymple let out a loud, guttural smoker's laugh and hacked uncontrollably for a moment while slapping me on the back. "I got you, man!" He took the pistol that had been resting against my temple and brought it to his face. When he pulled back the trigger, it spit out a short blue flame that he used to light his pipe.

"What the fuck, Teddy?"

Unholy laughter and coughing. "Had to make sure you wasn't some kinda narc or undercover fed. You think I'd give you a loaded gun? Shit, you ought to see your dang baby face, Al Capone."

I was both relieved and pissed at this giant hillbilly who'd almost made me a killer in the first degree. "You're an asshole, Teddy." I cracked a tense smile as I dropped the butt of the heavy weapon into his wide open lap, hitting him hard in the nuts in the process.

He yelped and doubled over. "Owwweee! Why the hell'd you go do that for?"

"Just had to make sure you weren't some kind of queer," I quipped. My arms felt like Jell-O as I wrenched open the screen door to head back inside the shack. "I needed to know I didn't have some sort of a faggot fighting next to me when the time comes." I wiped my brow.

I came away from the trip feeling both anxious about my involvement in the movement outside of Chicago and certain that the time had come for me to start loading up on weapons myself. I was convinced there was a race war brewing, and soon. I needed to be prepared. If we didn't protect ourselves, we'd be overrun. I was a white warrior willing to stand as a vanguard against that threat. I'd be ready. And heavily armed.

Sometime during the subsequent months, a fellow Hammerskin from Montreal visited Chicago and wanted to set up a meeting to introduce me to Wolfgang Droege, a radical Canadian KKK leader who'd been heating things up across the border. He tried to draw me in by saying that Libya's Muslim dictator Muammar Gaddafi had sent a government attaché to meet with Droege about giving North American neo-Nazis some financial backing. "Wolfie wants the Chicago Hammerskins in on it," he said.

I suppose I didn't particularly care if Gaddafi wasn't white. He despised the Jews as much as we did. And this could help bankroll a weapons arsenal. After all, an enemy of the enemy—the Jews and Israel—could be an ally. Gaddafi wanted to meet serious anti-Israel American radicals. Wanted to fly us over to Libya to discuss a strategy and support our cause by seeding us with cash.

This was big time. As serious as it could get.

I said I'd think about it, uncertainty hitting me like a cinder block. The Canadian Hammerskin hounded me, pressured me, insisting this was our big chance. I knew Droege had previously helped organize a failed military coup on the Caribbean island of Dominica and had gone to prison for it. That kind of adventure was intense and appealed to me. I was pumped at first; I could indeed be part of something huge. International.

But what if I got caught? What if it was a set-up? I didn't know this Droege guy or the Canadian skinhead very well. If I agreed to the plan and the feds caught wind of it, I'd certainly be convicted as a traitor to the United States. A crime punishable by death, not prison time. I loved my country, I just didn't agree with those currently in power—the System that held us down. I was willing to take on the government on my terms, but this wasn't the way to do it. Plus I didn't even like these Middle-Eastern ragheads; why should I trust them?

"He wants to give us a million dollars," pleaded the Montreal Hammerskin. "Think of all the weapons we can buy with that kind of money. The damage we can do."

He was coming on too strong. "So, why don't you go?" I asked.

"Wolfgang specifically asked for Clark Martell. When I told him he was in prison, he asked for the next in command."

"Tell Wolfgang I appreciate the offer, but I'll have to pass this time. I don't have a passport," I lied.

So I respectfully declined and kept my involvement domestic for the time being.

Damn good thing I did. A year later Droege and his cohorts ended up in federal prison because the whole Gaddafi deal had been a sting operation set up by Canadian Intelligence.

I'd dodged a major bullet.

There were plenty of conflicts to focus on closer to home. Like the pack of niggers who had been accosting Pecker and Chili, two of the Beverly guys, every day on the city bus they rode home from school. This infuriated the hell out of all of us, so we planned our ambush. Pecker and Chili would stand up to them on the bus, talk trash, and get them all riled up. They'd lure them off at their stop to fight. And we'd be there waiting.

Worked like a charm. Half a dozen of us hid around the corner behind the diner near the bus stop. When the three gangbangers got off the bus, we waylaid their black asses and beat the shit out of them in the middle of rush hour on busy Western Avenue. Cars screeching to a halt all around us, we hauled those useless niggers out to the middle of the street, beating them without mercy. Kicking. Dragging. Punching. Low blows. Bastards had it coming. You don't mess with us. Not in our backyard.

Car horns blared. People screamed. Didn't give a shit.

Kubiak grabbed a handful of afro on one of the guys and was swinging him around, off the ground, like an Olympic hammer thrower.

Three Beverly Boys had another pinned down and pummeled him with a barrage of kicks to his stomach, face, and back. His wails were louder than the car horns that were begging them to stop.

I chased the remaining gangbanger on foot and caught him in the alley behind the diner. I football-tackled him into a row of garbage cans and drove my elbow into his nose, breaking it with a resonating crack, as my feet suddenly shot out from under me. I'd slipped in a slick puddle of discarded restaurant grease, lost my grip and the guy got away. Lucky for him, as he'd ruined my bomber jacket and jeans in the process and I would have killed him if he'd stuck around. Disgusting. I was smeared in gelatinous yellow fryer fat and reeked like a fast food restaurant's backed-up toilet.

The rest of the guys didn't back off until they heard the police sirens approaching. Then we all climbed over cars—denting their shiny hoods with our boots—to get the hell out of there. Last thing I needed with assault charges already looming over me was to be busted for a race-inspired fight. A felony hate crime.

We made it back to my house without incident, laughing all the way, mimicking the niggers begging for us to stop. The Beverly guys and Kubiak ribbed me for weeks, calling me a "greasy Italian." Suffice it to say, those kids never rode that bus again.

Not long after the Western Avenue bus incident I appeared in court for sentencing on the trumped-up charges against me for allegedly assaulting that spineless spic Hector Diaz. Again, I dressed appropriately. Used my finest manners. "Yes-judged" that black-robed clown to death. I was sentenced to six months of court supervision, which pissed the hell out of me since I hadn't done a damn thing. I'd take what was coming to me, but that was a travesty of justice and proved how the courts favored minorities.

Because I was under court supervision, I had to refrain from getting arrested during that time. So, I shifted my focus and injected more venom into my music, got downright aggressive about rehearsals, and in May of 1991, we proudly gave our first live concert in a place called The Barn, a community center in Blue Island. At a birthday party of all things. I didn't particularly care for the venue, but it was exciting having people responding to our music, getting revved up, cheering for us.

The tiny place was jam-packed with a couple dozen kids, and the crowd was loving us. The scent of pine from the wood-clad walls was overshadowed by the pungent odors of floor wax and teen sweat. The unsuspecting parents were getting drunk in the parking lot while we entertained the sixteen-year-old birthday girl and a roomful of new recruits with our rendition of several Skrewdriver anthems and a few WAY originals.

We're the warriors of the street
With shaven heads and boots on our feet
We stand tall like a stone wall
Against all evil we won't fall
Streets and homes are never safe
Because there are niggers committing rape
WAY's our name, white power we follow
We're the White American Youth of tomorrow!

The room whirled with teen angst and perspiration. Choppy guitar rhythms and the rousing choruses drove the moist juvenile bodies violently into one another from every direction.

We're White! Strong and free!
White supremacy!
White! We preach the truth!
White American Youth!

The work, the frustration of getting practices together and figuring out how to operate as a single well-oiled machine, had all been worth it. There was no doubt we'd make something happen musically. Again, I'd proven I could do whatever I set out to do.

With only a month left until graduation, I drove to Ombudsman in the clunky 1984 Chevy truck my parents helped me buy so I could travel the extra distance to alternative school. As I pulled into the parking lot, I saw my old skinhead pal Craig Sargent—who by now had also been kicked out of Marist and Eisenhower for his racist activities—locked in a shoving match with two niggers. I jammed on my brakes, skidded to a stop, and jumped into the fray.

Craig and I beat up this fat dude named Pooky and his wiry sidekick Juice before they even had a chance to so much as utter our names. I pulled the bigger of the two off Craig, while he continued to pound the other. As a crowd—including the teachers—gathered in the parking lot, we continued to volley blows after they attempted to retreat into the building. We threw them against parked cars and knocked them to the ground repeatedly.

Having no doubt our efforts would mean we were both kicked out of yet another school and the cops would be looking for us, we hopped into my truck and took off, spending the rest of the day parked in a forest preserve drinking the warm beer I had stashed under my seat.

Four weeks to graduation.

And once again, I'd been expelled. Fifth time. Five schools. In four years.

My parents begged the school board president for a favor one final time and were granted a special reprieve to enroll me in the local community college to finish my remaining two high school credits.

"You're ruining your life," my dad said. "I know you think you know it all and believe you have everything under control, but…"

"Stop pretending like you fucking care. You don't! You never have." I managed to get the words out while holding back tears of anger at his very suggestion that he knew a damn thing about what I was feeling. "I do what I want, when I want. And you haven't earned the right to tell me what to do."

Just then seven-year-old Buddy walked into the room, holding a mangled wrestling action figure. He'd pulled the head off it and the plastic body was riddled with cut marks, rendering it almost unrecognizable as the former figure of black WWF professional wrestler Junkyard Dog.

"Look, Buddy," he beamed, "It's a dead nigger."

My mother grabbed it from his pudgy fingers as both she and my brother wailed.

My dad's angry eyes penetrated mine. "See what you've done?"

Knowing my time in school was coming to an end, I considered joining the military. I'd receive excellent combat training there. My fighting skills would only improve and I'd get to handle the best weapons known to mankind. I knew I could rise to a leadership position quickly and influence trained warriors to join our movement. Moreover, the Gulf War was going on and I could kill mud races legally. And get paid for it. Sweet deal.

I headed over to the army office to enlist. "I want to be an M.P.," I told the recruiter.

He took one look at my skinhead clothes and tattoos and shook his head. "You can't be Military Police. People like you have one choice. Infantry."

"People like me?"

"I know your kind. Tough, brazen, and you have a taste for blood. Front line for you all the way."

This grunt wasn't going to send me packing. "Fine. Infantry it is. I'll work my way up the ranks."

"Of course you will, Private," he said, and signed me up for the ASVAB test, the aptitude and enlistment exam for the U.S. military.

When my scores came back, the recruiter changed his tune. I'd scored higher than any of his previous enlistees ever had. "Son," he said, "you still want to be an M.P.? Let's get you that job."

Only problem was, I wasn't old enough. At seventeen I still needed a parent's signature. And for once, I couldn't forge it like I had for my less than stellar report cards at St. Damian.

When I told her I wanted to join the army, my mother was beside herself. She didn't want me killed. "You have a long life ahead of you. Why go fight in a war that has nothing to do with us?" My father agreed. Buddy liked the idea of having a brother who was a soldier and brought out his G.I. Joe toys and asked me to show him how I'd kill the bad guys. My mother snatched them away and told him to go watch something nice on television.

My mom brought my grandparents in as a last resort to try and dissuade me. She knew I still had a soft spot for Nonna and Nonno and wouldn't lose my temper if they were there.

My grandmother tried to convince me to change my mind. "Christian, why don't you go to school or find a nice job instead? You're such a good boy," she pleaded. "War is not a good place for anyone. Ask Nonno.

He can tell you." Her motherly warmth and calmness were always so comforting. I missed it.

As Nonna played my surrogate mother growing up, the adopted fatherly responsibilities fell to my grandfather, Nonno. But not even his dreadful firsthand accounts of his time in the Second World War could dissuade me once I'd made up my mind to enlist.

A man of few words, Nonno interrupted my grandmother. "It's not a place for you. You have a good heart." I wasn't so sure. "You will come back different."

I was counting on that.

Respecting my grandparents and their wishes was something I did without question when I was a small child, and I also understood that they were wiser than either of my parents—or me for that matter. But the world was a different place than the one they'd known in the old country at my age. I envied my grandfather for going to war, fighting as a bombardier in the Italian air force under Mussolini in exotic and far-off places like Egypt and Libya and Belgium. I respected that and I wanted to earn the same type of respect he had.

We were in a constant war within our own borders now, regardless of whether we wore military camouflage and desert boots or a bomber jacket and Doc Martens. I would go to the army and come back stronger. Tougher. Smarter. And more equipped to fight my own battles. I railed hard against my family's wishes, driven by the belief that I knew something they didn't.

Eventually they all caved. Big surprise.

And so the day came. I waited for the recruiter to pick me up and take me in for my army physical and have my parents sign off on my enlistment form. But he was late.

Half an hour late.

An hour.

I called the recruiting office to see what the holdup was. Seemed my recruiter had been reassigned to another station in Albuquerque two days earlier. "But don't worry, young man, we'll send someone else to come over to pick you up right away," the staff sergeant assured me.

"Don't bother," I said indignantly. "Fuck you people."

It felt good saying that to the government.

Meanwhile, at the community college where I'd started my final course to earn my high school diploma, to my amazement, school was actually interesting. I was taking a Criminal Justice 101 course to fulfill my remaining two credits. Struck me as cool to have a class ending in 101. For the first time, I was treated as an adult inside an institution of learning. It was college. An open campus. Nobody was shoving rules down my throat. Teachers never insisted I show up. Or forced me go to detention for not doing homework or for cutting a class that bored me to death.

Without much effort, I aced the course. I, a mere high school senior—a truant and delinquent and menace—was the only one in my entire college class to get an A. It felt good. Real good. The first time in my whole student life a grade meant something to me. I had to bite my lip when the professor talked about the demographics of race in the prison system and the lopsided incarceration ratio of blacks to whites, but it was tolerable. I could have explained the reasons for this better than him. But I didn't.

At the end of the semester, I'd completed the credit requirements and I was eligible to receive my high school diploma.

But I could not participate in the graduation ceremony, which was taking place at Eisenhower.

The school had filed for an order of protection—a restraining order against me. The directive was to arrest me on sight if I stepped foot on school property.

And so my high school years, those golden days that are supposed to be the best life has to offer, came to an end. Good riddance.

I'd learned about leadership. Instilling fear. Intimidation tactics. Organizing people. The law. Justice. Playing the system. How to use a weapon. The power of violence. Standing up for my beliefs. Marketing my brand. Putting my words into action. But it hadn't been school that taught me those skills.

What a joke the American school system was. It didn't teach anything valuable and it had no idea how to keep kids engaged.

Clark had explained to me in one of his early letters how the modern school system hadn't changed much since the 1950s, except that the instructional theories administrators used now favored uneducated minorities and kept white students at lower reading and comprehension levels. It made no sense that teachers were being forced to teach at the level of the lowest common denominator, rather than challenging the bright kids while the dumb ones got held back.

Yet somehow I managed to graduate, despite being kicked out of four different high schools, one more than once.

While the other subservient robots stood on stage getting their diplomas, I enjoyed my own private liberation from the shackles that had bound me for far, far too long.

14

GO AWAY

Finally. No more school. I hadn't given a rat's ass about it anyway, but still it had loomed over me like a noose. Happens to all kids. It dominates our lives. The only freedom we have is summer.

But I'd graduated.

Independence stretched out like a pure endless sky, despite the gnawing fact that I wouldn't turn eighteen for yet another five months. Gone were the dark clouds of gutless teachers and administrators and homework and exams and being forced to sit in a classroom full of ridiculous ideas and people I'd never associate with by choice. I hadn't wasted time on homework and I'd cut classes and entire days and weeks, but there was always some kind of consequence. Whether I ignored the consequences or not didn't make them go away. They annoyed me. But all that was over now.

My life was becoming my own, and I could devote myself full-time to being the man I was destined to be.

I had to expand my base. It wasn't enough to pick up kids around Blue Island anymore. Not even enough that my name had spread to skinhead groups across the country and into Canada. Time to focus on my band. No doubt music could make me stronger than ever. With school a thing of the past, we could start performing at rallies outside of Chicago, inciting people on a larger scale. Maybe even Europe.

So I threw myself into WAY, lining up whatever gigs I could. We spent hours writing new lyrics, figuring out beats, piecing together songs. Music was a means to an end, the end being more control.

Our second show was in the living room of a fellow skinhead's home—lots of teenagers, cheap wood paneling, linoleum floors. Small place had a tough time holding that many people. A mix of Blue Island skins and Beverly guys. Kubiak was there entertaining some of the younger recruits. Punk girls. WAY had only been together for six months, but it didn't matter. We just had to play fast and loud and get people moving and we'd be fine. There'd be beer, too, which always helps make marginal musicians sound good.

Took only a verse of inciting words and a few power chords into the first tune to win the crowd's approval. They were slamdancing, thrusting out their arms in Nazi salutes, nodding their heads aggressively to the beat, motivated by our songs. My words. Tremendously powerful feeling. We were a gang united through music and I'd never felt anything like it.

I could have sung all night.

But around midnight a beer bottle came crashing through the front window of the house. We dropped our instruments and filed out into the front yard looking for revenge. Across the street appeared a cadre of dark silhouettes, wearing hoodies pulled over their heads and hockey and ski masks to cover their faces. Bats, chains with padlocks, lead pipes, and hockey sticks clutched in their hands. Ambush.

Fucking Antis. Young and old, male and female. Skins. Punks. Straight Edge kids. SHARPs. Two dozen or so about thirty yards away, backlit by a glowing amber porch light as if their souls were on fire. The rest of our troops from inside joined us on the lawn. The tension hovered, approaching DEFCON Level One, fingers at the ready on the nuclear button. At least twenty of us lined up, ready to do battle, the fury of the music still drumming in our heads.

Another bottle crashed at Kubiak's feet, spraying shards of glass against his fourteen-eyelet oxblood boots. We breathed one deep collective breath and, as if a battle horn sounded, charged the enemy. Our Doc Martens stampeding, we marched at full speed into the night, across the black pavement. One line of warriors set to clash with the enemy.

Most of the opposition retreated, scattering at the sight of fury on our faces. We flew full-speed and caught up before they made it to the corner. Some had shown up solely to intimidate us through a show of numbers. They had no courage to fight. They fled like cowards.

Others turned and stood their ground. Put up a solid fight. Knuckles connected with noses, jaws, and cheekbones. Cries of pain and attrition filled the night as we struck each other down, like avenging angels in Doc Marten boots.

I turned from one person to another, punching with all my power. This was the enemy. No mercy.

I swung around and came face to face with April Crenshaw. She and her husband Jerry were the leaders of SHARP in Chicago, but he'd run off and left her there to fend for herself.

She read the rage in my eyes. Tears and mascara mixed and began rolling murky, black streaks down her face as she backpedaled, pleading for me not to hurt her.

I'd never hit a girl, but she needed to learn a lesson. So instead I tore her SHARP patch from her bomber jacket. My trophy. Better than drawing blood. And to humiliate her further, I made her take off her boots and hand them over to me in a final recognition of her defeat. I took a box cutter to the laces. Made her slide them off and hand them to me. A crowd of my soldiers gathered.

No skinhead ever gives up his or her boots.

Until then.

She rose, barefoot in fishnet stockings. I resisted an urge to kick her symbolically in her ass as she retreated. Off she went, a skinhead specter disappearing into the solitary night.

They'd lost.

We'd beaten down her crew. Our main skinhead adversaries in Chicago. And without so much as laying a finger on her, I'd humiliated their leader. More of a blow than any physical injury we'd caused.

Police sirens ripped through the darkness and when the first wave of cops arrived they arrested what remaining SHARP skins were laying around, for criminal damage to property. The ones who didn't run were covered in bruises, some unable to get to their feet.

Kubiak's friendly hand reached out to pull me out of the fray. "Get inside. Away from the cops. Danny's on his way and said he'd take care of it."

I retreated inside the house. Not out of fear, but because my freedom was essential. My crew needed me. I'd be no good to anyone locked up. Going to jail was for soldiers, not generals. Everybody knew this. I wouldn't get pinched like Clark had.

When the police banged on the door looking for me, I was nowhere to be seen.

"We didn't do anything, officer," I hear one of our girls say. "Just having a small get-together, and then a bottle flew through the window…"

"Where's Picciolini, smartass?" the lead detective asked, pushing his nose past the girl in the doorway to find Kubiak.

"Haven't seen him, Danny," Kubiak replied.

"You better get home before Mom and Dad find out what you've been up to tonight," he whispered. "And tell your idiot friend hiding in the closet to stay off the streets for a while."

"Yessir, Officer Kubiak," the younger Kubiak quipped.

"Have a good night, Mein Führer," I said from behind the closet door. It helped to have someone on the inside looking out after us.

Seemed like days before I came down from the high of the show and brawl. If this was where I could take people with music, we'd be invincible.

A few days later I decided to make a mark of a different sort. Every kid in the area knew me. Respected me. But I wanted the respect due me from adults. The very people whose children I was trying to protect.

I entered a car in the spectator's derby held at Raceway Park. The same racetrack where I'd flyered cars in the early days before Clark was sent to prison. Good attendance. Excellent exposure. And rednecks loved racism.

I bought an olive green, four-door Chevy Caprice junker from Kubiak's neighbor and set to work making my car the most striking heavy metal hate machine anybody would ever see. I'd gotten a small raise at the pizza job and picked up a few extra nights a week. The car cost me a hundred and fifty bucks—half of a week's pay—but the attention it would get would be worth so much more.

I painted it matte black with a roller and flat house paint, except for "88"—Hitler's number—in white on the doors. Nazi SS lightning bolts were in red spray paint on the rear quarter panels, two crossed hammers rising from flames on the hood. "White Pride" in large letters lay across the back bumper. A badass car with a powerful message. Like Carmine's. I had no doubt I'd win the derby and my cause would be further spotlighted in the news. White power would rule.

One of the few requirements for getting on the track, aside from removing all windows but the windshield, was that cars had to have a metal bar welded along the inside of the driver's door for safety. This presented a problem because, oddly enough, there wasn't a welder among my wide range of blue-collar acquaintances. I can't tell you how many people I asked, how many leads I followed, how many phone calls I made or doors I knocked on. I was determined to get my car into that derby and broadcast my message and, by doing so, spread the notion that white people shouldn't be scared to stand up for their race.

While I worked on the heap and continued my search for a welder, the car sat in plain view in my parents' driveway. My parents weren't remotely happy about it, but, as usual, they backed down.

The marked-up race car attracted a ton of attention, though, exactly as I wanted it to, and soon enough a CBS news crew came out to the house to do a story on it.

Nonno, my elderly grandfather who lived across the street, was outside tending to his yard when the news van showed up and a cameraman and reporter piled out.

He dropped his gardening tools as they surrounded my car in the driveway. He barely spoke English. They descended on him. Shoved a camera and microphone in his face.

"Do you know who this car belongs to? How do you feel about having this type of hate in your neighborhood? Is this crossing the first amendment freedom of speech line?"

My grandfather might not have understood English well, but he certainly understood the frenetic attitude, and he knew they weren't there to give me any awards for my artistic creation. It had been four years since I'd paid much attention to him or Nonna. I had work to do. I was too busy to look after them or visit, despite there only being a hundred yards between us.

But I was his grandson. Nothing else mattered. "Go," he said in his broken English. "He is good boy. Go away. Leave alone! Go! Now!"

And this frail old man from Italy drove the buzzards away.

They didn't come back.

He never said a word about it to me, and my car continued to stand proudly in my parents' driveway, steadily gathering public nuisance citations from the city. I eventually gave up on finding a welder and sold the car for fifty bucks to another kid on the block who painted over everything I'd done and raced it in the derby.

I didn't bother to find out how he'd finished, but I was sure he hadn't done well. He'd robbed the car of its power.

15
POLICE OPPRESSION

I PURCHASED MY NEXT GUN UNLAWFULLY and without a permit. Ironically, I bought it off the street from a Mexican illegal. A .380 caliber semiautomatic handgun. I threw the old, busted .25 that Kubiak had given me into the Blue Island canal one night after failing to get it to load ammunition properly.

Until you grip a loaded gun in your hand, you don't know power. It's a surreal feeling. Dangerous. Exciting. Exhilarating.

Holding my pistol, I felt I could conquer the world.

I loved it.

I talked to Bill Rudolph—an older Chicago neo-Nazi who I'd originally met through Carmine—about getting more guns. He worked in a bread factory, like a true blue American would, and responded by giving me a co-worker's stolen wallet, complete with Illinois driver's license.

"Use this," he told me. "First thing you gotta do is get a permit to buy a gun."

I didn't look a thing like the Mexican guy on the stolen license and pointed it out.

He scoffed at my inexperience. "You think anybody gives a shit if that's you or not? You fill out a firearm application and go to the ghetto to

Christian, local newspaper clipping, 1991

have some fat nigger bitch notarize it. She won't even look at the picture on the license. They collect the money and don't ask any questions."

I couldn't believe that would be the case, but I'd be damned if I'd show any fear. What's the worst they could do? Call the cops and charge me for having a stolen ID? It's not as if the cops and I were strangers. They didn't scare me. Instead, I must have worried them. They routinely stopped me on the street for doing nothing more than walking on the sidewalk on my way to buy smokes or standing on the corner waiting for a ride from one of my friends. I'd even heard that when the local Blue Island and Chicago city councils held town hall meetings, my name came up as an agenda item to discuss. These morons didn't exactly know what white power skinheads were all about, but they knew trouble when they saw it. And, to them, I embodied the spirit of the trouble that skinheads were bringing to the area.

Like Bill promised, the black lady behind the currency exchange counter didn't so much as glance at the ID. She took my money and stamped her approval on my firearm application.

I showed Bill. "So now what?"

"Send the application in to the Illinois State Police and…"

"State police?" I interrupted, "What do you mean state police? I thought that was it. She stamped it…see?"

"Don't worry about it. It's not your name or photo. The address won't even be yours."

"But isn't that a federal crime? Like mail fraud or something?" I could tell he was starting to lose patience with me.

"Look, just give me the damn application and I'll send it in for you." He took me to the window and pulled aside the curtain. "You see that vacant house across the street? We'll use that address. When the mail gets delivered, I'll grab it for you. Don't worry."

"Alright." It sounded like a valid theory. "Then what?"

"Go to a gun show, Jose Ortiz." We both laughed.

I swear I looked nothing like the guy in the stolen driver's license. And for two solid months I worried the feds would knock down my door and arrest me for a federal fraud violation.

It would have been simpler to buy guns illegally on the street like I had with the .380, but that meant the money would make its way into the hands of niggers and wetback gangbangers. Our enemies. That wasn't an option.

Gun shows were everywhere. I found one soon after Bill received "Jose's" firearm permit in the mail from the Illinois State Police and we headed to the show without a qualm. I had my gun license and Bill's reassurance that the racist hillbillies at these shows didn't give a damn who they sold the guns to. It was about the money. So long as you looked white.

Bill was right again. The people at this—and every other gun show I attended—couldn't care less who they sold weapons to. The guy he introduced me to, an old family friend of his, barely looked at the permit, aside from scribbling its info on the receipt. As long as you weren't a minority and had cash, you were golden. Even the mandatory federal waiting period didn't seem to bother this guy. The seller handed over the gun the second he collected my money.

I left that first show with a brand new Beretta 9mm pistol tucked into the waistband of my jeans, electrified by the sheer power of it. I was ready for anything now.

Only one thing I lacked. Training.

So I went to the shooting range. Again, no questions asked. Nobody cared. Give them the money, flash your permit and white smile, and we were all equal.

I picked up shooting quickly. My finger squeezed the trigger with ease, my arm supported the weapon without flinching, my eye zeroed in on the target within a fraction of a second.

Like most sports I tried, shooting was relatively easy for me. But shooting would not be a sport.

It was a part of my survival plan. I was prepared to battle to the death to save the white race from destruction.

I acquired more firearms from these gun shows. At seventeen years old, my arsenal consisted of a military-issue .30 caliber M-1 carbine rifle with a folding carbon stock, a new Russian-made AK-47, a Beretta 9mm, a .380 semi-auto handgun, and, for good measure, a sawed-off 20-gauge shotgun.

By fall, I was a decent shot and had collected weapons and ammo to spare. I was ready. I didn't brag about my cache, but word somehow got around. Cops suspected I had illegal weapons, but couldn't prove it based on only hearsay. They had no concrete evidence to search my house.

I usually kept a loaded handgun on me when I was away from home, but this had a strange effect. In addition to making me feel powerful, it made me very paranoid. Anything could happen. Circumstances could turn ugly fast and I knew it wouldn't take much provocation for me to stick it in someone's face. And I knew that if I were forced to pull it out I'd have to use it—I wouldn't dare not use it and appear to be a coward. That scared the shit out of me.

One evening I got home from work long after midnight, stripped down to my boxers and got into bed. But as I began drifting off, a noise outside my window jolted me awake.

Kubiak and I had kicked a lot of ass in the previous week. Had one of those Anti race-traitors come by to get revenge? That'd be like them. In the dark. When I was sleeping. Defenseless. Maybe it was the cops. Or the two Latin Kings we'd accosted behind Burr Oak Bowl last month.

I rolled out of my bed and crawled across the floor to my dresser. I reached behind it and moved my hand along the wall until I felt the wood stock of my sawed-off shotgun.

From a distance, I saw the intruder's backlit profile against the window. Someone was trying to break in. Creeping along the wall, I contemplated every possible scenario. What if they had a gun? What if it was the cops? I took in a deep breath and filled my lungs. Exhaled. I flung the curtain open, weapon ready to explode.

The frightened eyes meeting the barrel of my shotgun weren't those of an Anti. Nor those of a nigger or a Latin King or a cop.

It was my mother.

Sudden anger filled me, anger and horror. What was she doing spying on me in the middle of the night? Why couldn't she leave me the fuck alone? My finger was heavy on that trigger. A hair-trigger away from Buddy and me being half-orphans. I had almost shot my mother in the face.

"Christian," she cried. "It's me! Mamma. My God! Don't shoot! Please...don't shoot."

I lowered it. Trembling, I lifted open the window.

"Goddamnit! You can't sneak around like that! What the hell are you doing?"

She sank down into the bushes weeping and quivering. "Why do you have a gun? What life are you living? What have you done?"

My mother dropped to her knees and wailed, covering her face with her trembling hands. She prayed to God.

"Don't worry about it. It's for protection. That's all. Just in case." I was genuinely sorry.

"In case of what?" she cried, her eyes pleading. "Why do you need protection?"

Any angry feelings I felt for her evaporated. Her fear and concern were so sincere, so heartfelt; I felt a sting of empathy. She could be annoying and there were times I felt like strangling her, but she was my mother. I felt her sadness, I wanted to reach out and comfort her, hold her and tell her it would be okay, that I loved her. I knew she cared about me. I knew my father did too. But their lives were so full of things that didn't matter. I wanted more for them, to be happy, to not worry about me, but they refused to lift their heads out of the sand that had kept them buried for so long.

And I was outraged. They were the adults and I was *their* child. They should have known better than to abandon their son. Buddy told me they always fought over me and it had been years since I saw either of them show each other any affection. I felt pity for them and their miserable lives. But more than anything, I felt a deep sense of fear—of regret. I'd come so close to killing my own mother. Just a nervous twitch away from blowing her head clean off her body. My God.

"Go to bed. It's late. No more crying now. Everything's okay." I shut the window and heard her continue to sob, followed by a fit of retching. What if, instead of my mother, it had been Buddy at the window?

I stayed awake for hours trembling—shaken to my core and remorseful about how I almost blew a hole through my mother's face. But every time I started to drift off, exhausted from my mind racing, the idea that I needed more guns woke me right back up. Tonight had proved that somebody could come for me any time. I had to be ready.

16
MARTYR

In the midst of all the rallies and music, violence and guns, something very unexpected happened. I fell in love. Crazy wild in love.

Her name was Lisa and she wanted nothing to do with me and what I stood for.

We met through mutual Beverly friends. I wasn't looking for anybody. My life was full of responsibilities to my crew, my time taken with writing and performing white power music, and my head full of concerns about the white race and the serious risks it faced.

I had a survival pack. Guns and ammunition. An escape plan. When ZOG's secret, Jew-run shadow government launched their attack to enslave us, I would be ready to battle it head-on. To lead a revolution like a martyr. Exactly how Earl Turner had in *The Turner Diaries*:

Among those uncounted thousands, Earl Turner played no small part. He gained immortality for himself on that dark November day 106 years ago when he faithfully fulfilled his obligation to his race, to the Organization, and to the holy Order that had accepted him into its ranks. And in so doing he helped greatly to assure that his race would survive and prosper.

A love affair wasn't necessarily part of the picture.

Sure, I had my fair share of girlfriends and casual sex, but nothing serious.

When I first saw Lisa, I didn't pay much attention to her. She hung out on the periphery of the Beverly group. A nice little mod rock chick who showed up at parties now and again with some of her Catholic high school girlfriends. She'd been a year behind me in school, so our social paths hadn't crossed often, but this time she caught my eye. Hard to say why. Her auburn pixie haircut? Emerald green eyes? Plaid schoolgirl uniform? Maybe her reticence, her shy, downcast gaze and soft innocence?

Whatever it was, I was drawn to her.

So I asked her out.

"I was wondering if…maybe…I could take you to a movie or dinner or something. I hear that *Terminator 2* is supposed to be really awesome…"

She said no.

No was a word I was unaccustomed to hearing. The people around me always said yes, and they said it quickly and followed it up with whatever action needed to happen.

And she told me *no*?

I lost sleep over her response, trying to figure out how I'd put her off. Was it because she was still in high school for another year and I'd already graduated? Perhaps it was distance—we didn't live all that close to each other. Maybe she didn't like skinheads or my reputation as a fighter. Was it the movie? Maybe I should have suggested *Sleeping with the Enemy* with the chick from *Pretty Woman* or *Point Break* with that surfer dude Keanu Reeves instead.

But what was all of that compared to what I could offer? I was handsome, intelligent, streetwise, tough, admired. A leader. I succeeded in everything I'd ever set out to do. I was driven. I laughed at the thought that I might even be a doctor if my mother had her way.

Who was she to say no?

She refused to give me a chance.

Every time I asked her out, her answer was the same: a resounding no. I was pissed.

"Send her some flowers, you jerk," one of my close female skinhead friends advised. "Show her you're more than a hardass. And stop suggesting guy movies. Ask her to see something nice and funny like *City Slickers* or some romantic comedy. She's probably a sweet girl. You're running around kicking people's teeth in and getting in trouble with the cops all the time. You gotta convince her you're a good guy."

"Want to write me a letter of recommendation?" I joked. There weren't many skinhead girls around, and the ones that were always had a swarm of guys hovering around them regardless of how cute they were. It never bothered me, because I wasn't attracted to the skinhead "Chelsea Girl" look. The tattoos were sexy, but I preferred more feminine girls like Lisa that wore Mary Janes instead of Doc Martens. Aside from that, it was nice having females around to bring the high levels of testosterone down.

"Seriously. I'm telling you. Try sending flowers."

I'd been toying with the idea anyway. The only reason I hadn't was because I thought it might be too corny.

But what the hell, it couldn't get any worse. What could she do? Say no again?

So I sent a bouquet of red roses to Lisa's house. I'd like to say I sat back and waited, but that'd be a lie. I obsessed over what to do next. Wait for her to make the next move? Call her and ask if she'd gotten them? Show up at her place like I had a right to be there?

I got my chance a few weeks later when Lisa invited the Beverly gang over to her house for some beers one night when her mom was out of town at a sales training seminar for her job. I saw this as my opportunity to cozy up to her and convince her I had a soft side. I asked her what she thought of the roses I'd sent. She said they were nice, a sweet gesture. After a night of hanging out and talking about things that interested us both, like music and drawing, she decided to give me a chance and agreed to go out on a date the following week.

Late in the evening of our first date after I drove Lisa back to her house, we sat in my Chevy Blazer in her driveway, kissing, listening to a music mixtape I'd made for her after her party. It had songs on it we both enjoyed, tunes by The Smiths and Ramones and Social Distortion. Words about young love and passion and heartbreak. Conspicuously, there were no white power songs on the tape. Not even my own.

A steady rainfall had begun and the rhythm of the droplets pitter-pattering against the roof created a soothing cadence for our makeout session. Lisa's skin felt like silk on my fingertips and I worked hard to summon up my soft side, touching her face when we kissed. Cradling her gently in my arms.

The humidity of the muggy August night and our steamy lip-lock caused the car windows to fog up, revealing several crude swastikas that Kubiak had traced with his finger on the windshield the week before, while we'd been staking out a house in Blue Island that a group of SHARPs had rented. The Antis had claimed they wanted to move their operations closer to ours, so they could monitor our activities from close range. We knew they moved into our territory simply to spite us. And it did piss us off. Though they had no idea how closely it also allowed us to keep an eye on them.

I leaned in and pulled Lisa close to shield her eyes, so that the markings wouldn't upset her. Not fast enough.

"Can I ask you something?" Lisa spoke timidly, pulling herself out of my arms. "Promise me you won't get mad."

"Of course." I reached to caress her face and held her hand. "What's wrong?"

Lisa sighed and moved her gaze away from mine. I could tell from her hesitation that she was about to ask me something that had been weighing heavily on her mind. "Why do you have so much hate inside of you?"

The stickiness level in the car felt as if it had quadrupled once the question left her lips. I couldn't help but adjust myself in my seat to fend off her unsettling glare. At that moment, I would rather have been hit in the jaw with an uppercut than been faced with that question. Especially from Lisa. It caught me off guard, but I knew I had to give her an answer if we were going to have any chance for a second date.

So, I lied to her. "I don't hate anyone. I just love what I stand for so much that I'm willing to protect it from those who want to do it harm."

I knew my answer was bullshit. Instead of being honest with Lisa, I'd replied with the standard one-size-fits-all party line. It was a common practice within the movement to always spin our hateful agenda and wrap it in a pretty little "white pride" bow for the general public to consume. The truth was, we hated everybody that wasn't like us.

Without flinching, Lisa replied, "But, then why aren't you doing anything positive? All you do is say such hateful things and get in fights and hurt people. That's not love. That's violence and destruction and hate." Her eyes pleaded with mine for the truth. "But when you're with me, you are so caring and gentle. Which one is the real you?"

The question, when posed by Lisa, made me uncomfortable. Nervous. Even though I'd answered it without much effort dozens of times before, when thrown at me by teachers and coaches and adults. When responding to them, the answer was not quite as romantic—the word "nigger" often punctuating my reply. When the question left her soft lips, I suddenly couldn't muster the words to string together an answer that made much sense to me.

The cassette in the car stereo clicked and flipped to begin playing the first song from the second side of the tape. The familiar tone of Social Distortion's guitars drew me in and it wasn't until the verse hit that a sick feeling pitted itself in my stomach.

I sit and I pray in my broken-down Chevrolet...
I'm lonely and I'm tired and I can't take any more pain...
Take away this ball and chain...
Take away this ball and chain.

Lisa continued, "When you love something, how can you possibly do so at anyone else's expense?"

Her voice was tender. Caring. The dampness in the air turned the fogginess on the windows into streaking rivulets of water that raced down the windshield and erased the symbols on the glass. But not the thought from my mind. Her eyes looked deep into mine as my stomach wrenched tighter. I looked into her eyes and said, "I do it because it's important to me."

"Am I important to you?" she pleaded.

"Yes." The wind picked up and shook the truck violently, startling Lisa.

In the foreground, the porch light lit up and we heard her mother call Lisa's name. "They've issued a severe weather warning. You should come inside, Lisa."

"I better go before the storm gets any worse. You should go, too." She leaned in and kissed me on the lips. "Thanks for my tape."

With that, she threw open the Blazer door and darted for shelter. I watched as she gracefully dodged the raindrops and disappeared into the house. The wild storm battering my truck was no match for the tempest brewing inside of me.

I spent every waking moment with Lisa and never wanted to leave her side. She was smart and creative. Aside from our politics clashing, we were perfectly matched. She was headstrong, but she trusted me and felt safe with me around.

Lisa eventually brought me home to meet her family, and they also began to like me. Her mother had been a hippie in the early '70s, but somehow me being a racist skinhead didn't seem to bother her much. Besides, she'd never tell Lisa no to anything. She treated her like a companion, not her daughter. She wouldn't want to upset her by disagreeing with either one of us.

Being accepted into Lisa's home made me feel like I was stable and part of something normal. Her mother had remarried, but her new husband was a bit of a slug, so Lisa and her mom thought it was nice to have a real man in the house who could repair things and help with the yard work. And it wasn't long before her little brother dressed the skinhead part. I had made my way in and influenced my surroundings like I'd done in every other area of my life.

Lisa was the first person I totally opened up to. I'd even held back from the High Street Boys, and sure didn't confide my innermost feelings to any of the skinheads. Leaders don't do that.

But Lisa and I had so much in common; we understood each other on a deeper level almost immediately. So we opened up and talked about our innermost feelings.

Like me, she had been more or less raised by her grandparents, and her parents had played no significant role when she was a child. They were flower children who'd split up when it wasn't fun being together anymore. Lisa was only three at the time and her brother less than a year old. Her dad never looked back, so Lisa had no recollection of him.

Once she was on her own, Lisa's young mother had no choice but to adapt to responsibility. She found her way into a corporate job that meant long hours and little time with her children.

Like me, Lisa spent most of her time with her grandparents while her mother, like mine, dedicated all her time building a professional career instead of spending it with her family.

Long before either of us ever thought of having children, we had both promised ourselves we'd never be like that with our own kids.

"I'll go to every single sports game they play," I told Lisa.

"And I'll be there for all their events at school. Do you know how embarrassing it is that my friends don't even know what my mother looks like? I think half of them thought my grandmother was my mother and that I had the oldest mother in town," Lisa would say.

"I know exactly what that's like," I lamented. "My mom never had time to go grocery shopping, or she would forget to send me to school with lunch altogether, so I'd have to hide from the other kids who made fun of me when she'd remember to bring some fast food later." I laughed. "Looking back now, I guess my lunches *were* always better than anyone else's. I was eating French fries when the other kids had to eat carrot sticks."

"Sounds like they were jealous," she giggled. "My mom thinks we're girlfriends. I mean, it's great that she's easygoing and all, but there's some details of her life I'd rather she didn't tell me. Why can't she just be a mom like other kids have? You know, tell me when to study and normal stuff like that."

"Would you listen?"

She shrugged. "I don't know. I'd give it a try. How about you?"

I shook my head and scoffed. "My parents have been scared to say no to me since I could walk. I've never listened to a damn thing they've said or told me to do. Why should I? Don't you have to be present in somebody's life to earn the privilege of playing role model and making the rules?"

"Good point."

We talked for hours about the mistakes our parents made and how we'd be way smarter than them the day we had kids of our own, although we were speaking in general terms—Lisa hadn't even graduated from high school yet, and I sure as shit didn't have any intentions of becoming a father before I'd even reached eighteen.

Lisa had a stepsister who was ten years younger than her, the same way Buddy was ten years younger than me. Buddy liked Lisa and would spy on us, his full cheeks becoming flushed when we kissed and held hands.

"Buddy, I saw you kissing that girl," he said one day, his shy eyes smiling.

"You did, huh?" I laughed. "Someday you'll have a girlfriend, too. And you'll probably want to kiss her like I did."

He scrunched up his face. "No way! That's gross." He said it was gross, but I knew he just thought it looked funny.

"And when you meet that girl, you might even marry her and have babies someday," I joked.

Buddy's expression became gloomy. "I heard you tell her that you love her. Does that mean you don't love me and Mom and Dad anymore?" He stared at the ground nervously.

"No, of course not, Buddy. Why would you think that?" I crouched down to meet his downcast eyes. "You can love more than one person at once. I love you a lot and I always will. Just don't love more than one girlfriend at once or you'll be in big trouble." We laughed.

"Can we go outside and play catch?" asked Buddy, raising his eyes to mine. There was so much in this apparently simple question.

"I can't right now. I have to go pick up Lisa. But I promise you this weekend we'll go outside and play."

He knew it wouldn't happen. Another broken promise from his big brother. "Okay, Buddy."

What I saw wash over him in that moment made my heart stop. I'd let him down again. He just wanted to belong. I'd make it up to him.

In addition to being raised by our grandparents, Lisa and I were both smart, had a strong sense of responsibility, and were old for our years.

In Lisa, these traits led her to a realization that she wanted to become a schoolteacher. "I want to make a difference," she told me more than once. "You know, be there for kids. Help them learn and make good choices in life."

I encouraged her, ignoring the fact that I hadn't made time for my own kid brother, didn't trust teachers, and the choices I'd made were anything but good in her book. But the world needed more people like Lisa. Her kind heart couldn't steer children wrong.

Even if she wasn't a racist.

Or a fighter.

In fact, she detested prejudice and violence of any sort. She wasn't crazy about the lyrics I wrote either. She didn't mind the music that much, but refused to acknowledge the words at all. She did a good job of pretending the things she didn't like about me didn't exist. And somehow, they practically didn't when I was with her.

When Lisa and I were together, I didn't want to talk about white power and revolution. It felt out of place. I wanted to discuss personal things, so I confided in her about my feelings of loneliness when I was younger, how I'd basically spent the first twelve years of my life drawing and daydreaming alone in my grandparents' coat closet; how I'd blamed my parents for abandoning me; how hard it was to straddle two completely different worlds like I had to do when I was bounced back and forth between the contradictory cultures of Oak Forest and Blue Island. How I hated being bored and felt called to do something special. Important. Noble, even.

Lisa found it odd that I had opted not to go to college. "You're so smart. What are you going to do with your life without a college degree?"

"I plan to start a business," I told her. "You can't learn what you need to know about being your own man in college. I've been figuring out ways to make things work since I was a little kid. I don't need a worthless piece of paper to prove that I can."

"You could get a degree in business, though."

"It's not my path."

"What is?"

"This is," I said, leaning in and kissing her tenderly on the lips.

We spent as much time as we could together. Day and night.

It didn't take me long to get comfortable with that. Aside from the joy of falling asleep with her in my arms and seeing her first thing every morning, it made all the other goals I'd set for myself seem trivial.

For the first time since my brother's birth, I felt totally aligned with one single person.

We built a world of two where nothing and nobody could reach us. Touching her cheek, feeling her hand in mine, her head on my shoulder, making love to her every night filled me with a sense of completeness and peace I'd never known. I knew her every look, knew what she was feeling before she verbalized it by catching the way her lip curled when she had something on her mind. No words were necessary to tell me what she was thinking. Our time together was beautiful. Vulnerable.

And she knew me—my lonesomeness, my longing to leave my mark on the world. She respected that, which is why, I think, she didn't try to stop my skinhead activities even though she was wholly opposed to the racist world in which I was living. Without compromising her own beliefs, she still found ways to support mine. And I began to fall deeply in love with her.

Lisa had been the ingredient to happiness I hadn't even known was missing. I couldn't mess that up.

Shortly after Labor Day of '91, that spineless Anti Hector Diaz had his Jew lawyer petition the court to have my suspended judgment revoked and the assault charge against me reinstated. Claimed I'd threatened him during my period of court supervision. Goddamn fucking liar. That meant possible jail time if they could convince the judge I'd defaulted. I'd own up to it if I had, I wasn't scared, but I hadn't even seen the scumbag, let alone threatened him.

The cops took me into custody when I pulled into the EZ–Go gas station on Western Avenue to buy cigarettes. Towed my truck into the impound lot. I spent the night in the Blue Island lockup, next to a cell with a drunken nigger bum who kept me awake all night snoring like a jackhammer, and was released on my own recognizance at daybreak. Not even a crumb of food or a smoke for twelve hours. I was on edge, to say the least. Another court date was set.

I dressed respectfully again, acted polite and humble, bit my tongue until it bled, and clearly stated my innocence. Judge didn't believe me. Or, maybe he did, but knew I was bad news and so decided to sentence me anyway.

Lucky for me it wasn't a harsh sentence, though, still avoiding jail time so far. One hundred hours of community service. Five days a week, Monday through Friday, I had to report to the county courthouse at eight in the morning. Other guys sentenced to community service would be there too, mainly for driving drunk, misdemeanors, skipping out on child support, major traffic violations—that kind of stuff. There were ten of us altogether. We did janitorial work around the courthouse or were hauled off in a prison transport van with two county sheriffs to pick up garbage along the roadway or pull up weeds in empty city lots. Painted a couple of fences. I did this every weekday for a month for six to eight hours a pop to work off the time. Made pizzas in the evening. No big deal. Annoying more than anything.

I was concerned with how Lisa would take this brush with the law and was relieved that she took having an archcriminal for a boyfriend in stride. She believed I hadn't done anything wrong. At least as far as threatening Hector Diaz.

As the fall months came and went, I looked back on them as an affirmation of progress despite the legal speed bumps. I'd been to a bunch of skinhead festivals throughout the South, my band had made a name for itself in our home region and even beyond, I'd thrown my share of knockdown punches, had proven to the Antis my crew wouldn't take their shit, and had met the girl I knew I'd someday marry.

Concerts and rallies would slow down once the weather grew colder, and I couldn't imagine how I'd spend the long days missing Lisa while she was back in school.

Of course I found a way.

ROCK-O-RAMA
Herbert Egoldt
5040 Brühl, Kaiserstr. 119
Tel. 02232/22584

OU 49

MIT LUFTPOST
PAR AVION

MIT LUFTPOST
PAR AVION

W.A.Y.
Chris Picciolini
P.O. Box 734
Midlothian Ill. 60445

RoCK-o-RAMA
RECORDS

HERB
KAISE
D-5040

TEL.

POSTGI
KÖLN 16

IMPORT · HARDCORE · NEW WAVE · PUNK

W.A.Y.
Chris Picciolini
P.O.Box 734
Midlothian Ill. 60445
U.S.A.

DATUM

Hello Chris,

thank you for your letter + demo-tape.
Yes, if you like we would produce an lp with your band.
Please tell me any phone-no. I can get you.

Best regards,

17

HAPPY DEATH

I SPENT THE NEXT MONTH lining up interviews for WAY in a couple of skinhead newsletters, "zines" as we called them. The publications themselves were crude—badly made photocopies on poor-quality copiers—but that didn't matter. Skinheads were used to getting information that way and read everything they could from the few printed things remotely resembling magazines.

When interviewed about who influenced me politically I didn't hesitate to answer. "Politically we are influenced by the National Socialist German Workers' Party of the 1930s, and by contemporary English political organizations such as the National Front and Ian Stuart's Rock Against Communism. In America I support former Klansman and politician David Duke."

I answered questions about my views on specific subjects with earnestness, not remotely reluctant to have them known. *Blind Justice*, a British skinhead zine, had printed some of these views in its newsletter the previous year. At the top of the interview, an image of a Hitler Youth eagle with a swastika emblazoned on its breast and sword and hammer clutched in its talons accented the page. Wings spread wide open, ready for attack. Perfect symbol for me, if not everyone who supported WAY.

Here's what I had to say in the article on various topics:

Gays: I think all queers should be sent to Mexico and blown to bits along with the Mexicans.

Jews: I despise Jews for one simple reason. They corrupt society with their evil lies. The Jewish parasites manipulate us and control our government, the banking system, and the media. I dislike Jews for the same reason that every civilization over the last three millennia have hated and banished them. They infect and kill every healthy thing they touch.

Race Mixing: I think race mixing is possibly the worst, most sub-human act against Mother Nature. We will soon see an end to this disease, because the Day of the Rope is returning.

Drugs: Drugs are for weak people who feel insecure about themselves, therefore they need the drugs to numb their feelings and enter an alternate reality. I am proud of who I am and don't need the false self-confidence that drugs provide.

Religion: I'm an agnostic and tend not to trust organized religions because they are as money-hungry as the Jews. If anything, I'd consider aligning myself with the Norse Odinist beliefs of warfare and reward. The principle of Victory or Valhalla resonates with me.

Zionism: The Zionist Jews stole the Holy Land, enslaved its people, slapped a Star of David on it and called it Israel. In spite of that, I'd be satisfied if every Jew just moved there and stayed out of America.

Capitalism: Capitalists can all rot in hell with their dirty blood money.

The press we'd been receiving put us in the spotlight overseas and in America, but it was just the tip of the iceberg.

Something much larger was brewing.

During my last week of community service for the phony Diaz beef, I assembled my WAY band mates and we cut a demo tape of six of our original songs. Very crude. Raw. I set up a microphone on a table during band rehearsal and we laid down a few tunes in one live take.

The next morning I rushed to the post office and mailed copies to the famous French white power record company Rebelles Européens and Rock-O-Rama Records, the legendary German label that handled all the prominent European skinhead bands, including Skrewdriver.

The French label offered us a record deal almost immediately, but I was gunning for Rock-O-Rama. So confident was I that when Gaël Bodilis, the owner of Rebelles Européens, called me to follow up on the offer he'd sent us in the mail, I politely turned him down without having heard from the other.

I tried following up by calling the Rock-O-Rama office in Germany repeatedly for the next two weeks to see if they'd received my package. After more than a dozen attempts, staying up late at night to call because of the seven-hour time difference, I finally got through and managed to talk to Herbert Egoldt, the owner of Rock-O-Rama. He was jovial. Lighthearted. Said he'd gotten our tape and continued to speak the sweetest words I'd heard since Lisa first told me she loved me. He promised to fax over a recording contract within a few days.

Luckily I'd lifted a fax machine a few weeks back from a neighbor who was being evicted from his apartment. The sheriff's deputies who displaced him had piled up all his stuff in the parking lot behind the building. Nothing else was worth taking, but I spotted the fax machine and thought it could come in handy. Turns out it did.

The contract arrived as promised a few days later. In German. None of us in the band could follow a single word of it, but what the fuck did we care? It meant we could make a record. Exactly what I'd hoped for. We had a deal on the table in early October and I got the band to sign immediately on the dotted line and faxed it back.

Within a month, I arranged to record our first album in a studio called Square Bear Sounds in Alsip, a suburb just outside of Blue Island. The owner, Doc Beringer, grew marijuana plants in the back room and was always stoned. He mainly recorded ghetto rap acts, although he looked like a mundane white guy who you'd never expect to be hanging around gangsta street thugs. He got a kick out of our blatantly racist music even though he wasn't particularly bigoted himself. I think he thought the band was an over-the-top gag. Like a vulgar version of Weird Al Yankovic or something. He even made suggestions for sound bites that we could sample and add in to our songs to make them even more vitriolic.

In the studio we cranked through song after song—thirteen in all— including a rousing rendition of Skrewdriver's anthem, "White Power." We altered the words slightly to make more geographic sense for our American and hometown Chicago fans.

Multiracial society is a mess
We ain't gonna take much more of this
What do we need?
White Power! For America
White Power! Today
White Power! For Chicago
Before it gets too late.

As more "accomplished" musicians, Larry and Rick may have liked being in the studio, but I *loved* it. Despite the embedded pot stench in every piece of broken-down furniture and the lack of toilet paper in the grimy, roach-infested bathrooms, the process of recording all the different instruments onto separate tracks fascinated me.

Mixing the individual sounds independently, tweaking the levels just right, achieving the exact tones the songs deserved. The spinning sound of the giant wheels of recording tape—where the music magically lived—flapping when the reel-to-reel console hit the end of the tape was a joy to my ears. The glowing vacuum tubes, bulbs, and meters, reminded me of bright city lights. Inspired me. Everything waiting to be mixed together like a giant art puzzle without a reference picture—piece by piece—was like solving a foreign spy mystery. Piecing together the various bits into complete songs with mighty anthems that thousands would sing along to were the end result.

Glorious.

Before we hit the studio Davey had told us he was out. He had a real shot at becoming a professional skateboarder and putting out a racist record would negatively influence his chances. We didn't want to hold him back, so we parted ways and brought in a new bass player, Skinhead Mark, to fill his role. Though, unfortunately, this didn't happen before Davey "wrote" a song that we inadvertently recorded and put on the record without knowing he'd entirely ripped off the main hook lick-for-lick from a New York City hardcore band called Sick Of It All.

Despite that, the mood in the studio was electrifying. Literally.

Well into a long midnight session, while I was recording my lyrics I accidentally knocked over and spilled a beer on the vocal booth floor. Trying not to interrupt our flow, as time and money were limited, I gripped the microphone and was instantly sent flying back violently against the wall. My boot had been resting in the puddle of beer when I gripped the shoddy microphone, nearly killing me via electric shock.

If you listen closely to the track "Happy Death"—which we cheekily decided to name the song after my close call—you can hear a faint pop where we were unable to fully scrub the sound fluctuation from the track without having to redo the entire song.

I didn't care. I would have died happy.

We recorded and mixed the entire record in five days for exactly $1,372, paid for by Rock-O-Rama. The album was pressed first as a vinyl LP and later made into a compact disc when that format hit the mass market the following year. The album was officially listed as Rock-O-Rama #123: White American Youth, *Walk Alone*. It was primarily sold in Europe, though a few record stores in Canada also carried it. But mainly, if you lived in the U.S., you had to order it as an import by airmail and postal money order from Germany. I was incredibly proud.

From a financial standpoint it was a lousy deal for us. We didn't make a single dime and didn't even get free promotional records like bands typically do. Without knowing it, we'd essentially signed over one hundred percent of the rights to our recorded music in perpetuity to the label. Feeling both angry and foolish, I scraped up some cash and ordered fifty copies of the record at the wholesale price and sold them to our friends at cost to save face. The label handled all mass distribution.

Everybody in Blue Island and the surrounding Chicago area knew we'd recorded the album. We were celebrities, even though I didn't get treated all that differently since I'd been treated pretty well already, but it was the cherry on top of the white power sundae for me. Another notch in my belt.

Even some of the Antis were surprisingly cool about it and defected to our side because of the record. Local kids loved that somebody in their neighborhood had actually released an album and they wanted to be a part of the fun.

Despite the hodgepodge way Rock-O-Rama promoted their releases and managed the relationship with us, it didn't take long for the record to become popular among skinheads. We officially joined the ranks of America's first few white power bands. Along with Bound For Glory, Bully Boys, Arresting Officers, Max Resist & the Hooligans, and Midtown Bootboys, we were in good company. Exalted company as far as I was concerned. Aside from WAY, Bound For Glory was the only other active American band on the legendary Rock-O-Rama roster.

Getting to play on a bill with Bound For Glory continued to be important to me. Hailing from the Twin Cities of Minnesota, they were the white power musical outfit that had every skinhead talking. Many had pegged them as the "Skrewdriver of the States," after Rock-O-Rama released their first album *Warrior's Glory* the previous year to critical skinhead acclaim. Their style was different than most of their British or American Oi! counterparts, bringing more homegrown thrash metal flavor to back up their pointed lyrics. Bound For Glory quickly became the band everyone wanted to emulate and associate with. I made it a priority to get our bands to play together.

Rehearsals were awkward at first. Before we cut the record, half the group didn't know how to play our instruments and none of us had performed in a band before. But we worked hard and built something tangible with no roadmap or instructions. Few white power skinheads had traveled this road before us. And we persevered. We had the confidence that came along with having an album and a legitimate label behind us, a group of friends intent on making music that meant something, and a desire to succeed against all logical odds.

The whole experience was exciting beyond words. I'd put our band together, written the lyrics of every song, and in two short months after we recorded our demo I'd landed us a record deal that allowed us to eventually sell tens of thousands of albums worldwide. We'd performed a dozen concerts, mostly in smoky Knights of Columbus halls or in friends' musty basements. But now we had the royal stamp of validity. We weren't just *on* our way.

We *were* the WAY.

Not long after we released the *Walk Alone* record in early December of 1991, I was arrested yet again. To keep the movement alive—to make sure my name was seared into the brain of every kid in high school—me and one of my associates showed up at Eisenhower one morning to protest in support of white students. We waved large signs emblazoned with "White Pride," demanding "Equal Rights for Whites." I'd coordinated a dozen or so white kids in the school to join us by staging a cafeteria sit-in, refusing to go to class until the school agreed to grant them a white student union to rival the various minority student groups already in existence.

Car horns beeped both approval and disdain. Passersby threw supportive shouts and disapproving projectiles at us. A news crew showed up. Cops came. The young protesters inside the school succumbed to the pressure of impending suspension and were shuffled back to class. Even though I had never left the public sidewalk, I was arrested and charged with criminal trespassing on school property since I was no longer a student there. The previous restraining order against me didn't make it any easier. The demonstration made the local newspapers, and a Blue Island police sergeant identified me in an article as a "white supremacist mob boss."

"And proud of it," I would have added if the reporter had bothered to interview me.

18

VICTORY MARCH

Finally, after months of hard work, we'd been booked to play in the same venue, on the same stage, as Bound For Glory, my favorite American white power band. I'd corresponded with them some, but the interest was more on my part than theirs. WAY had been lined up to perform with them twice before, but skinhead concerts and fests were routinely shut down when some half-wit concert promoter got scared that we'd start trouble.

But now we were slated to play with Bound For Glory in Muskegon, Michigan. And not just in some basement or at some kegger party. We were playing in a real club. The Ice Pick. It was in the middle of a ghetto, but it was a legit punk rock venue. The interior of the place had seen its fair share of rock and roll abuse, every inch of the walls covered with nihilistic graffiti. The smell of piss and stale beer was overwhelming.

On the day of the concert, The Ice Pick was overrun with at least three hundred white power skinheads from around the Midwest and East Coast. A whole shitload of young hooligans full of rage and fury, waiting for an excuse to erupt into violence. The club was so packed I was surprised the fire marshal wasn't summoned to shut the show down. But nobody wanted to mess with us.

I played it casual when I met Bound For Glory the first time, intent on not letting any traces of anxious fan-boy energy show through. It was important to be perceived as an equal, even if I was slightly starstruck and much younger than them.

Despite my nerves, Big Ed Arthur, the guitarist and leader of Bound For Glory, and I hit it off immediately. Felt like we'd known each other for years. We became fast friends, bound by the fact that we were both first-generation Americans. His family had emigrated from Croatia around the same time mine had come over from Italy.

But as soon as WAY took the stage, one of the drunken East Coast skinheads in the crowd threw a beer can toward Rick, our guitarist, and accosted him for his long heavy metal hair.

"Hippie scum," he babbled, headed for Rick, fists in the air. "I'll kick your fucking commie ass!"

Incensed anybody would go after Rick, I jumped in front of him, ready to beat this drunk asshole to a bloody pulp right there on stage for all to see.

Big Ed hopped up in a swift, sure move and wedged himself between us. His stare communicated to this dude so much more than what came out of his mouth. "They're with me."

The drunk backed down without hesitation. Everyone respected Big Ed. He was a massive, fully-tattooed bear of a man. It was hard not to be intimidated by him. I liked the way he'd handled it. Made a note of it. Quiet power and choice words could come in handy. Silent strength. I tucked the concept away for future use.

But all wasn't well. After our set was over, Rick was in a hurry to leave.

"This is crazy," he said. "That fucking guy wanted to kill me!" I tried to calm him down, but he was having none of it. Being a part-time racist, Rick wasn't used to the violence that came with the territory.

With Rick still stewing on our drive home from Michigan, things got worse when we stopped at a rest area to call home and received word that a skinhead mate from our crew, Jason Silva, had stabbed his girlfriend twenty-one times in a lover's quarrel. Shit. We'd all been close friends with Jason and his girl. We often joked that all they did was argue like jealous lovers so they'd have an excuse to fuck like rabbits and make up. Maybe we should have seen it coming. Jason was overly possessive, but we never thought he'd physically hurt her. For them, it was ultimate passion or shameless aggression, but never violence. They loved each other.

Now he'd stabbed her twenty-one goddamn times?

Jesus fucking Christ.

I felt sick about it, hoping that she'd pull through. She'd survived, but the horror of it was surreal. We were all speechless the rest of the drive home.

I knew between being confronted on stage and now this news, Rick wasn't going to be with WAY much longer. And if he quit, Larry, our drummer, would follow. They were best friends. Had been forever. They'd stick together. As friends should. I couldn't fault them for that.

I immediately began thinking of who could replace them. I'd only recently come out in the Belgian skinhead zine *Pure Impact* saying we were planning to release a second album with nine new tracks. I'd be a laughingstock if the band disappeared shortly after we'd gotten started. I had to assemble another band. And fast.

Meanwhile, my personal life couldn't have been going better. Even though high school took up Lisa's days, we spent our nights together. We never ran out of topics to discuss. I wanted to hear everything about her day. Nothing she said bored me. I kept most of my skinhead activities to myself, not wanting the ugliness that sometimes erupted to touch her. I shared the victories—progress with writing new songs, an interesting conversation I shared with somebody I admired—but never discussed the fights or the drama. And sure as hell never used the language with her that I used on the streets. Our love was pure, and nothing remotely dirty had any part in our world together. It was a nice reprieve from the constant madness.

One night as I lay in bed watching her sleep, a profound sense of peace washed over me. We hadn't made love that evening, but my passion for her didn't need physical union to flood me with feelings for her. As had become our habit, we pledged ourselves to each other before drifting off to sleep. Leaning over her on one elbow, I watched her chest move up and down with each breath she took.

How could I be so fortunate? I loved everything about her—her sweetness, her sincerity, her intellect, her loyalty, her kindness. We'd talked many times about spending the rest of our lives together. We both wanted children someday, and I loved that she could only imagine having them with me. I admired that she was serious about helping kids and I'd grown more comfortable with her plans to become a teacher. Maybe she'd find a way to change the system. Not all teachers had to push a false agenda. Lisa would be different. I was sure she was smart enough to not let college brainwash her.

As that thought hit me, a sharp realization accompanied it. If she were to go away to school, we would be apart. She would live in a world that didn't include me. A blow far more powerful than any I'd received in the many fights I'd been in.

I could lose her—I *would* lose her—if she went off to college.

Without me there to protect her, the experience would change her. And I would be alone again.

But it wasn't just being alone again that terrified me: It was being without *her*.

The thought was unbearable and I struggled to breathe. I panicked and was overcome with fear.

Life without her was unthinkable.

There was only one solution. I had to keep her here.

I had to propose to her.

It wasn't enough to tell each other we would be together forever. It had to be official. She had to say yes, she must marry me.

I blocked out the voice condemning me for such a selfish act. That knew marriage might mean a major change in her plans for college, for her own future. I wanted her with me; what she thought she wanted was secondary. And we'd be together. That's what she needed most, right? I knew what was best for both of us. I was the strong one. I was the leader. It was my destiny.

I began planning my proposal. All worries about losing her faded as I began to visualize our lives together.

I bought her a chip of an engagement ring with what little money I had saved making pizzas, not at all certain how or where I'd ask her to marry me. She was still in her final year of high school. But I knew I couldn't wait until she graduated.

A multitude of scenarios passed through my head. The when and where of it. What I'd say. The expression on her face. If I'd be able to hold it together when I asked her.

The time came unexpectedly in December, just after my eighteenth birthday. Lisa and some of our Beverly friends threw me a belated surprise birthday party, and as I was surrounded by people who loved me and who I loved, people who thought enough of me to plan this whole special event, I knew the moment couldn't be more perfect.

In front of everyone, I held Lisa's hand, got down on one knee and declared, "I love you, Lisa. I can't imagine my life without you in it."

She was shocked, looking around at the equally surprised faces of our friends, not saying a word. Excited gasps became contagious in the room around us.

"Nobody makes me happy like you do," I managed to say before getting choked up. I cleared my throat. "Will you do me the honor of being my wife?"

She was taken aback. Sure, we'd spoken about marriage before, but never anything definite. We hadn't even been dating a year yet. Not even half a year. But she didn't hesitate. "Yes," she said, "Yes!"

I took her gentle face in my hands and kissed her on the lips. The hushed silence in the room was shattered by cheers and beer bottles clinking. The girls in the room wiped their teary eyes.

I was eighteen. In love. And engaged to be married to a girl I cared deeply about.

I would make sure she never regretted joining her life with mine. Lisa would be proud to call herself my wife, and I began to see my actions through that lens.

Through the skinhead grapevine, I heard Bound For Glory was heading overseas to Germany in March of '92 to play a concert. Doing so would make them the first white power band from the United States to ever play a show on European soil. They'd make history.

I had to be part of this. Didn't matter to me that WAY had broken up when Larry and Rick left the group. I'd started a new band without missing a beat—Final Solution, in homage to the original band Clark, Carmine, and Chase Sargent had formed for a brief time in early 1985, at the genesis of the whole U.S. white power skinhead movement. I had three months to prepare the band for our trip.

After some initial hesitation, I decided to write to Clark in prison about it. Asked his permission to resurrect the Final Solution name. Two years had passed since we'd corresponded and the materials that did still randomly trickle in willy-nilly from him bordered on nonsensical and repulsive. It had become clear to me that Clark was indeed seriously mentally ill. Relatively benign pornographic descriptions of women had turned into sadistic, rambling accounts of sexual violence and torture.

When a letter from Clark finally came back with his blessing on the use of the name, I didn't respond to thank him. Thinking, even for a moment, how those sorts of twisted thoughts could enter someone's mind and escape their lips turned my stomach and made me feel dirty. I quickly put it behind me and moved forward.

This time every member of my band was a skinhead. Two new guitarists, Mack and Hugo from the Indiana Hammerskin crew. Their friend Kenny Flanagan rounded out the group on drums. The only member of WAY that was part of my new band was Skinhead Mark, the bass player, whom we'd replaced Davey with a few months earlier when he'd bailed to follow his skateboarding dreams.

With some digging, I found out who was promoting the German concert. I phoned him late one night and said I'd toured with Bound For Glory previously in the States and insisted my new band travel with them to this concert as well. No resistance whatsoever from the promoter. He more or less said fine, if we could get there he'd let us play.

So I called Big Ed from Bound For Glory and told him we'd be going along to Germany. They were getting paid to perform and set up with a place to stay. I let him know we'd fund our own trip and find our own place to bunk, but would be meeting them there. He seemed glad we were going.

I couldn't wait to tell Lisa the news. She'd go with me, of course. Spend her eighteenth birthday with me. I wanted to experience this milestone together, even if she'd want no part in the concert itself. She loved to take photographs and sketch architecture and I thought we could travel together and split up when it was time to take care of band business. Germany had an abundance of historic landmarks and breathtaking scenery to keep her busy snapping photos and drawing for weeks. Who cared that the concert was in March and she'd still be in school? I wanted her to be part of that history.

Getting booked to play in Germany might have been simple, but don't think for a minute I hadn't earned the right to be there. I'd been attending rallies, pumping out printed material, and recruiting people for our cause for over five years, much longer than most skins had even been in the movement. Out of everyone I met nationwide, I was often the youngest—but almost always the most active. I'd put together not one, but two, well-known white power bands, knowing being in a band was a sure way to rise up in status and make a lasting impression. What I might have lacked in musical talent I had in guts, and the two bands I put together garnered instant fans. Which translated into more skinheads, more soldiers, and more attention.

The recruiting tactics for my Hammerskin chapter had shifted focus from printing and distributing flyers to strangers, to producing music and using it as a targeted marketing tool to keep the flooding masses of new recruits—that were now coming in on their own volition—happy and engaged.

I'd lost almost all interest in throwing fists since I met Lisa, content in simply conducting the chaos like a maestro leading a symphony. Earning the crossed hammers patch for their bomber jacket became an obsession for new recruits and I was the local gatekeeper. There were strict rules like abstaining from drugs and respecting your brothers. A brief probationary period allowed the cream to rise to the top and the wayward most to be skimmed off. I was satisfied with my position at the top of the Illinois Hammerskin pyramid, still leaving enough time for me to focus on the band and my beautiful fiancée.

A surprising thing about skinheads, though, was that for all the fear the media propagated, membership was actually pretty small. Across the nation, there were probably fewer than five thousand racist skinheads—of which only about five hundred were Hammerskins—yet we were considered a formidable force. From local cops to the FBI, law enforcement soiled their panties thinking of what we might be up to or where we'd pop up next. Minority adults saw a kid with a shaved head, tattoos, and Doc Martens in their town and they were running to realtors and having earnest conversations about pulling their kids out of the local public school.

While we got the nation's attention after Marty Cox called Oprah a monkey on national television, we'd cemented the public's fear and loathing two years later when a skinhead busted Geraldo's nose on his talk show. We still laughed about it amongst ourselves.

Every time a skinhead threw a punch or desecrated a synagogue, the media picked up on it and vilified us as extremist right-wing radicals—domestic terrorists. So we didn't need a whole bunch of us to strike fear into the heart of America. Fifty of us partying together was reason enough to call in the SWAT team, the FBI, and the National Guard. As our numbers grew, so did our violent behavior.

Back in the summer heat of 1990, two Houston, Texas, skinheads stomped a fifteen-year-old foreigner from Vietnam to death. According to one of the killers, the kid's last words were, "God forgive me for coming to this country. I'm so sorry."

The following year, some other Texas Hammerskins took out a race-mixing nigger in a drive-by shooting. He'd been hanging out with some white traitors.

A few months later, Aryan National Front skinheads from Birmingham, Alabama, beat a homeless black vagrant to death on Christmas Eve. Shortly after, four other skinheads stabbed and killed another transient waste of life. Cleaning the streets of all the filth, as far as I was concerned.

And yet, while my skinhead brethren were out patrolling the homeland and taking care of much-needed movement business, I couldn't help but acknowledge the lurking gratitude that I felt for my hardworking immigrant parents and all that they had fought to accomplish since coming to this country. Though we were hardly together to enjoy the creature comforts that their efforts provided, they consistently put food on our table, a roof over my head, and I was afforded luxuries that were often beyond our financial means. They found ways to give me a leg up in society—a way to rise above the filth—despite the absence of their physical affection. I'd found a proxy to fill the remaining void. And the two halves formed an abundant whole.

While our numbers weren't big compared to other street gangs, white power skinheads were spread out far and wide and tucked into every corner of the country. We took turns hosting rallies and fests to get together to exchange information and motivate each other to keep fighting the good fight. Not a whole lot of people would travel long-distance for some boring meeting, but add old friends, aggressive white power music, and beer to the agenda, and it was a guarantee skinhead guys and gals would drive hundreds of miles to get drunk and hear music from the few bands singing their tunes.

Skinhead gatherings were like white power pep rallies. The energy at these events reignited our weary fires and put us in the right frame of mind to continue battling the enemy. It gave others who came solely to experience the music another chance to join our intrepid efforts to save the white race. It's pretty damn hard to listen to hours and hours of aggressive music preaching about the need to fight those trying to destroy the people you love and not to come away pissed off, ready to do something about it.

Music was usually preceded by speakers. Sometimes I was one of them. We'd get up on stage and set the tone through communicating that our nation was in jeopardy. "Heil Hitler," we'd say.

Hands would shoot up with the precision of a well-trained Nazi brigade. "Heil Hitler," the devotees would shout back.

"Our goal today is simple. We're here to listen to a little white power music."

Whistles, cheers. Stiff-armed salutes from those who weren't double-fisting bottles of cheap beer.

"And we're here to secure the existence of our race and a future for white children!"

The response was invariably deafening.

"I'll bet you know there are people who don't want us here today. Who tried to stop this peaceful gathering."

More cheers and boot stomping.

"But they can't stop us," the speaker would scream into the microphone. "It is our birthright to assemble here and exercise our right to speak freely. The meddling Jews who run this country and own the media would love nothing more than to shut us up because they know we're onto their secret ZOG scheme to destroy the white race and rule the world. They know we've got their number. We have got the guts and the motive to hunt them down and take them out.

"The niggers are right alongside them, and they won't be happy until we are all in chains. If we'd run them out of our country like we should have when slavery was abolished, strung them all up by their filthy necks from the nearest bridges, they wouldn't be here now to pollute our cities and sell crack to innocent white kids. They wouldn't be raping our women and living off our hard-earned wages."

By that point, it didn't even matter what the orator had to say. The crowd would be going wild, the words lost in the fervor. Ready for the music.

The band would start. Guitars deafening. Drums pounding. Nefarious words of faith spewing into the microphone.

Glory be to the white man and woman.

But not without a price.

By the end of the show, fights would break out all over the place. The skins from Atlantic City against the skins from Buffalo. The old school skinheads feuding with overzealous fresh-cuts. You could bet there'd be a catfight, too. And with an overwhelming ratio of men to women in the movement, you could be sure someone would try and screw your girlfriend and a brawl would ensue.

It was a drag.

Pathetic.

While things in Blue Island couldn't have been going better for me and my crew, I began to have nagging bouts of rational thought regarding others within the movement. The flawed gamecock mentality—the inherent aggression that skinheads expressed against even their own kind—so often presented itself at these gatherings and didn't mesh well with my own sensibilities. Unity and respect were paramount back home. Friends helped each other and didn't dare cross one another. There was a sense of loyalty to your team. From the CASH skins way back to my Eisenhower teammates and even the High Street Boys, we relied on that special bond to move us forward—together. But outside of our tight-knit Chicago bubble, it seemed as though others operated with a complete absence of reason. I wasn't used to the behavior I witnessed, especially when it was so-called brothers and sisters beating each other's faces in over trivial things that meant little in the grand scheme of what we were supposedly fighting for.

I found it harder and harder to convince myself that most of the skinheads I'd met over the years weren't ignorant, white trash thugs. They weren't interested in saving the white race as much as guzzling their courage and vomiting words they could never back up without a pack of bloodthirsty attack dogs at their side to overcompensate for their own lack of courage and fighting chops. Stupidity and alcohol inevitably burst into a flash of skinhead fists and fury.

I'd stand back and watch. Disgusted. How the hell were we going to achieve glory for the white race when we couldn't even protect ourselves from our own petty insecurities?

Goddamn, it was going to be an uphill battle.

I was willing to bet European skinheads had it more together. For one thing, Europe was where the whole skinhead movement began, in the '60s. They had decades of experience on their side. The time had come for their American counterparts to operate at the same level. I wanted to be part of that. I knew this concert in Germany was going to be an historic event, and no way would I be left out. I'd taken the initiative to make damn sure of that.

By the time I'd cemented our appearance overseas, Final Solution had already built a decent fan base there. WAY had served its purpose and left its legacy, no doubt about that. My forethought and obsessive work ethic had positioned us legitimately in the top echelon of the founding American skinhead music scene, and we'd made some noise overseas by aligning ourselves with Rock-O-Rama. We'd built our following, playing mostly in basements crammed full of forty, fifty, sometimes a hundred kids. We played a show in Minneapolis with Bound For Glory to standing-room only, a couple hundred skinheads. Again, these numbers might *seem* trivial, but this was a gathering of some scary people, seen as violent terrorists by the rest of the country. So a few hundred of us together packed a whole lot of weight and caused significant aggravation.

I was totally hooked on performing and continued to write lyrics while the rest of the band collaborated on the actual music. Final Solution had already played all over the country—Georgia, Tennessee, Michigan, Minnesota, Illinois, Indiana—at rallies with more than five hundred skins and neo-Nazis, a large number in terms of attendance at skinhead concerts in the U.S., and inevitably spooked everybody in town who were unsure what we were about. It was a guarantee that wherever we played, you'd find FBI and local law enforcement there taking snapshots of the attendees and adding more info to their already overstuffed files.

One of the more hilarious instances of police harassment occurred when I was pulled over by a state trooper while driving home from a get-together in Atlanta, Georgia. Upon searching my vehicle, behind my driver's seat, the officer uncovered a wooden coffee table leg with a long, pointy lag bolt sticking out horizontally from its end.

"What's this for, son? Do you intend to use this as a weapon for your Aryan revolution?"

"No, sir, officer," I replied. "I intend to add it to my three-legged coffee table as soon as I get home. I'm tired of it tipping over every time I put my copy of *Mein Kampf* on it." Even he couldn't help but laugh at that.

We performed in all types of venues—warehouses, anybody's private property where we could throw up a makeshift stage and plug in our gear. The Detroit Hammerskins had their own private social club and charged five bucks to get in. We played on their stage a number of times. Always a good party. Until the drunken assholes started fighting again.

Climbing the rungs of the American white power ladder felt as natural as sacking a quarterback or punching someone in the face. And with it came applause, respect, and admiration.

My life had been a struggle at times. I'd known loneliness and battled with my fractured identity as a kid, but that was in the past. I now had a beautiful fiancée, hundreds of loyal associates, clout, a band about to make history, and I was headed to the land of Adolf Hitler and our National Socialist predecessors to loudly profess our faith and once again march victoriously through their streets.

Could life possibly get any better than this?

Eighteen years old and I had the world by the balls.

19

OPEN YOUR EYES

Weimar, Germany. I knew little about the place. Had no idea famous writers Johann Wolfgang von Goethe and Friedrich Schiller had lived there. Not a clue that one of history's greatest pianists, Franz Liszt, had spent part of his life in the city. Didn't know philosopher Johann Herder had called it home or that Friedrich Nietzsche lived out the final years of his life there. I didn't even know that artist Paul Klee, who the Nazi party had denounced for creating "degenerate" art, had been a resident of this eastern German town.

Nor did I know that, nearby, the Nazis had set up a concentration camp—Buchenwald. More than fifty thousand inmates, including Jews, gays, Catholics, criminals, and children, met their deaths in this camp. Conditions were said to be so horrendous that many died of typhoid and starvation. Others were shot in the back of the head. Thousands of inmates were slaughtered by lethal injections and countless others were victims of medical experiments that included the use of the deadly Zyklon B gas.

The camp displayed human tattooed skin as "modern art" in an area called the "pathological block" after prisoners were skinned alive and their hides tanned like animal pelts.

Adolf Hitler was a leader I admired, and this was more evidence of his vision to purge the world of inferior races, parasites, perverts, and misfits.

But I didn't know a damn thing about Weimar.

When we arrived, I paid little attention to the people or history of the town. I was oblivious to the fact that in this city of little more than sixty thousand people, there were twenty museums full of art, literature, and music. Some of the finest minds of numerous eras had lived there, created there, thought lofty thoughts, and pondered questions about the nature of human existence.

What did I care? What the hell did the past have to do with me? With the exception of the proud legacies our Nazi forefathers left behind, only the present and future were important. All that mattered was that white skinhead warriors from all over Europe were getting together for one epic concert in Germany. Hitler's stomping ground—in more ways than one—and I was going to be an undeniable part of this historic event.

Despite the swelling support from the thousands in attendance, it felt solitary. I'd be the only remaining original skinhead from back home in Blue Island who'd made it this far, who'd embraced the lasting legacy we created and fought so hard for. Carmine Paterno and Chase Sargent had drifted away. The Manson girls had moved on, likely to idolize some other charismatic leader. The superfluous few had vanished. And Clark Martell had lost his mind.

But I'd found the way. Still inspired by the first words of Clark I'd ever read:

We must throw ourselves, blood, bone, sinew, and soul, behind the skinhead battering ram as it rolls with the splitting of wood through the gates of power into the evil one's domain, now ours to reclaim, with the skinhead anthem upon our tongues and the flag in our hearts.

The Weimar concert was beyond a doubt the most unforgettable experience of my life up to that point. Four thousand racial comrades—assembled from all over Europe—effectively invaded the quaint German burg. Every beer hall, restaurant, and street inundated with white heroes and heroines from far and wide. As if 1930s Nazi Germany had squeezed through a wrinkle in time to the present day. All gathering and descending upon an ancient stone cathedral to celebrate an event that would go down in the history books as the first time an American white power band stepped foot on European soil to play a concert. Rumors flourished that Ian Stuart might even attend and perform some acoustic songs.

Lisa had stayed behind at the hostel in Munich to wander around and take photographs of the architecture. I'd catch up with her as soon as the concert ended. But for now, my mind was focused. Clear. The buzzing energy was palpable.

We were second to last on stage that evening—preceded by the most popular German skinhead bands like Radikahl, Wotan, Märtyrer, Kraftschlag, and Störkraft—and the crowd was ready to hear some truth. When our time came, I grabbed the microphone and didn't waste time on small talk. As soon as our instruments were tuned, our equipment turned on, guitars plugged in, I motioned for the band to start.

Ear-splitting, stirring beats filled the walls of that once-upon-a-time hallowed church faster than a candle could be lit in effigy for our sins. Or blown out. Any holy souls still lingering among the memories of mass and Christ sensed vengeance was upon them as my voice echoed through the loudspeakers:

We are skinheads, the vanguard today
Our rifles are cocked, so get out of our way

We will cut you down with no remorse
We'll die for our race. Our pride is our force
Our flags raised high after this fight
We shall overcome our foes by might
We're the new stormtroopers, the SS reborn
From our lands we shall never be torn!

The applause began midway through our first song and never died down.

At last, I was the hero of the baseball team being carried off on the shoulders of my squad, by crazed fans drunk with appreciation.

If I had lingering doubts about my message, about the skinhead scene, if I had reservations about the white race's superiority—or if what I was doing was right—at that moment I didn't care. This was what I had been born for.

"Heil Hitler!" I shouted.

The crowd was out of its mind going insane around me. Four thousand skinheads on their feet, boots stomping. Arms outstretched in glorious salute. Beams of sharp-edged white light washing over shaved heads. Sweat breaking over swastika tattoos black as sin, awash in pulsating strobes.

Me on stage. Leading it all.

"Heil Hitler!"

Spotlights daring to glare through what was once a sacred house of prayer. Weimar. Former East Germany. 1992. Borders down. That communist wall tumbled, crumbled. Gone.

Dense stage fog filtering around and up, skyward, like a cobra undulating to a snake charmer's flute. A new dawn rising.

"Heil Hitler!" I screamed again into the microphone.

Swirling around, feet swinging free in midair, I raised my clenched fist to my band to begin the next song. Veins popping on my tattooed arms, muscles rippling, rivers of sweat flowing down my face, my neck, my back. My eyes manifest with supreme conviction.

The band burst out with the force of a stampeding bull breaking free of immobilizing restraints. Music shattering any ancient echoes of holy hymns that had ever harmonized in this stone sanctuary.

The white race was at war and God couldn't help.

Thank whoeverthefuck was in control of our celestial destinies that I was there to fill that gap.

My voice filled the room.

There's white pride all across America
White pride all across the world
White pride flowing through the streets
White pride will never face defeat.

The night was mine. Ours. Arms outstretched in solidarity. Our music. Me leading the *first* American white power band to *ever* play in Europe. Me in charge. Dictating how history would remember me. Complete control.

I was stronger than Clark Martell had ever been.

One message delivered.

White power.

White power.

"White power!"

Me. Adolf Hitler resurrected, as far as the crowd was concerned.

And if not Hitler himself, I was the embodiment of his spirit. His ideas flowing through my arteries, pumping my heart to one hundred times its natural human size. Beating louder than drums. Louder than the deafening crowd. Eardrums breaking with the force of it.

The complexities of German National Socialist politics may have been largely beyond me, but I knew enough about Nazi doctrine to recognize that our proud European heritage was being threatened on all sides by muds. In front of me lay an undulating sea of white warriors, proof we would never let that happen without a fight.

Hitler. Julius fucking Caesar. Me. The new holy trinity.

Eighteen years old and on a mission to save the white race. Age was irrelevant when the issue was truth.

Jesus Christ had nothing on me. If someone were to be stomped to death in the frenzied crowd, with the energy pulsing through me I could raise them from the dead like Lazarus.

I had the power.

The power.

The power.

Next song broke so quickly who could say where one began and one ended.

Why don't you open your eyes?
Why don't you open your eyes?
Why don't you open your eyes?

The afternoon following the concert, I traded goodbyes with my band in Weimar and boarded a train to meet up with Lisa in Munich, the city where we'd started our European journey together.

By the time I arrived, I was exhausted. I could see her from across the train platform, searching for me in the distance. The moon's silvery glow cast an iridescent outline around her body. It was dark but I could see the soft silhouette of her face. I approached quickly and as I got closer, she turned and opened her arms to embrace me.

Her eyes were gentle. Comforting. Her hand reached to caress my cheek and I pulled her in close, lifting her to her toes and giving her a passionate kiss.

"I missed you so much, babe. Weimar was *crazy*. I have so much to tell you." Her body melded with my arms and our eyes connected. "But first tell me that you missed me as much as I missed you."

Lisa whispered breathlessly, "Let's go," and she led me down the long and narrow platform out to the adjoining cobblestone square.

I hoped I'd never have to let go of the moment. She smiled and I could see in her eyes a flash of yearning that was so inviting.

After a short, brisk walk, we arrived at her private room at the hostel. We couldn't tear each other's clothes off fast enough. I hadn't ever wanted or needed her as badly as I needed her in that moment. I pressed my lips against hers, and nothing else mattered—not even one second on that stage in Weimar even crossed my mind. Nothing but the love between us meant anything.

We made love slowly that night as we held each other tight.

"Lisa...you know I love you, don't you?"

She pulled me close. "Yes, I know you do. And I love you."

After spending a glorious few days with Lisa picnicking on hillsides and visiting museums and parks around Munich that she'd discovered before I'd arrived, I left her once again and took a standing-room-only overnight train alone to Cologne. I showed up without an appointment to Rock-O-Rama headquarters in Brühl where I dropped in unannounced on owner Herbert Egoldt, a round, jolly old man who I quickly realized wasn't even a racist.

Seemed he didn't give a damn about much of anything but making money. He was a capitalist pure and simple.

As he led me into his office, I met his shallow eyes with a steely stare, letting him know I was onto him. He'd pay my band album sales royalties, never mind that Rock-O-Rama was widely known as a non-paying label. I would be the exception to his rule. I'd lead the way for him to start paying the bands he'd fleeced for years. Slime ball. He may have given us a platform to promote our message, but he'd be giving us our hard-earned money, too, if I had anything to say about it.

Not for a lack of trying, I never got a dime from Herbert or the label. His bulky warehouse goons made sure of that. But I did manage to leave with a small box of about thirty various white power CDs before I left, which I happily sold when I got back to the States.

After spending only an hour at the office, I took a taxi back to the train station and headed back to Munich to spend my final days with Lisa.

The high from the trip lingered once we got back home. But daily life immediately interfered with my renewed commitment to fight for the white race. To rule the world, actually. Somebody asked me once what I'd wanted to be when I grew up. I told them at ten I wanted to be a doctor; at twelve, a detective, an explorer, a spy; but by fourteen, I wanted to rule the world.

I might have been half-joking about it then, but I was serious now. I'd had a taste of power and loved everything about it. Acceptance. Freedom. Fear. Respect. Control.

So what the hell was I doing still working in a pizza place? I was better than that.

Something had to give. I needed a better job. A persistent voice inside me began to wish I'd taken formal education more seriously. But I shut that voice down and used my lack of decent-paying employment opportunities to my advantage. I spoke to my recruits with great fervor about the work ethic, the importance of providing for our loved ones, and ranted against the Jews who were controlling all the money and making it impossible for good, clear-thinking, hardworking white people to put food on their tables and feed their families.

"There is honor working in factories, making goods for our fellow Americans. We don't need to import a bunch of foreign junk from slant-eyed, yellow-skinned chinks. Buy goods made right here by white Americans who get out of bed every day, who go to work to support their loved ones, to put clothes on their backs, and food in their stomachs.

"There is no shame in driving trucks and getting these American-made goods from local factories to stores owned and operated by white moms and pops who know what we want, who understand our needs. And at the end of the week, after paying the bills through our sweat and labor, it's good to relax and enjoy ourselves like we're doing here together now.

"Be proud to serve your brothers and sisters by working in restaurants and the service industry. I am proud to say I make pizzas. I see exhausted white folks come in after a long day's work and I'm honored to provide them with food for their family that is made with my own hands. It's a labor of love, and we don't need any capitalist Jews with their vile fast food chains destroying our health with their poison. Let the uneducated animals eat that garbage. We need to stay fit, eat right, and prepare ourselves to be the righteous freedom fighters that our destiny demands us to be in this battle to reclaim our rights!"

I made it a point to attend every rally I could, no matter how small. I performed music, keeping the energy flowing as younger skinhead candidates joined us. But I took less of an active role in any confrontations. I'd already done my fair share of knuckle dusting. Made a name for myself. I had nothing left to prove. It was time for somebody else to deal with the cops and bruises. That's what soldiers were for. And by this time, I had an abundance of warriors ready to obey my every order.

I was a good commander. I taught my recruits how to respect themselves. Many of them had been marginalized or disenfranchised kids with low self-esteem, searching for identity. The traits that made them loathe themselves made them easy targets and gave me a reason to save them. They'd do anything they were told in order to have something to belong to. And if they got arrested for carrying out a mission or if they got hurt, there were others ready to take their place and pledge their support. Those risks were assumed when they signed up.

Meanwhile, my love for Lisa kept growing, and when she told me three months later that she was expecting our child, I was overjoyed.

"I'm pregnant," she cried.

"We're going to have a baby? Lisa, that's amazing!"

She sobbed. What about her plans? What about college? What about becoming a teacher? Needing to comfort and reassure her, I took her gently into my arms.

I am ashamed to say that part of my happiness over the pregnancy was that it meant she would stay with me. She wouldn't be going off to college, making new friends, having a new life I wasn't a part of. All her reassurances that college wouldn't change her love for me hadn't ever stopped the fear that she'd fall for somebody else and leave me. At the very least, if she attended college she would live in a world I was not part of. Abandoning me. Like my parents had.

I held her tight and tenderly kissed her tears away. "This is wonderful. What we've wanted all along. Maybe it's earlier than we planned, but that doesn't matter. We are going to bring a child into the world. And we won't be like our parents. We'll do this right. It's fate that we have this child now."

I nestled Lisa close, stuffing her fears away. "I love you. And I love this baby," I said, assuring her that everything would be okay.

My mother was not pleased.

I hadn't been sure how to tell her. I still technically lived under my parents' roof and I might need their help financially until I found a better job. While she didn't spend too much time in church, my mom still considered herself a devout Catholic, and a child born out of wedlock was a mortal sin. It was a disgrace amongst old-world Italians who were obsessed with the notion of protecting their public image—*la bella figura*, as they called it. What mother would raise a boy to have a child before he was married? Nonno and Nonna would be disappointed. Of course, Buddy would be thrilled to be an uncle, even if he was only in third grade.

I tried easing my mother into the idea. Lisa and I clearly needed to live together now. It was my duty to protect her and our unborn child.

There wasn't a graceful way to break the news. "Lisa and I are going to be living together."

"What are you talking about?"

"We're going to have a baby."

I don't know which came faster, her tears or the rapid-fire throwing of her shoes at me from across the room. "What have you done? You're only a child yourself! You aren't a man yet! She's still a schoolgirl! How could you do this?" My father left the room without saying a word.

I waited patiently, letting her get it all out.

But then she said something I hadn't expected. "This can be fixed," she declared, eyes wild as a loon, wiping away her tears. "She can have an abortion."

Rage filled my veins. I rose like a dust storm, swept over to her, my face casting a shadow over her now fearful eyes. "How dare you suggest something like that to me? This is my child. Your own flesh and blood. You think I should destroy my own child? If you ever say anything like that again, even so much as think it, you will never meet my baby. And you'll never see me again. Ever. Understand?"

I left the room, seething, fists tightened, to get my temper under control.

My mother came around. She always did, and by the time Lisa graduated from school and our wedding in June of 1992 approached, she had accepted that not only would she have a daughter-in-law, she would also soon be a grandmother. Even became proud of the fact.

Our wedding was intimate, held in a quiet, non-denominational ceremony in a quaint little chapel in the woods.

Thirty people attended. Lisa's family. My parents and grandparents were there. The groomsmen—my band mates from Final Solution—all had their heads freshly shaved and their muttonchop sideburns aptly trimmed for the occasion. They shined their boots to wear with their black tuxes. The contrast between them and Lisa's bridesmaids—all friends of hers from her Catholic high school—was hysterical.

Little Buddy, looking cute as the stout little ring bearer in his mini tuxedo, led Lisa through the chapel doors and down the aisle. As he passed me, I bent down to kiss the top of his head. He may have been only eight years old, but I wanted him to know he'd always be my best man.

Lisa was radiant. Stunning. Her emerald eyes glimmered as she passed across the rays of sunlight beaming through the narrow, rose-hued chapel windows. When her gaze caught mine, time paused in a moment of suspended reality. Blink. I pledge my life to you and to our child growing inside of you.

Kubiak—my best man—snuck a flask of whiskey from his jacket pocket and passed it along to the other groomsmen. They all had virginal bridesmaids on their minds and some indulging of spirits was in order to celebrate the occasion.

As Lisa and I looked into each other's eyes and proclaimed "I do," the time that had been standing still recalibrated and the three of us were one.

But if the wedding was small, the reception more than made up for it. My parents wouldn't allow us to have the small gathering we wanted for fear the other Italians would badmouth them as cheapskates, so they sprung for a large Italian affair with more than two hundred guests. Relatives from both sides. Skinheads and Catholic school girls. All eating and drinking together and having a grand time. Traditional Italian tarantellas rang out, interspersed with punk rock ballads my drunken friends strong-armed the wedding deejay to play. The High Street Boys weren't there. We hardly saw each other anymore; even passing each other on the streets of Blue Island's East Side was a rarity. A few of the Beverly guys were there, but they, too, were mostly part of the past. The Bound For Glory guys, on the other hand, had their own table.

The cops patrolled the parking lot of our wedding reception. Certainly not because they were invited or even because anything got out of control, but because they'd been told I was getting married and they wanted to document who'd shown up. More notes for their files. I didn't let it get to me. I was too happy. I even brought some cake out to their unmarked cars.

While our honeymoon was short—I couldn't get time off work—and the location less than romantic—we stayed at Lisa's grandparents' mobile home on a small lake in rural Michigan—we couldn't have been happier.

I carried my beautiful bride across the trailer's threshold and set her down on the sofa bed. In typical Italian fashion, we'd been given stacks of cash by our wedding guests. We sat on the bed and counted it. Fourteen grand! We were rich.

We threw it in the air, watching it drift back onto us. Rolled in it.

We were going to start our lives out right, as the happiest couple alive.

20
AMERIKKKA FOR ME

I SETTLED INTO MARRIED LIFE EFFORTLESSLY. I was bringing in a steady salary, working full-time at the pizza place. And Lisa had begun working part-time at a furniture store in town. With some semblance of financial stability, and because we figured having my mother close to help with the baby might be nice, Lisa and I rented the smaller of the second-floor apartments in my parents' two-story building. With the money from the wedding, we'd also begun talking about buying our own place somewhere. We now had enough for a down payment.

I loved Lisa. She loved me. Both of us loved the baby growing inside of her. Like all couples in love for the first time, we believed our bond was stronger and more special than anything anyone had ever known.

Our time together *was* special. We rarely argued, and everything we did was new and exciting. To prove our unity, she let me give her a tattoo. By now tattoos covered my arms and legs, chest and back, and it was only fitting she had one too.

Her trust that I would do a good job, that she would be safe, was absolute. As a way to make a few extra bucks, I'd given my friends dozens of tattoos in the past couple of years. I'd done the first few using a homemade tattoo machine I created using a little motor from Buddy's remote-control car. I used a guitar string and a hollow plastic pen tube for a needle contraption and bottles of colored India ink for the pigment. I saved my tips and eventually ordered a real tattoo kit from the back of a biker magazine for two hundred bucks. I'd been a decent artist growing up, honing my drawing skills in my grandparents' coat closet, and now underage friends came to me for their ink. Most of the tattoos were racist, naturally, although my Irish Beverly friends were partial to shamrocks and Celtic crosses.

Lisa opted for a small outline of a daisy on her ankle.

Along with our wedded bliss came my commitment to support my family. The Rock-O-Rama deal had proven to be a bust, with the label refusing to pay sales royalties to any of the bands it signed—besides Skrewdriver. And working in a pizza place may feed the deserving hardworking white masses, but it sure wasn't going to allow me to earn enough money to care for my family in the style in which I wanted us to live. It was time to look for a real job.

I eventually found work on a road construction crew, with a company making and distributing road barricades and doing traffic control—setting highway lane closures, detours in construction zones, that kind of stuff.

When I started the job, I made a little over four bucks an hour, but with overtime, I knew I could make more than minimum wage. The job suited me. I had the physical strength to do it, and what could be nobler, better to prove myself as a hardworking white man than joining the working-class stiffs doing manual labor?

After about six months of assembling road construction signs and traffic barricades in a warehouse and loading them on trucks, one of the foremen noticed I was a hard worker, so he let me go out on the road to assist one of the drivers with setting lane closures. I'd pull the flashing traffic horses off the truck and set them in place to detour traffic.

I did this well, too, and before long my boss made me the permanent road assistant for a shift supervisor on a long-term highway resurfacing project in the city. This meant putting in long days, but I didn't complain. Even though I'd become increasingly distant from the Chicago skins since I found out Lisa was pregnant, I knew the job would allow me to lead by example, even if it meant sacrificing time with the group. My crew meant almost everything to me, but not at the expense of my new wife and our family-to-be.

At first I struggled with the separation from my gang, as my leadership role had become my identity and the movement my family. But I justified it knowing I was doing something far nobler for our cause—being a productive white man.

My role in the movement had begun to change over the last year and I couldn't stop it from happening. What had meant everything to me for the last five years was competing with what had given me renewed life, my family. But I was convinced the two could somehow continue to live simultaneously in harmony.

As a skinhead, I knew that no job was too menial when it came to supporting my wife and child. I would have believed this even if I wasn't a skinhead, but I might not have taken as much pride in being a blue-collar worker. I knew I had the intelligence to do more than labor, but being a skinhead made it easy to be satisfied with a job that was physically demanding and offered no real reward other than bringing home a decent paycheck to support my family.

So I buried my growing desire to work for myself, to be an entrepreneur like my parents. I stilled the voice inside me that wanted to put my imagination and talents to work, telling myself I had bigger responsibilities now and couldn't risk our wellbeing by pursuing interests that might not put Top Ramen noodles in a pot.

I threw myself wholeheartedly into my road construction job, being a model to other skins—doing my work with pride and honor, and this dedication caught the attention of my manager. Within a year of starting my construction job, I became a driver, had my own truck, and was entrusted to manage an overnight road shift of my own. In six short months I'd labored my way from a little over four dollars an hour to almost fifteen dollars an hour.

While I didn't advertise my skinhead activities on the job, I didn't hide them either. My work boots were Doc Martens, my tattoos clearly visible on my arms. But I worked hard and I was white—two factors that were readily apparent on a construction crew dominated by lesser-paid, unskilled minorities. I toiled away daily with every intention of proving to my bosses that I was more worthy of the work than my counterparts.

Coincidentally, I wasn't the only racist around. Chuck Johansson—a rotund, older gentleman with a salt-and-pepper handlebar mustache—had worked for the company for thirty years and made no secret of his long-standing membership in the American Nazi Party. He sat in the warehouse break room openly reading racist literature and wore white power T-shirts under his overalls, but he never started any trouble at work even though his tenure with the company was bulletproof. We hit it off immediately. He gave me stacks of new books to read, which I devoured during work breaks, even though I knew most of the content already.

Whenever I could spare the time off from work and Lisa was busy with her job, I still traveled to rallies out-of-state and spoke vehemently against our non-white and Jewish enemies. Lisa wanted none of my racist rantings, nor did I want her or the child we would have to be any part of the hostility that surged through the gatherings. It was unthinkable that hate could be any part of our world. Instinctively, I didn't want the dirtiness of the movement to destroy our family purity. I would wade neck-deep through that mire on my own and carry them on my shoulders so they could benefit from my sacrifice.

I continued to spread my vitriol with a vengeance. While I gave my wife puppy dog eyes full of love and put my head to her stomach and whispered lullabies to our child and the two of us giggled when he kicked so hard we could see her stomach move, I was still a committed racist intent on doing damage to anyone unlike us.

In September of 1992, two months before our child was born, I headed to Pulaski, Tennessee, to attend the Aryan Unity March, a Klan rally held by the Fraternal Order White Knights of the Ku Klux Klan. The location was significant—the original KKK had been founded in Pulaski on Christmas Eve in 1865.

This wasn't my first Klan rally. But it was a rare opportunity for me to spend time with many of the skinheads and fellow white power associates I'd known and been corresponding with from around North America. I drove to Pulaski alone. No one from Chicago had the backbone to go with me. They wouldn't leave the comfort of their homes to get away for a weekend of white solidarity. I began to doubt my crew's loyalty. If they truly believed the future of the white race was in jeopardy, it was their responsibility, their duty, to pick up and go. They could lie to their parents or girlfriends or wives or bosses or whoever they were afraid of to take care of important movement business.

If they were intent on being cowards, then I'd represent Blue Island, the birthplace of the American neo-Nazi skinhead movement, at the birthplace of the Ku Klux Klan by myself. Together, we were the front-line fighters of the coming revolution, and there was no way in hell I would stay home and be complacent.

The day of the rally was hot. Sticky. The smell of steamy asphalt and thick musty air hung like the hordes of law enforcement officers that lingered on rooftops. Sweat gathered on my forehead and at the base of my neck. I wore a "Rest In Peace Robert Jay Mathews" T-shirt to show my respect for one of my fallen heroes. Mathews had been the leader of The Order, a covert white nationalist militant group—inspired by *The Turner Diaries*—that successfully staged armored car heists and counterfeited money to fund the white revolution. Federal government bastards had taken his valiant life on Whidbey Island, Washington, in 1984. Trapped and burned him alive. They'd murdered Mathews for his beliefs. Spawned a martyr. The government who'd taken his life was the enemy and here they were, all over these Tennessee country roads. Watching. Waiting for us. But we would outnumber them. We would demonstrate our unity and make our voices heard.

We didn't care if they tried to stop us. We were going to stand on the city hall steps and proclaim our faith whether they wanted us to or not. We were here to show the world what white power meant. Gathered from all corners of North America here in bumblefuck Pulaski, Tennessee.

I was dressed for combat. My fourteen-eyelet black Doc Martens shone deep and slick. My jeans were rolled up so the blood that was sure to flow through the streets would not stain them. My head was shaved to a close crop, and I took the thin black braces off my shoulders. They hung at my sides, a statement to my enemies that I was ready to fight and defend my race with my sweaty, balled-up fists. The boots were heavy on my feet and sweat rolled down my back. The humidity was dangerous, and so was the tension in the air. Feds were not-so-subtly stationed all over the streets, taking our photos with cameras bearing lenses as long as their arms.

Hundreds of skinheads, people dressed in Klan robes and Nazi regalia, and racists of a more general ilk congregated at the designated staging area. Men with bullhorns barked orders for us to come together and shouted motivational white power cheers, which were followed by arbitrary stiff-armed salutes.

There were men and women. Children. Hugs and embraces from

folks who only saw each other a few times a year, but were kindred spirits in a vast family.

The air was thick with banners. Confederate flags, Nazi battle flags, hand-painted placards with sayings like "God Hates Niggers," "Join The KKK," and "Save The White Race. Unite!"

The attacks of September 11th, 2001, hadn't happened yet, but the American white power movement was in full swing, and people were paranoid about every move we made. We were the most dangerous extremists within our borders, as far as mainstream America was concerned.

And we were ready for action. Eager for battle. Some of us had makeshift wooden shields with swastikas painted on them. Some had God's cross. There were militiamen in camouflage with riot helmets and Nazi armbands. The Klan leader, the Grand Dragon of the Fraternal Order of White Knights of the Ku Klux Klan, was there along with several dozen different Klan factions from across the United States, all of which fell loosely under the purview of the Knights of the KKK.

Despite my enthusiasm for action, I couldn't help but notice all these organizations had different leaders. The groups were splintered and independent by design. Within the movement, we'd started to teach the concept of leaderless resistance, the idea that small independent cells of activists could inflict much more damage to the system and stay invisible if they weren't connected to a larger group. Lone wolves. But this gathering was the antithesis of that. These groups were assembled and driven by greed. Too many clusters, too many leaders, too many loose ends and confusion. The rally was a disorganized jumble of people brimming with hate, sweating it from every pore. Barking orders over each other in spite of the goal to come together.

There was no way of knowing who was in charge. Was it the Klansmen or the skinheads? The two groups didn't even look like we belonged together. Skinheads were militant, natural stormtroopers, like Hitler's

SS. These redneck Klansmen in their white robes spoke of God and the Bible. This was the precipice of war, not a pulpit. And they looked pathetic, downright silly, wearing sheets that looked like dresses and those stupid pointy hats on top of their heads. It may have looked intimidating to people a century and a half ago. But now they looked like clowns. No way anybody could come off as tough, wearing an outfit like that. Who would take you seriously if you looked like a buffoon? But I got a grip on my judgmental attitude.

Despite the chaos, we were all here to fight for the future of our people.

I spotted friends. The guys from Bound For Glory were there, as were some skinhead pals from Toronto and Dallas and Pennsylvania. We rushed toward each other, exchanged bear hugs, and felt comfort in each other's presence.

"These Klan guys look ridiculous," I said.

"Tell me about it," one of my Canadian friends replied. "Whose brilliant idea was this? It's not like skinheads and the Klan have a good history with each other."

True enough. They thought we were thugs, and we pegged them as dumb hillbillies.

We were prepared for war and all they could do was recite bastardized Bible passages to prove their claim that God hated fags.

"We have to put our differences aside," I said. "It doesn't matter right now. Today we show the world our unity."

Everybody agreed, and off we marched through the streets of this backwoods town.

We responded to chants led by the Grand Dragon of the local Klan chapter:

"What do we want?"

"White power!"

"When do we want it?"

"Right now!"

Rebel flags and Nazi swastikas waved furiously in the air. As we turned the corner of our gathering place, nervous energy crackled around us. A wall of thick, humid air pounded us in the face like the pressure from a blast furnace.

So did the chants and protests from hundreds of people who had gathered to oppose us. Black and white. Old and young. Male and female. United by their commitment to stop us from marching. They were clamoring for us, only held back by a thin blue line of Pulaski policeman and Tennessee state troopers. We hated these cops, these ZOG marionettes. It wouldn't take much for one of them to "accidentally" let a protester through to attack us.

How's that for quintessential irony? The very people we despised and distrusted were there protecting our civil liberties. The mob of counter-demonstrators grew by the second. They were loud. Far louder than us, and we had a bullhorn.

Our mighty flags unfurled and our white power chants grew to meet their opposition. They held up peace fingers, and we flipped them off, taunting them with racist epithets and a barrage of "die, race traitor" and "faggot cocksucker" obscenities.

Several of the skinheads engaged with groups of rowdy protesters that were more intent on confrontation than others.

They carried peace signs.

We carried the weight of the world.

They were wrong.

How could they be so gullible to think peace and love could be achieved with the muds burning down our cities and the Jews controlling our government, the media, destroying our lives?

Not a chance. More than anything we wanted a white society.

Didn't we?

And then it dawned on me: I missed Lisa more than anything. More than I wanted a white homeland. For a brief moment I became lost in love and I didn't care if the blacks and Jews still existed or were rounded up and killed like the rest of my comrades wanted. I'd probably even be satisfied if whites just peacefully lived separately from other races. We could have our own territory. Maybe we could inhabit the Pacific Northwest and isolate ourselves like my hero Bob Mathews prophesized. Let the others keep their inner cities.

But what would it really matter if some blacks and gays lived around us? I wasn't gay and knew I wouldn't magically become gay. From my experience, gays seemed pretty clean and kept mostly to themselves. They didn't bother me much.

As for blacks, the ones I knew from school didn't want to be around whites. Most of them were as racist as we were.

Jews? I'd never actually met one. To me, it seemed like they numbered in the hundreds and a powerful few secretly sat in rooms, rubbing their greedy Zionist hands, trying to figure out how to play a perverse game of chess where we were their pawns. What match were they for us anyway?

And goddamn, I hated the Klan. Why would I want to live with them as my neighbors? They *were* white trash. Straight up unintelligent Southern rednecks that couldn't string together a sentence without the words "dumb ass nigger" in it. The thoughts and words from the last five years of my life suddenly tasted foul.

Why was I here and not at home with my pregnant wife who I adored? With my ear against her belly, taking in every beat of our unborn child's heart? I suddenly felt guilty and out of sorts. I didn't respect these people, the Klansmen, the racist clergyman wearing a priest's collar around his neck and a KKK patch over his heart, the mother carrying her infant baby with a tiny Klan hood on, the inbred hick with missing teeth and a beer-stained "Niggers Suck" T-shirt.

But there were skinheads here, too. Brothers. And sisters. I related to them. They came from neighborhoods like I did. Urban jungles, not Southern swamps. They knew what this struggle was about.

It was about…well…I didn't really feel certain anymore. It was about pride, I guess. Being proud of our white culture and standing up against those who wanted to take that away from us. That's not hate, that's love. Right?

Doubt rushed in and my thoughts drifted back to my earliest memory of holding Lisa in my arms, her pleading eyes searching deep inside me for my truth. "Why do you have so much hate inside of you?" she'd questioned. "You are so caring and gentle. Which one is the real you?" Suddenly I wasn't so sure.

But one thing I was damn sure about was that when I was pushed, I pushed back. We marched onto the steps of the city hall in small-town, humid, hot-as-hell Pulaski, Tennessee. Klan leaders proclaimed this was once again the birthplace of a white revolution. Niggers, queers, and Jews were the enemy.

Yeah, yeah, we all knew that—niggers were raping our women and forcing drugs on our youth. It didn't happen in my town, but maybe it was more prevalent in theirs. Jews controlled our lives and queers destroyed white propagation, or so we believed—who really cared? But maybe the crowd didn't know it.

We could change them.

Yeah, right. Here are these peace-loving protesters gathered by the hundreds, waving peace flags and holding hands singing folk songs, and we instilled *so* much hate and revulsion in their soft hearts that they resorted to ripping up chunks of concrete from the sidewalk to violently pelt us with.

What was wrong with this picture? We inspired so much animosity in those who believed in only peace that they were trying to hurt us with violence.

Confusion overwhelmed me and I felt as if someone had landed a solid blow to my solar plexus. Along with my breath, my commitment was knocked out of me for the first time, and for a brief moment I clearly saw there was a serious problem with my reality.

My head spun in all directions and I began to feel sick to my stomach.

The Nazi salutes had tired my arm and the cries for white power had strained my voice.

I was weak from a day of heat and hate. We'd barely made it out alive.

When the march came to an end and my comrades were celebrating by getting hammered with booze, I was hit by the disturbing thought that maybe the whole thing was simply an endless cycle of excuses to fight and drink and commiserate. To belong to an exclusive club of other people more fucked up than you.

How superficial could it get?

I left breathless and disillusioned with what I had been doing with passion for the last five years. But I couldn't let myself give up. Not yet. I had to make sense of it all.

Maybe the problem wasn't with the principles, our beliefs. Maybe it had been that rally. With the Klan. We still needed to set the world straight.

And I needed to get home to Lisa and our unborn child. Between work and my lingering responsibilities to the skinhead movement, we hadn't been spending enough time together. I vowed to change that. If there was one thing I was sure of, it was that our family was what mattered.

I'd already more or less given up on music, even though Rock-O-Rama had offered Final Solution a follow-up recording contract after we played in Germany. After finding out how shady the label was, we had no problem walking away from the deal and putting a record out under our own vanity record label, Viking Sounds. Not long after, the band broke up. Final Solution didn't have the same spark, didn't fill me with the same spirit as White American Youth had. Weimar had been a high point, but in reality, being able to keep the band at the top of my growing list of priorities diminished. My mind was elsewhere. My heart belonged to my wife and our child. And it showed in the substandard recording we released. The album sold a few thousand copies and flopped. I hadn't had the time or the energy it took to keep it together.

Now it was time to cut down on rallies and other distractions as well. I'd have to find another way to promote my pro-white agenda. I didn't know what shape that would take, but I was in way too deep to climb out. Even if I wanted to. This life was all I'd known through every single one of my formative years. Who would I be otherwise? This was my identity. Where would I go? This was my family.

I returned home ready to try harder than ever to prove my worth as a man. I threw myself wholeheartedly into my construction job. The hours were long, the work at times grueling and other times mind-numbingly boring, but we needed the money. Aside from the wedding money we'd earmarked to buy a home, we were broke and expecting a child in two months.

We lived on forty-nine-cent packages of oriental noodles and macaroni and cheese. I had no health insurance, so Lisa was on public aid for her prenatal care. I didn't let myself dwell on the fact that I was dependent on taxpayers' money to bring my child safely into the world, something I had ripped into blacks about hundreds of times over the last few years.

I did far more than my share of work. Putting in sixteen-hour days was normal. Sometimes I worked even more hours than that. In fact, the night Lisa went into labor, I'd just come off an eighteen-hour shift. I was dead to the world when her contractions began at home. Lisa's mom cared for her through her labor pains while I napped until it was time to go to the hospital.

I was far too worn-out to be the overanxious dad on the way to the hospital, but I came alive when I got into the delivery room. I watched Lisa's every expression intently. I hadn't been able to go to birthing classes with her because of my hectic work schedule, but I was confident I'd be able to do my part during the delivery.

Labor was long, and every hour on the hour ancient nuns came on the hospital's loudspeaker to read verses from the Gospel of John. It drove us nuts, but being on public assistance had not put us in a bargaining position, and this was the hospital we'd been assigned to by the welfare agency.

After an eternity or two, our son Devin was born.

I have one word for the experience. If you've had kids, you'll know what it means. If you don't, you will the moment your own child is born. *Magic.*

I held that tiny, helpless, beautiful, flawless infant, not much bigger than my own two worn and battered hands—hands that had been curled into vengeful fists since I was a child myself—and I promised him I would be the best father in the world, no matter what it took.

Lisa squeezed my hand and saw in my eyes that my hard outer shell had begun to crack.

Caressed by the soft, gentle breath of our fragile son in my strong, tattooed arms, I was carried away momentarily from the uncertain reality of being a nineteen-year-old father shouldering the vestiges of a fraying cause. My child's sweet, precious scent filled my lungs. I inhaled deeply and felt it permeate my soul.

My son's life was in my hands, both literally and figuratively, and never had I been charged with a greater purpose.

For the first time in my adult life, I broke down and wept.

21
FINAL SOLUTION

THE BIRTH OF OUR SON CHANGED MY LIFE. Hardly an original statement. I know a child's birth has that effect on millions and millions of parents every year in every corner of the globe. The world stands still, everything else fades into the background, and time stops the first time you gently hold your newborn.

So pure, so untainted, so absolutely unsullied by any of the world's influence. Babies know nothing of differences. The color of someone's skin is meaningless to them. They have no concern for someone else's beliefs. Not money or power, creed or sexual preference matters one little bit to an infant.

Not only don't these innocents care what someone's pay grade or position is in the world, they don't even understand the concept that those non-essential things exist. Education level, financial success, owning a home, a luxury car, having stock options, are completely without meaning. All the worldly trappings mean absolutely nothing to a newborn. The only thing that matters to a baby is love, and they cry until they are embraced by it.

My son opened his eyes and looked into mine, and I saw nothing but complete and beautiful innocence. A love purer than I imagined

Christian and Devin, 1993   **253**

possible pulsated through me, pulling me into a world of splendor I had long since abandoned, claiming me with a power and responsibility greater than anything I'd ever experienced.

And in that moment, the animosity I had felt toward strangers for half a decade was so inconsequential it was not even a minor thought in my head, a germ of an emotion in my heart. Love blocked out all the venomous anger and prejudice I'd been living with for the previous five years—all but one of my teenage years.

If I could have held on to that sense of clarity, if I could have honored it in my every act and deed from that moment on, tragedy may well have been prevented.

But I was young and careless. Unenlightened in ways that horrify me still. Instead of respecting the power of love my son had brought into my life, my signals got crossed, and I convinced myself more than ever that I had to make the world safe for my child by protecting him from the dangers I believed existed. Blacks. Jews. Gays. Anybody who wasn't white, who didn't contribute to my family's wellbeing. Anything that came from a culture I refused to understand. I saw threats to my family's safety everywhere.

My mission to protect the white race and ensure a safe future for my child became even more critical.

So, too, did the need to provide for my family.

Lisa and I decided it was time to buy our own home. We found a modest, three-bedroom duplex that suited us, used the money we'd received from our wedding as a down payment, and moved in shortly after Devin was born. That's what it was all about, right? A family. A house. A job. A future.

My parents said they were proud of me. Finally. Here was their nineteen-year-old son with a good job, his own home, and a family. What a good boy. My grandparents were pleased with me, too. Only nine-year-old Buddy wasn't happy. "You hardly ever do anything with me when you live in the same building," he cried. "Now I'll never see you."

"Sure you will," I said. "I'll be over here all the time to visit with the baby."

He pushed me away and thumped his little fist down on the kitchen table. I'd never seen him upset like this. "You just love the baby. You don't love me anymore." My heart tore with those words.

"Buddy," I pleaded. "How can you say that? Of course I love you."

He ran to his bedroom crying and slammed the door so hard that a framed picture of the gondolas of Venice hanging in the hallway fell to the floor and shattered into a million pieces. It might as well have been my soul. "Buddy?" I knocked gently. "Buddy, please open up." No answer. "I love you."

"Go away! Leave me alone." I'd heard that before, but it had been from my own lips.

I'd watched my shy and innocent little brother grow up from a distance. And only now had he become visible to me through the murky glimpses of my own selfish determination. But Buddy was no longer the wide-eyed pudgy nuisance that I once so easily brushed away without consequence. Hearing his words reminded me of what I had been at his age. Lonely and angry. Wanting desperately for someone to pay attention.

With work and my own family now, I knew I hadn't given him much attention over the last year. But how could I have? There were only so many hours in the day.

I continued to coordinate the Chicago Hammerskins—albeit from a more remote position than I had in the past—while I dutifully worked my construction job six or seven days a week. Pulling double duty with both the movement and my job, not to mention my wife and kid, was a difficult task. But despite the fact that I prided myself on working harder than everyone around me, I still didn't go home at the end of the day with any real feeling of accomplishment. And I desired that. Desperately.

I needed to work a job that didn't shut down during the harsh Chicago winters like mine did. It was tough enough living on unemployment wages for four months every year when there were only two of us to support. With an infant, that was virtually impossible. Devin was born on November 11th, 1992, and I'd be laid off by Thanksgiving two weeks later.

It didn't take me long to figure out I could supplement my unemployment checks by importing and selling music on the side to my growing number of skinhead friends. White power music was extremely difficult to come by. Most people settled for third-generation audio dubs of whatever they could find. Record stores wouldn't sell it, so you either had to trade tapes with your network of friends, or you had to order from Europe. Sometimes it would be weeks before your CD arrived and the customs taxes almost made it not worth the cost.

I recognized that the opportunity to save money on shipping and taxes existed if I was able to place a larger order. So, I revived my relationship with Rock-O-Rama and bought a handful of titles at wholesale prices from them and marked up the prices a few dollars. I began peddling a variety of white power titles—old and new—so I always had something fresh to sell.

Anyway I looked at it, this was a golden opportunity to seamlessly work on two of my commitments at once—I brought in an extra three hundred dollars a week for my family by selling music while I was laid off from my job, and I was able to keep promoting the white power message. For once, the two worlds seemed to blend together nicely.

In the spring of 1993, HBO aired *Skinheads USA: Soldiers of the Race War*, a documentary about white power skinheads living in the South. The film opened with a scene showing my band Final Solution performing live during a celebration commemorating Hitler's birthday at the Aryan Youth Front compound in Alabama, a mountainous plot of land owned and run by an older neo-Nazi guy named Will Manfredi, whom I'd never met. I figured it would be incredible exposure for the movement, though the film ultimately focused on the negative aspects and depicted skinheads as a bunch of lunatics. Even if there was an element of truth in that, it certainly didn't describe the scene as a whole. Did it?

I'd gotten the band back together for one last show and drove down to play the concert on two days' notice. The Aryan Youth Front, which Manfredi ran, had a large membership base of militant skins that loved to party, and that meant a good crowd for Final Solution's farewell concert. Skinheads from all over the United States were set to travel to the fest, and we'd been asked to perform at the last minute when it dawned on the organizers that there wasn't enough planned in the way of entertainment. I didn't hesitate. Rounded up the guys for our last hurrah, packed my Chevy truck with our equipment, and we headed down to Birmingham.

Upon arriving at the compound, we set up our equipment on the only piece of flat land that existed on the property—a small strip of dirt next to the lingering stench of an overflowing outhouse, during the peak of an Alabama heat wave—and ran through a rousing musical set that included both Final Solution and WAY favorites. The temperatures were stifling, almost unbearable, but the crowd loved it. I have to admit it was fun getting behind the microphone one last time.

After we finished performing, curious to know why the fellow whose property we were playing on was not in attendance, I asked when we'd get to talk to Manfredi. I was eager to meet the man who'd built such a large skinhead following and ask him if he'd have any interest in a bulk purchase for his crew of some of the CDs I'd been importing. I was promptly informed by a skinny, red-haired boy who lived on the property that "that asshole" Manfredi wouldn't be attending because he had been arrested for illegal weapons charges the night before and was being held for further questioning in several cases involving sexual indecency and forced sodomy on a minor.

"Excuse me. What the fuck did you just say?"

"Yup," said the freckled teenager, "Will's been molesting most of us and we finally turned him in."

Jesus Christ.

Turns out that dozens of underage boys—many of them disenchanted runaways—had been living with Manfredi on the compound. He gave them food, water, and shelter, and in exchange, they provided sex. The story I was told was that after he rescued these boys from a life on the streets and indoctrinated them over time to worship him, turning them into burgeoning skinheads, he'd sexually abuse these kids and then threaten to expose them as homosexuals if they said a word.

Had I known about this sick bastard before the band was asked to come down and perform, I would have not-so-kindly told him to eat shit and die, while exposing him to the rest of the movement as a child molesting scumbag. Now that I'd found out, I just wanted to shove one of his illegal guns up his ass and pull the trigger. More than happy to watch him disintegrate into bloody vapor. Manfredi didn't know how fortunate he'd been, being in that holding cell instead of at the concert. Had he been there when I found out, he would not have made it off his own mountain alive.

By now Lisa had begun pressuring me heavily about my lingering involvement with the movement. She'd always been afraid for me, but now she was also feeling underappreciated. My responsibilities as a leader were taking time away from her and from our son.

She was right. Despite my efforts to keep my life with Lisa apart from my skinhead activities, the two worlds were colliding. The first incident happened not long into the marriage.

Again I'd been arrested when I was named as party to a fight I hadn't been involved in. I was driving some skinheads visiting from Milwaukee to get some late-night food when they started a ruckus in the restaurant with a few inebriated jocks. When the stealthy undercover cops who'd been tailing us from my house to the restaurant showed up with flashing lights and guns drawn, they all fled and I was left holding the bag. Literally. A take-out bag carrying my dinner, a foot-long pastrami sub and some butter and garlic French fries.

Luckily, the prosecutor couldn't prove I'd physically assaulted anyone, so I was only found guilty of Mob Action and Disorderly Conduct instead of Assault and Battery. I was placed on house arrest for thirty days. Had the Pakistani storeowner not testified on my behalf that I wasn't party to the fight, it would have meant certain jail time. Again, my prejudices collided with reason.

At the police station, the cops took away my food and for two hours they pressured me to give up the names of the others involved, in return for dropping the remaining charges. I had no interest in cooperating with them. I was pissed at the Milwaukee guys for coming into my town and starting trouble that I was left to clean up, but I was no rat.

A second incident that had understandably freaked Lisa out happened when Devin was five months old. I'd been tipped off by one of our double agents that a rival anti-racist gang was planning to detonate a pipe bomb on our home on the anniversary of their founding. I rushed home from work, sent Lisa and Devin to her mother's house where they'd be safe, and rounded up six of my most loyal associates. We stood watch all night with loaded rifles and shotguns pointed out of the windows, ready for someone to approach in the darkness.

Around midnight, we saw a figure appear from the shadows. Instantly, we turned our guns on him. My finger lay poised on the hair trigger of my AK-47, waiting to squeeze it.

"Don't shoot!" one of the gunmen yelled. "It's Steve!" Steve was a young probationary Hammerskin, arriving late for the vigil.

I set my weapon down, leaned my back against the wall. For the third time in my life, I'd almost shot someone. Each time, someone innocent. I shook to think how closely we'd come to opening fire on a friend. This only increased my anger that someone was threatening my family.

How dare they put me in this situation?

Fuming, I ordered everyone back to their positions. We resumed our patrol. Hours passed, but nothing ever happened.

By morning we were exhausted from lack of sleep, aggravated from the pointless watch, and Lisa was furious at me for worrying her for no good reason.

Without being able to pinpoint when it had begun to turn bad, married life wasn't all that much fun anymore. I adored Devin and still treasured my marriage, but Lisa and I rarely agreed on anything any longer. We began arguing all the time about my extracurricular activities. I looked for reasons to go away because the fights wore me down.

One such weekend in the winter of 1993 I drove to a concert in Buffalo, New York, to blow off some steam from another one of our arguments. A high-energy skinhead show promised to give me a break from all the domestic drama. No Alibi from Buffalo set up the show and invited The Voice from Philly. Aggravated Assault from Atlantic City joined the bill. Music and beer propelled the crowd and, before we knew it, some skinheads took advantage of the copious amounts of liquid courage they'd ingested and a ragtag army of drunken warrior wannabes took to the tenement building across the street from the venue. They busted down doors and beat and dragged some black and Latino families forcefully out of bed in the middle of the night. Just for fun. Police sirens sliced through the darkness. I exited the bar from the back door and retreated into the shadows, inching my way to my car parked down the street so I could safely disappear back home to Chicago. I had no interest in partaking in the senseless brutality of the night. And I couldn't afford to get arrested. Again. The next time I got pinched would surely mean prison time for me.

Whether or not I still had reservations about the whole white power skinhead movement, I found it very hard to let go. It had been my entire identity from the age of fourteen and I still savored my role as a leader.

By August of 1993, Big Ed from Bound For Glory had pegged me to take over management of the Northern Hammerskins organization. It meant I'd oversee the Hammerskin Nation operations for all of the northern U.S. states. Nearly two hundred skinheads would be under my direct command.

Big Ed had been leading the group for four years already, but wanted to focus more on his band's exploits, since they'd been touring and recording almost non-stop since our groundbreaking concert together in Germany. It was his sole responsibility as existing director to name his successor and he had no qualms about passing the baton to me. He knew I deserved it. I'd even stepped in from time to time to help him manage the role when he was busy on the road or in the studio with his band. Although it was never made official, I had more or less assumed the interim position of director for the Northern Hammerskins in his absence.

The next month, while I was at Big Ed's home in St. Paul, Minnesota, transitioning the role, we received a call from the Blood & Honour skinhead crew in England with unimaginable news. Skrewdriver's lead singer and driving force, Ian Stuart, had been tragically killed in a car crash that morning. We were stunned. Ian Stuart was an inspirational folk hero to many skinheads, including a huge role model for me. I'd never had the opportunity to meet Ian in person, but the few letters we traded back and forth were always cordial and inspiring. He was intelligent, influential, and an undisputed pioneer for skinhead music, racist or otherwise.

There was some suspicion the British government or anti-racists were involved in orchestrating his death by tampering with the car he'd been driving in, but no evidence ever surfaced to back up these theories. Nevertheless, Ian Stuart's death kicked white power skinheads all over the world back into motion, focusing our mission and binding us more tightly for a while. But I think we all knew the movement would never be the same without Ian's voice.

I thought for a moment about Clark Martell. The man who'd been responsible for introducing me to the boisterous music of Skrewdriver and the skinhead lifestyle when I was a young boy, all of thirteen-and-a-half years old. Where might he be? I'd only stayed in contact for a short time with Clark during his lengthy incarceration, but I'd heard he'd since been granted an early release to a halfway house far north of the Chicago city limits.

The letters he'd sent had gotten too bizarre and his artwork too lewd. I stopped responding after the first few years. His mail continued to arrive like clockwork for four years until it eventually tapered off to nothing. The last bit of correspondence I remembered opening came with a Polaroid picture of his new prison tattoo—on the center of his forehead was a freshly inked German eagle holding a swastika. In it, Clark looked old. Haggard. Sick. On the back of the photo was a simple, hand-drawn smiley face with the barely legible words, "See ya when I see ya! Long live the Aryan Goddess! 14/88. CM." Before long, I discovered other folks had been receiving similar disturbing packages from Clark and his once mythical cachet quickly evaporated.

While I sat and mourned the passing of Ian Stuart, I wondered where the man who had promised to save my life would find his own safety. Word spread that shortly after his release from prison, Clark had fled the halfway house and made his way into Michigan where he'd gotten into a row at the Detroit clubhouse and stabbed a Hammerskin with a screwdriver. The irony wasn't lost on me.

22
ORGANIZED CHAOS

C OLLECTING AN UNEMPLOYMENT CHECK and selling a few compact discs may have taken some of the sting out of being laid off from my road construction job every winter, but Lisa and I were still barely scraping by financially. Sometimes hardly even speaking to each other, both exhausted from the constant fighting. The wonderment and magic of being newlyweds and a having a baby as part of our family had been eroded by the harsh reality of diapers and more bills and little money and time for each other. Marriage wasn't the bliss we so naively expected when we'd first gotten together as teenagers. Our mobile home honeymoon vacation was over.

When she got angry, Lisa would let me know she wished she'd gone to college instead of marrying me.

"I'm home all day long doing laundry and cleaning the house and I never leave to do anything but buy baby food and diapers!" she'd argue. "Why don't you pitch in and help instead of going to your stupid skinhead meetings and running around with your useless friends?"

"You mean the ones I hardly get to hang out with anymore because I'm working seventy-hour weeks? Those friends?" I would counter.

Inevitably she'd cry. And then the baby would cry. "God, I wish I'd gone to school so I could go out and get a real job. So I wouldn't have to depend on you to raise my child."

"Your child? Your child!" I got so angry I threw my dinner plate in the sink, smashing it to pieces. "He's *our* child, Lisa, and I support you both so you don't have to work. So you can sit at home on your ass all day." I didn't really believe that, and things would always spiral down quickly from there.

Lisa would begin shrieking at the top of her lungs for the whole neighborhood to hear.

"You are an absent father and husband! You don't know what it's like to raise a child," she cried. "Everything has been handed to you your whole life and you don't even appreciate it. You are a spoiled brat. I know you resent your mother and father for not being there and now you've become exactly like them. Grow some fucking balls and be a man! You're just a child. You don't deserve a family. Devin doesn't even know who you are and, frankly, I don't want him to!"

And on and on she would go, her voice rising in volume with each poisonous jab, without so much as taking a pause to breathe.

That was usually my cue to grab the car keys and slam the door on my way out. Her words hurt me and I was afraid of not being able to control my temper. I never hit her, but I could begin to feel myself wanting to. So I'd leave for fear of losing control and physically hurting her or saying something I could never take back.

A few hours later I'd come home after finding one of my skinheads to drink and commiserate with. Lisa would be locked in the bedroom with Devin and I'd sleep it off on the couch until it was time for work the next morning.

I found it painstaking to look for work, or toil all day at a job that I felt was getting me nowhere, and then have to go home to a resentful wife and fussy baby. We fell into the same pattern most young couples do when the real world calls. Forget about flowers and romance and dreaming of the future and the rosy life we'd have together. The reality was that we were too young and immature to handle the responsibility of marriage and raising a child. And while we both loved Devin with every single ounce of our being and wanted genuinely to be a loving, happy union of three, neither Lisa nor I had much enthusiasm for doing the things that would bring a healthy relationship to fruition.

Lisa claimed she felt trapped and that she never slept while I was away attending to movement business. She became resolute in her objections to anything at all I did with skinheads. Not only did she despise the racism, she worried constantly that I was going to end up in jail or dead, leaving her to fend for our child herself.

In our calmer moments, we talked about how we were growing apart. How we both felt overburdened with responsibilities. Both continued to imply that the other one had it easier. And after expending every possible avenue, our ultimate solution to save our marriage was to do yet another foolish thing. We selfishly rationalized that if we had another child, we'd somehow create an opportunity to bind us closer to each other and thus repair our fractured relationship. So, we began to make love with another baby in mind. This did rekindle our affection for each other and it gave us a new purpose, and when Devin was a little over a year old, Lisa was expecting again.

Big Ed called late one night, shortly after we received the news that Lisa was pregnant, to congratulate me and set a date to meet again. With his busy traveling schedule and the sudden news of Ian Stuart's passing, we hadn't gotten around to formally finalizing the leadership transfer of the Northern Hammerskins to me.

"The last thing we need to do to make this official is get you on the phone with Shane Becker." Becker was national director for the Hammerskin Nation and one of the Dallas Hammerskin founders who'd been at the Naperville meeting in 1988. "It'll be tricky since he's still in prison, but if we set a date and a specific time window for you to be by your phone we can make it work."

"Ed, I've actually been meaning to call you about that." I hemmed and hawed before actually getting to the point. "With work and the new baby and all, I'm going to have to bow out of the running."

"Well, that's disappointing." I could tell in his voice, without him saying the actual words, that he understood my dilemma. We were close friends and I'd confided in him multiple times about my marital woes. "I understand. Take care of that family and come see us soon in St. Paul. Julie and the kids would love some company."

"Will do, Ed. Please send the girls my love."

The next day, while I was packing a lunch before heading to work, I received a call from a Texas correctional institution. It was Shane Becker asking if I'd reconsider. After a few pleasantries, I politely declined the offer and wished him well.

I tried my best not to dwell on it too much, at least publicly, but walking away from the directorship role for the Northern Hammerskins pained me. I had worked so incredibly hard to establish myself as a prominent national leader within the white power movement and now, in one fell swoop, I had stymied my own hopes for making that reality happen. But I couldn't let the disappointment wash over me. Even if I hadn't turned it down, I'd be giving up so much more. On the home front, I had vowed to make my marriage work. And on the frontlines, I still had work to do. I had to find a way to make both work.

I was still importing white power CDs from Europe to supplement my income and selling so much of it on the side, the idea to open a record store and to be my own boss took root. Not only could my shop carry music, I could sell posters, T-shirts, boots and braces, and other accessories I knew skins and punks would buy. I could use my entrepreneurial knack to both feed my family and keep the local skinhead scene going strong, without having to leave either behind.

My leadership and steadfast involvement over the last six years had helped grow the American white power movement from its earliest roots—the legacy bestowed upon me by the founding triumvirate of Clark Martell, Carmine Paterno, and Chase Sargent—but between the responsibilities of working and taking care of a family and Lisa's fears for my safety, I found little time anymore for rallies, recruiting new members, maintaining the crew, and the things that had catapulted me into a leadership position in the first place.

With a store selling our unique brand of music and feeding our culture, I could contribute to the cause in a different, but still significant way. The music I'd sell would keep us straight on our priorities, it would inspire newcomers to join our mission, and the flexibility of being my own boss would allow me to spend more time with my family.

Lisa didn't initially object to me opening a store, although she wasn't so sure it would work. But she agreed we needed the money, so I was able to convince her my idea would ease our financial troubles and give us time to work on our marriage. After what seemed like months of debates, and me pointing out the advantages, Lisa decided to go along with it. It wouldn't be easy. And a small shop wouldn't guarantee us riches, but what more could we lose?

Hungry for professional fulfillment in my life, desperate to earn a better living, wanting an opportunity to prove my capabilities as a husband and father, I gambled our paltry savings and a small three thousand dollar loan from her mother and ramped up my idea quickly. I headed out to find the perfect spot for Chaos Records—the name I'd settled on months earlier—the rhythm of wild success pounding in my head. The thought that this would support my expanding family while still allowing me to remain connected to the movement filled me with purpose once again.

I signed a cheap lease for a vacant storefront near a busy intersection just west of Blue Island's border. The space had been sitting empty for a while, a fact I used to negotiate a favorable deal on the rent. I built out the inside of the store myself, from counters to racks to shelving, and paid an artist friend from high school fifty bucks to airbrush the walls with apocalyptic images better suiting the giant neon "anarchy" sign glowing in the window. I hung dozens of busted vinyl records from the ceiling with fishing line, plastered my old punk rock posters all over the walls, and tiled the floor in a black and white checkerboard ska pattern. I spent weeks carefully choosing and ordering my music inventory—all independent or underground music you couldn't find anyplace else in the area, at least not at mainstream record shops like Record Town or Sam Goody. I had no interest in competing with mainstream consumerism.

While selling white power music was my bread and butter, I also carried more run-of-the-mill Oi!, punk, ska, hardcore, rockabilly, and black metal music. This was a business, after all. I needed a diverse inventory that would bring paying customers through the doors. But it was the white power inventory and my regular skinhead customers that were my mainstay and kept me in business.

Cops were onto the store the moment it opened. Squad cars routinely lurked in the parking lot, the police expecting trouble. I was selling subversive music that few, if any, other shops in the country sold. They were no doubt concerned my store would be a front for bad stuff. Perhaps it was one of Chaos Records' two taglines that I used in print advertisements and spray-painted on the walls inside the store that roused their ire: "The Revolution Starts Here" and "Fuck Peace. I Want Chaos!"

Had they known me at all, they would have seen that while I was still looked upon by the movement as the chief Chicago figurehead among white power skinheads, I had little involvement with any daily activities. I had transferred most of those activities to veterans in my crew. I no longer wrote letters or sent out pamphlets. Hadn't been to an out-of-state gathering in almost a year and I'd stopped recruiting altogether. The glory of both my bands had faded. I stayed in the background while the remaining crew floated unattended for the most part. I'd been leading from behind for some time, and while there were others within my crew still pounding the pavement, our diminished numbers were evident.

I had a hard time letting go. My selfishness and insecurity made damn sure I hadn't groomed an heir apparent to take over the gang in my absence. Sure, there was pressure from Kubiak and some of the other guys to be more involved, but for the most part they understood I had a family to support. After all, a main tenet of the fourteen words that we lived by was to build a future for our children.

I'd pitched it to my crew as more of a retirement from the streets, but the truth was I'd run out of gas, leaving me idle and fatigued. Still, nobody questioned my allegiance.

Not long after I opened the record store, a couple of undercover cops wandered in. Talk about conspicuous. In waltzed two narcs in their early thirties wearing street clothes, apathetic and clean-cut as soldiers in boot camp.

Smirking, I walked over to them, held my hand out, and said in my politest tone, "Nice to meet you, officers. Let me guess, you're either here to pick up the new Cradle of Filth album or to buy tickets for the Anal Cunt in-store acoustic show we're having next week. Either way, I can help you. Cash or credit?"

Red-faced, they looked at each other, shrugged and said, "You got us." They turned around and left.

Before I opened my shop, I would have given them hell. Told them they had no right to trespass on my property and kicked them out for being traitors to their race. I'd have thrown my constitutional rights to serve who I pleased into their faces.

But I chose not to do business that way. I bit my tongue and treated everyone who walked into my store with respect and fairness. My kids' livelihood depended on it.

And because it did, I unwittingly became more tolerant of those people whose views didn't line up with mine. Until the day Sammy, the black anti-racist skinhead, entered my shop.

I kept a loaded 9mm handgun behind the counter. Just in case. When Black Sammy and three of his fresh-cut minions walked in, it didn't take long for the pistol to find its place tucked within reach behind my belt.

I'd been paging through catalogs of upcoming new releases, jotting down titles I wanted to stock the following month, when Sammy strolled in with his crew. My blood froze when I casually glanced up and saw him standing there in the doorway, his black bomber jacket hanging off his skinny frame, dark eyes brooding, his henchmen unflinching behind him. It was a standoff for about fifteen seconds. Short, wiry build, the whites of Sammy's eyes were faded and lifeless. Our stares held each other, suspicious and ready.

"You got any Skrewdriver in this joint?" Sammy quipped as he made his way through the front door of the record store. "How about some White American Youth or Final Solution?"

Sammy was a well-known old school skin who had co-founded the anti-racist group SHOC—Skinheads of Chicago—with Dwight, another black skinhead who'd grown up in Chicago's rough ghetto housing projects. They found each other as lonely, young punk rockers going to shows on the North Side of the city, dark-skinned anomalies among an ocean of white suburbanites in studded leather and tinted mohawks. After CASH members began passing out Romantic Violence flyers in front of punk shows at clubs like Cabaret Metro and Medusa's in 1985, the two decided they would counter Clark and his crew by forming a rival anti-racist skinhead gang—pre-dating the Chicago SHARPs by half a decade.

"I think you're in the wrong place, Sammy," I replied, staring him down as I stepped from behind the counter. I was alone in the store. My hand was hovering behind my back, near my piece.

"Come on, Picciolini, I know you guys keep that shit behind the counter." He sounded serious, despite the curious ink on his forehead. Sammy was an enigma. He was a virulent, black anti-racist skinhead who was deranged enough to have a giant swastika tattooed on his forehead. A reviled Nazi symbol on the forehead of a black anti-racist skinhead? That's right. It never made sense to any of us white power skins, but we chalked it up to his frequent alcoholic blackouts and a touch of insanity. Even his own cohorts thought he was nuts. I wasn't taking any chances.

"Sammy, you and your crew are welcome here," the words came out of my mouth before I realized I'd said them. "But I don't want any trouble."

"Good, now give me all your motherfucking Skrewdriver." He approached as my hand nervously adjusted my waistband.

"Alright, I'll bite," I said, snapping into action. "Which album do you want?" I moved my way back over to the counter, creating a barrier between me and the four goons who were now littered about the shop.

"All of them. I want everything you've got." Fuck. Here we go, I thought. Don't make me shoot you, Sammy. Not in my store. Not today.

As I knelt behind the counter to grab the box of CDs, I carefully slid the already racked pistol from my belt and held it at the ready behind my back. Scenarios flashed through my head of how I would have to put two bullets in Sammy first and still have time to track the other three Antis and put the remaining 9mm hollow-point rounds in them. Surely it would be justified self-defense in response to a robbery.

"How much are they?"

My itchy finger located the trigger as I slowly rose up with the gun hidden beneath the box of CDs.

"Do you take credit cards?" Sammy asked.

"What?" I wasn't sure if I'd registered what he said.

"Do you take credit cards? I ain't speaking Swahili, motherfucker." His guys laughed.

I carefully returned the readied gun behind my back to my waistband. "Yeah. MasterCard and Visa. No American Express." I turned to scan the barcodes into the computer. Hesitantly, I turned to him. "Sammy, why the fuck are you buying Skrewdriver?"

"Why the fuck do you sell it?" He paused. "That shit is dope, nigga!"

I didn't bother to ask about the Nazi tattoo below his receding afro as we spent the next thirty minutes discussing other "dope" skinhead bands and reminiscing about the early days of Chicago skins and my time in WAY and Final Solution. I laughed when he told me that he hated Bound For Glory because their music was "too goddamn metal," but WAY was "aight for some white boy music." I jokingly told him I'd pass along the feedback to Big Ed.

Before they left, Sammy and his pals spent over three hundred dollars buying music and T-shirts that afternoon. By far the biggest receipt for a single customer since I first opened the store. Before I knew it, we were shaking hands, and a bizarre smile was forming on my face. What could I say? My beliefs were crumbling right before my eyes. This guy wasn't less than me: In the head, he may have been a few beers short of a six-pack, but he was just another lost soul, trying to find his way in a tough, mixed-up world. That thought stuck with me.

Once they were gone, I unloaded my gun and locked it in the safe in the back room. I'd come too close to murder again that day and I didn't want to make that mistake again.

Over time, dozens of Antis came in to buy the more apolitical Oi! and ska music they would otherwise have to trek twenty miles deep into the city to get. They may have been my sworn enemies for nearly the last seven years, but I offered better prices and a vast selection to choose from. I carried titles that record shops in the city wouldn't stock. Even some of the anti-racist skinhead bands. That seemed to occasionally trump their negative feelings about me.

Regardless, I couldn't put a gun in their face or chase them out of my store or not sell to them if I wanted my business to succeed and provide for my family. So I chatted with them. Made small talk. Remembered names. Answered their questions and learned about their personal lives by exchanging conversation. I was surprised to discover they were decent. Even more so, they were *people*. Period. Politics aside, we had many things in common and I began to humanize them. No longer were they just a target for my group to eliminate, they were human beings. Most of us weren't violent by nature. Many came from hardworking families. We all had our problems with each other and our fair share of street fights, but none of us were actual sociopaths. On second thought, Sammy might be a sociopath—and Clark definitely was—but most of us weren't. Regardless, we got to know each other over time. Bonded over music. Became friendly even.

Meanwhile, my white power customers dwindled. I started hearing less and less from Kubiak and the crew. I chalked it up to the fact that they were usually broke, or that none of them were married or had kids to support and they probably thought hanging around at a boring record store all day wasn't as exciting as being out on the street raining mayhem. I didn't think too much of it at the time. I was engrossed with keeping the business running smoothly and by the friendly new connections I was enjoying. If I had to be completely honest, though, my crew rarely entered my mind anymore. Business was decent and keeping me more than busy. And what little time I did have those first few months, I spent with my family. The guys seemed to be operating smoothly without me—at least that was the impression—so I put it out of my mind.

Surprisingly, my customer base was quite diverse. I began to meet gay and Jewish customers and increasingly found myself being genuinely civil to them, as well as other minorities. Our conversations were brief. Guarded at first, but slowly we got to know each other through our shared interest in music. And they kept coming back. Through music, we found some commonality, and I found myself thinking clearly, "These are good people. I don't want to hurt them." We talked about bands, laughed, swapped stories about concerts we'd been to. Related to each other in ways I hadn't thought possible.

The first female Jewish customer I met was a twenty-something punk rock girl who'd introduced herself as "Godiva." She was a stunning brunette with a great body and ample breasts. I know this because when she came to the cash register to pay for her Sex Pistols T-shirt, she took her top off right there in front of me to try it on, not only revealing her bare breasts, but also a huge Star of David tattooed around her left nipple. I'm pretty sure I forgot to charge her for the shirt, further distracted after she leaned over the counter and kissed me on the cheek, saying "Thanks!" before leaving. All I could do was smile.

I met punk rock customers of every color. Metal heads from Latin America. A rockabilly band from Algeria. A gay Christian couple shopping for underground death metal lounge music. I didn't have it, but I ordered it for them. And I met my first gay, half-Asian, half-Puerto Rican atheist Jew. Life became interesting in a way I never would have guessed it could.

The unexpected camaraderie I began to share with customers at the store jolted me back to the summer my family moved to Blue Island, between my eighth grade and freshman year in high school. A time only recently passed, yet it felt a lifetime away.

In my nostalgic reverie, I recalled being the insecure thirteen-year-old boy who loved playing sports with his High Street mates, being part of a team, belonging, having fun.

I missed that. And it felt good to get a little glimpse of that innocence back. To have friends who didn't care what your "beliefs" were. I suddenly became aware that the bitterness that had surrounded me had begun to atrophy. Empathy had trickled in, filling the resulting void.

In August of 1994, shortly before our second child was due, I decided to attend a concert that was being held in memory of Ian Stuart in Racine, Wisconsin. Resistance Records, an upstart American white power label whose music I'd sold through the store, was hosting the highly-anticipated event.

Lisa was far from happy I'd decided to go, but she knew I'd kept my promise to step back from movement activities to spend more time with the family. She recognized this concert was a one-time thing and especially significant to me. Stuart had been one of my musical idols, someone I'd corresponded with and emulated over the years. What worried her was that the concert would be well attended. And where groups of skinheads gathered, trouble was certain to follow.

I minimized the likelihood of that, reassuring Lisa I wouldn't do anything to jeopardize our mending relationship and that I'd drive the two hours back home as soon as the concert ended. I pointed out that I didn't consider myself an activist anymore. I'd even decided to stop selling white power music in the store. And I'd completely—and voluntarily—stopped using derogatory racist terms now that some minorities and gays had become my customers. Not because I wanted to sell more music, but because I'd become friendly with them, and I didn't want to insult anyone.

Reassured somewhat, Lisa hugged me and told me to come home safe.

When I arrived, the concert was humming with energy. Great music. Centurion and Das Reich from Wisconsin. Aggravated Assault and their AC Boys crew caravanned in from Atlantic City. Nordic Thunder from Delaware. Berserkr came from Tulsa. Rahowa from Canada. No Remorse from England. And Bound For Glory. Not to mention how close I'd been with the members of every band on the bill, the audience was also crawling with old friends. Embraces and shared stories filled the night.

"Well, look who it is. How's it going, stranger?" It was Big Ed.

"Hey man. Good to see you," I replied.

"How's that record store of yours doing? Are you carrying the new Bound For Glory record?"

"Actually, I've been thinking of scaling back a bit on the white power music. It hasn't been selling like it used to. Rock-O-Rama raised their prices and I have to charge more and I guess people just can't afford it," I lied.

"Really? That's too bad." He seemed to want to say more than he had. "Well, maybe you can bring in some of that jigaboo rap music to boost your sales," he laughed. He didn't mean anything by it, but it made me feel uneasy nonetheless. By now the first band had taken the stage and was ripping into their first song.

I let out a half-hearted laugh. "Well, hey man, it was good to see you. Pretty cool that No Remorse was able to make it, even if it is under somber circumstances."

"Yeah. I've gotta get ready for our set." He gave me a bear hug and started to walk away. "Oh, that reminds me, some guy claiming to be from your crew in Blue Island sent me a letter a few weeks back. I think you should read it."

"Really?" I was genuinely surprised. "What did it say?"

"He was saying all kinds of crazy shit about you. Julie's got my bag. I'll give you the letter after the show and you can take it home and stick it up his ass. You should read it." I said I would. "It ain't good."

"Oh, okay." I became worried. What the hell was he talking about? And, more importantly, who the hell was the letter from? Nobody had said anything to me back home. I hadn't been hanging out, but nobody seemed too upset by it. I knew a few of the guys weren't too happy about some of the music I sold in the store, but they'd been in the store since I'd started carrying it and never mentioned anything about it other than ribbing me a bit.

I couldn't get my conversation with Big Ed out of my mind. I ran through every possible scenario I could think of. Had I slighted someone? Said something to offend one of them? Just then No Remorse took the stage and the nagging voices in my head disappeared.

Before blasting into song, their singer Pete Burnside, who I'd shared some correspondence with and become friendly with over the years and whose music I had grown up on and learned from as a young skinhead, began his set with a moving speech about Ian Stuart. And for a moment, I let myself be pulled back in, high on the ephemera and intensity of the night. The music pounded in my veins. A thousand skinheads filled the hall. Outstretched arms carving the air in tribute to a fallen hero among skinheads far and wide. The worries and responsibilities of my family faded into the background again as the desire to be part of this fractured world filled me anew. Old comrades I hadn't seen in years were happy to see me, peppering me with questions about what I'd been up to.

"You know, the family…the store," I'd say.

But the extreme high was short-lived.

Less than an hour after the concert ended, tragedy struck. While buying beer in a nearby convenience store, Joe Rowan, a fellow Hammerskin and the lead singer of the band Nordic Thunder, was shot and killed in a skirmish with black youths. Joe was a friend. Someone I'd known for several years and had grown to respect. We'd spoken at the venue less than twenty minutes before he was murdered. He was shot just minutes after I'd gotten in my car to head home. Joe was so proud of his children and carried on affectionately about them and showed me their photographs that he kept in his wallet. Now he had left his two young babies fatherless and a young, single mother unequipped to care for them.

I didn't wait around for Big Ed to give me the letter. I no longer cared. I just wanted to leave.

I could no longer deny my ambivalence, my doubts about this miserable existence I'd created. This life wasn't for me. This fractured perpetual motion machine of unending violence and despair that I'd helped create was not something I was proud to be a part of anymore. I cried for Joe and his fatherless kids the whole ride home. Another part of me wept for my own two children.

23

WALK ALONE

Between my friend's hate-related murder, my disillusionment with the movement I'd helped build, and the fact that due to my experiences at the record store I couldn't reconcile hating the people I'd once wanted to eliminate on principle alone, I began to let go of my biases. I discovered so many commonalities that I could not in good conscience disparage anyone based on superficial differences. I simply couldn't justify or rationalize my prejudices any longer.

Memories of the past seven years flashed through my mind and they made me angry. I thought about the Ku Klux Klan with their ridiculous dunce caps and tablecloth clown costumes; the racist sovereign constitutionalists who carried automatic weapons to the grocery store and felt like man-made laws didn't apply to them; the Christian Identity nuts that distorted the Bible to suit their perverse dogmatism that turned God into a vengeful Aryan warlord who sought to slay the mud races which they say are reincarnations of the Devil; the revisionist historians who claimed the Holocaust never happened and six million Jews somehow magically evaporated from the earth; the laughable American Nazi Party stormtroopers dressed as if every day were Halloween—with their brown Boy Scout shirts and fancy culottes; the racial Odinists who believed that fairy Viking gods who lived in the clouds would strike down the dark-skinned infidels with bolts of lightning and a crack of Thor's hammer; and the neo-Nazi skinhead gangbangers who fooled themselves into believing that they had an ounce of courage running through their veins, when in reality they were filled with a volatile cocktail of cheap beer and self-loathing to fuel their hate. Now, when I looked into the mirror I saw a hollow shell of a man—a stranger—filled with all of those same toxic elements, staring back at me.

For one-third of my life I'd chewed and swallowed gristly bits of each one of those twisted ideologies and now all I felt like doing was jamming my fingers down my throat and vomiting them all up into the nearest toilet. I felt sick. Like a dope fiend detoxing from selfish power and control, instead of heroin—always needing more and blindly living my life on a razor's edge to score the next hateful fix.

The horribly misguided actions of my last seven years had begun with my extreme loneliness as a child and materialized themselves as vengeful hate and bigotry. I'd blamed everyone but myself for what I believed had been taken away from me as a young boy. I was angry with my parents for abandoning me for their careers and I took my misplaced aggression out on the world, blaming those who I failed to make an effort to understand, rather than taking responsibility for my own feelings and actions.

And because I was so blind, too overly ambitious to pay attention to my true emotions, I ended up blaming others—blacks, gays, Jews, and anyone else who I thought wasn't like me—for problems in my own life they couldn't possibly have contributed to. My unfounded panic quickly, and unjustly, manifested itself as venomous hatred and I became radicalized by those who saw in me a lonely youngster who was ripe to be molded. And because I was so desperately searching for meaning—to rise above the mundane—I devoured any crumbs I was fed that resembled greatness. Made them my identity, overshadowing my own authentic character. The same one that I'd grown weary of as a kid. And through my misguided animosity, I'd become a big, fat, racist bully. Morbidly obese from the countless lies I'd been fed by those who took advantage of my youth, naïveté, and loneliness. Toxins I'd eagerly feasted on. Now, I just wanted the poison inside of me to get the fuck out.

And I was exhausted.

Spending seven years willfully denying the truth of humanity drains an incredible amount of energy. At twenty-one, I didn't have the strength anymore to continue to engage in constant battle with my own conscience.

Now, people I had once terrorized knowingly put what I'd stood for aside and connected with me. I didn't feel like I deserved their kindness. They were aware of my entire sordid history, yet they never judged me nor did any damage to my business, which I'd feared they might. They never condemned me or kicked out my taillights or spray-painted obscenities on my store or hurt my family. They weren't the people I'd set out to serve when I decided to start my business, but the undeniable impact they made on me during that time gave me an intensely eye-opening perspective on life. They looked beyond my crumbling façade and sensed my pain before I even acknowledged theirs, and I understood now that it had been me alone inflicting damage onto the whole of us for so long.

Non-whites and Jewish people weren't evil or out to get me; gay people loved each other in the same ways I loved my wife and child; the people I'd thoughtlessly punished were all victims of the same pitfalls in life that I was. We were all in the same world—the same underdog's corner. Bobbing and weaving tirelessly against the ropes with our guard up as we fought to survive in a world full of pointless jabs—in the end, just wanting to be loved for who we really are. We had to *rely* on each other, not *hurt* one another.

This truth was at first excruciatingly painful and shameful, but it was the key that unlocked the heavily fortified barricade that had imprisoned my soul.

Everyone from my old crew had stopped visiting the shop. They grew certain that the jumble of outsiders who'd made their way into my circle were pushing them out. They'd grown weary of my excuses for why I couldn't come out and spend time with them: I was tired; the baby was sick; the store needed to be inventoried. Before long, I began to hear whispers that I'd lost my edge, that I was a capitalist looking to profit from white power music. I became nervous. Afraid to come clean about my feelings, worried that others might see me as a coward, I squashed the rumors as quickly as I heard them by making an example of those who spoke them. Shaming them. Discrediting them. Turning the tables. Even Kubiak and I had grown distant after his bachelor party. He'd only half-heartedly asked me to stop by after we bumped into each other at the gas station the night before.

"What the hell is that nigger-lover doing here?" I heard the young new face quip just after I arrived, as I descended into the wood-paneled basement of the shabby VFW hall. "Shouldn't he be at his shop, sticking his nose up some kike's ass?" A small group assembled around him silently chuckled behind the beer cans pressed to their lips.

I stepped over Kubiak who was already half in the bag, laid out on the steps. "What the fuck did you say?"

I hadn't ever noticed this kid before tonight, but the deadness in his eyes reminded me of something I'd seen in my own mirror a thousand times.

"I said you're a nigger-loving faggot who sucks circumcised Jew dick."

Operating on pure muscle memory, I pushed off the bottom stair and lunged at him. I'm not sure which came faster, the bile filling my gut over his words or my clenched fist crushing his glass jaw. Either way, my knockout blow meant he'd have an easier time spitting out several of his teeth than repeating that sentence again anytime soon. The crowd scrambled to separate us and Kubiak reached in from behind and put me in a chokehold.

"You have to fucking go," Kubiak grunted as he struggled to drag me away. "You can't be here."

Those who had once been fiercely loyal to me had begun to disparage my commitment behind my back. The fuse had been burning for months—they'd been whispering loudly about it amongst themselves— and tonight the spark had finally reached the powder keg and triggered the explosion. They'd been witnessing my change happen and decided amongst themselves to sever the head of the beast before I could swallow the poison pill and take the group down with me. I'd become a pariah. And as scared as I was of what the consequences might be for my perceived betrayal, it was also the first time in my life that I was satisfied with the feeling of *not* belonging. At once, I denounced my responsibility to them, unsure of what my future held.

I soon found myself preferring the solitude of the store to anyplace else and spent at least twelve hours a day there. Which did not sit well with my wife.

Neither the coming of our second child, nor the extra money the store was bringing in, was making much of a difference in our marriage. I began avoiding Lisa again, tired of the renewed fighting, weary of the accusations about not spending enough time with her and Devin; sick of the complaints that she was tired of the way we lived. Bitterness and melancholy engulfed me. I'd given up all my involvement with the movement. All I did was work to support my family. What more did she want from me?

I was too young, too blind and damaged, to realize that what she and Devin needed most from me was simple—they were starving for my time and attention. All I believed was that nothing I did pleased her. In retrospect, I realize now that I was extremely unhappy with myself, not my wife. I was a disappointment to me.

One of my biggest motivators for opening the store, aside from supporting my family, was that I wanted a chance to start my own business like my parents had done. While I may not have been able to articulate it at the time or even been aware of it, I desperately wanted acceptance and respect. From my parents. From friends. From the movement. From Lisa. This desire became stronger than any other motivating factor, ironically overshadowing any dedication to my family. The manifest irony that I was losing respect from those I was seeking it from, because I was so narrowly focused on my own selfishness, never dawned on me.

So I continued to find solace in my work, ignoring my pregnant wife's and small child's essential needs, certain that as long as I was providing for my family financially, I was in the right.

But Lisa and I continued to argue constantly over the same things. Lisa was incensed that I was never home to spend quality time with her and Devin. She was right. She needed a partner and I had checked out. I never did see that she just needed a break. A young woman, barely out of her teens, stolen from her own dreams, who was busy caring for a two-year-old and about to give birth again. I was too engrossed in my own selfish needs to help. I should have been there for the intimate times and the small things that often mean so much more. Irresponsibly, I had treated my own wife and son like my parents had treated me. This was a harsh blow.

Our second son, Brandon, was born on November 18th, 1994, just after my twenty-first birthday and almost two years to the day after our son Devin was born. His birth was every bit as moving and magical as his brother's had been, and Lisa and I instantly fell madly in love with him.

But his birth could not save our marriage. If anything could have, it would have been our children.

It was too late.

I knew we were doomed the night I came home late again to Lisa strapping Devin and Brandon into their car seats. Missing dinner, like I had the night before. One look at her swollen eyes that avoided mine like poison, I could tell she had been crying. She said she wasn't in love with me anymore. Not only that, "You make my skin crawl," she added, stabbing me with an icy, dead stare, clasping four-month-old Brandon to her chest. That bruised me the most of all the arguments we ever had. I knew at that moment all hope for our marriage was lost. I wasn't sure we could recover from that fatal sentiment. "I want a divorce. I want you to go," Lisa cried, slamming her car door.

Lisa left for her grandparents' tiny trailer on the lake in Michigan—the very same one where we'd spent our first night as joyful newlyweds—with our boys in tow. I stood in the street and watched my family vanish into the darkness before me. I'd set out to give them everything, but instead I had selfishly hijacked their lives. I knew I had no right to stop them from leaving.

I spent the next two solemn hours packing a canvas duffel bag with the only belongings I felt entitled to—a couple T-shirts, two pairs of worn-out Levi's, an armful of underwear and socks, and the heavy Doc Martens on my feet. It was all I deserved. I slept on the floor in the back room of my shop, next to a stack of broken vinyl records.

My marriage was over.

Quietly.

No pleas for forgiveness. No more promises to change.

At daybreak the following morning, I knocked on my parents' door and moved back into the basement apartment below them that I'd made my home when I was fifteen.

Just like that.

Back to my skinhead frat-boy dorm room. Dusty and stale. The air moldy and dank.

I'd outgrown it. And it served as a constant reminder of my failure.

Even eleven-year-old Buddy didn't want to hang out with me.

"Hey, Buddy. I could use some help doing inventory at the record store. Want to come to work with me tomorrow?"

"No. I'm going to the movies with Flaco. Maybe some other time."

I'd been too busy with the movement and my own aspirations to pay much attention to him. He was in middle school now with friends of his own. I'd thought of him often. Missed him. But when the holidays and rare instances of extended family time came, I paid too much attention to my own selfish needs and not enough to those of my young brother who had idolized me growing up, but who now resented me for abandoning him when he most needed me.

Leaning against the counter, tired and alone after work that night, I realized that I'd been exactly like my parents. I'd relived their failures, irrationally thinking that being devoted to anything other than the needs of the ones you love equated to being a good parent. Too busy making a living instead of making time for my family. And I'd even taken it further. If I had been completely honest with myself, I'd have realized that it wasn't the desire to put food on the table that had kept me away from my home and family. It was my egotistical dream of being somebody important, of making a difference. Being a hero. When all I needed to do, to be those things, was just to pay attention to what was right in front of me the entire time.

When all was said and done, the only thing I'd accomplished was to become someone I didn't respect. Fueled by hubris, detached from those I loved, planting lies and sowing seeds of hate to mask my own feelings of insecurity and loneliness. Creating fear, dividing people against each other. I had instead become someone I didn't even like. Exactly what I'd hoped, from the beginning, not to become. A villain.

Chaos Records would not fulfill my desire to provide for my family. Instead it broke us. After I pulled all the racist music from the inventory, which had accounted for the bulk of the store's sales, my income plummeted and before long I couldn't afford to keep the doors open. Two short months after Lisa and I split up I shuttered the store.

We decided she should keep the house and in our divorce proceedings the judge awarded her majority custody of our boys. I was destitute. I had no job, no home, no friends, no wife, and I no longer lived with my sons—the two most essential beings remaining in my life. My identity—the person I thought I was, who I'd fought for seven years to become—imploded.

Each harsh thrashing became a catalyst for the next.

At twenty-one years old, I'd lost everything.

Four months later, on the morning of April 19, 1995—the day before neo-Nazis across the globe would have celebrated Adolf Hitler's 106th birthday—white supremacist Timothy McVeigh drove toward the Alfred P. Murrah Federal Building in Oklahoma City, Oklahoma, carrying a 4,800-pound fertilizer bomb in the back of his rented Ryder truck. He detonated it, killing 168 innocent people—including nineteen children—and injuring many hundreds more. McVeigh had with him an envelope containing pages from *The Turner*

Diaries—the fictional account of Earl Turner and an army of white revolutionaries who ignite a race war by blowing up FBI headquarters using a truck bomb.

The same book that Clark Martell had given me when I was fourteen.

The same book that I'd read over and over.

The very same book that I kept stuffed in my coat pocket for almost seven years.

What the hell had I done with my life?

24

RAGNARÖK

For the next five years I withdrew from the world and sank into an ever-deepening depression that saw me wanting to sleep in just a little while longer each morning until, eventually, I would run completely out of daylight. I'd open my eyes, hoping the darkness surrounding me meant that I was dead. I didn't know who I was, what my place in the world should be, or if I even cared enough about myself to remedy my miserable situation.

I'd lost everything that held any real value in my life. My wife and children were no longer part of my daily routine. I'd long since alienated myself from my parents, grandparents, and brother. My social framework and business had both collapsed. I found it painful to muster the energy to seek meaningful employment, and when I did force myself to find work—because I wanted to support my children—the best I could do was to toil away in a part-time, minimum wage job without much promise of self-fulfillment. Once again, I felt completely alone. Isolated and empty. The same feelings I'd experienced as a lonely young boy sitting cross-legged in my grandparents' coat closet, gazing past my own reflection on the windowpane, wishing I were part of the vibrant cinema of life projected behind it.

Christian Picciolini (Photo by Meredith Goldberg) **295**

In my youth, during the years before I joined the white power movement, I'd watch the world from afar, detached from it like an outsider. My innocent hopes to belong to something floating on the horizon—out of reach—a million miles away.

In retrospect, everything seemed so perfect from a distance. So romantic. In my solitude, I daydreamed of being the hero, the leading actor, the protagonist, so that others would more easily accept me, instead of embracing who I truly was, who I was meant to be—an individual; one that was flawed and scared but had many great qualities in common with other wonderfully flawed and scared people. I imprudently took miscalculated risks and co-opted the stories of others as my own identity.

When I was a kid I wanted so desperately to be like Rocky Balboa or Han Solo or Indiana Jones. What little boy didn't dream of that growing up? I craved the same type of outrageous adventure I saw played out on the movie screen and thought that if I could be more like them, people would like me better and let me into their world. But then as I grew older and saw acceptance slip further out of reach, I started to gamble away that simple innocence—the fundamental quest to belong—hoping that I could more quickly force my own destiny if I took on the role of a tough, well-respected gangster character instead—à la Robert De Niro as Johnny Boy in *Mean Streets* or Vito Corleone in *The Godfather*.

When those small bets began to pay attention-garnering dividends, I wagered against even greater odds for a chance to further gain respect and thus began imitating the real-life people around me that I admired, like Carmine Paterno and Chase Sargent and Clark Martell. As my ego spiraled out of control and I became unsatisfied with simply being respected, I craved being feared, as well. So, I went all in and bet against the house, only to lose everything while thoughtlessly trying to fulfill the savage role of Earl Turner from *The Turner Diaries*.

I wanted a story to tell so desperately that I ignored all I had when it was already within my grasp. I started to gamble it all away, ultimately losing everything. The familiar sensation of despair I'd experienced in my youth—not unlike that of a solitary crow perched upon a broken tree branch, swinging in the wind, looking for a last-chance meal—rushed back and overwhelmed me. I'd become so emaciated from a lack of self-acceptance that I'd starved my soul just as one could deprive their body of food and nutrition. I'd become a paper-thin shell of skin and bones with no heart and no soul.

Throughout the seven years of my involvement in the white power movement, I worked tirelessly, not only to disrupt the lives of so many innocent people, but to sabotage myself, denying myself of what was absolutely essential—love, basic human goodness, and a clear purpose for living. For years after I abandoned the caustic crusade I'd helped define, I would suffer those losses of love, goodness, and purpose again and again. Even when I stopped ingesting and spewing the poisonous bigotry of the movement, I still denied myself the nourishment of redemption and the natural cleansing that happens when exposing toxicity to healing light and fresh air. I prevented my own truth from escaping my lips.

I found myself meandering lost inside the solitary world I'd built for myself. I trusted no one and avoided most. Only my own sadness offered me exile. A self-imposed death sentence. I couldn't begin to understand what I was feeling—so I let it prevail over me.

In the end, the only way I knew how to destroy the convoluted world I had created for myself was to suffer under the weight of it.

I needed sustenance. Both physical and spiritual. I was a father with children. I had a life to rebuild. A soul to repair. So when an acquaintance told me about a temp job with IBM in late 1999, I saw no other choice but to leap at it. Never mind I didn't know a damn thing about technology or computers or software. I had confidence in my ability to fake it until I made it. I needed to stand on my own two feet, and I had two young kids who still depended on me to be their father.

I'd blown it with them so far, but I was determined to make up for it. I'd be sure they never lacked for anything. I resolved to be the parent to them I'd always wanted mine to be for me. I'd spend time with them. As much time as I possibly could. Every weekend. I'd find out what interested them and do everything I could to encourage their dreams. If they played sports, I'd never miss a game and I'd be there to encourage them to get up when they fell down. I'd make time to coach them. If they liked science, I'd buy them chemistry sets and microscopes and computers and telescopes and we'd visit the best science museums so they could see what amazing things are possible if only they have the courage to dream them.

If they liked history, I'd take them to every historically significant site in the world and expose them to cultures as ancient as the dirt upon the earth. If it was music that inspired them, I'd get them instruments and lessons. If they were passionate about art, I'd encourage them to paint or sketch and expose them to the world's most important artists. They would never again lack for my love and support, my belief in them, my unswerving interest in all that was vital for them to lead productive, caring lives. Just as I had discussed with Lisa all those years ago when we first fell in love, when we'd made a promise to each other that we'd do better for our children than our parents had done with us.

I landed the job with IBM.

My first assignment was working as the project manager's assistant on a computer rollout job at Illinois School District 218. Ironically—or by some divine intervention—the same school district that Eisenhower and PIE belonged to. And who should I run into on my first week on the job but Mr. Taylor, the black security guard I had spewed all my racist bitterness to on the day I was escorted out in handcuffs.

"Damn," I said when I saw him, ducking around a corner. "What the hell…"

My IBM co-worker gave me a curious look. "What? You know the chief of police?"

I almost swallowed my tongue. "Chief of police? He's the security guard."

"Hardly. He's the top cop now and runs the security team for the district." My co-worker looked me over. "So, you in trouble with him or what?"

"I made his life hell when I was a so-called student here," I said. "We almost came to blows once. I was an ignorant…racist…asshole and caused all kinds of problems for him."

"Racist?" she asked, surprised. "You?"

Her disbelief washed over me like a cleansing rain. For years during my involvement in the white power movement, nothing made me prouder than my racist reputation, and now here was someone who was incredulous to hear that word associated with me. It had been five years since I'd left it all behind, though I had still not publicly confronted my past. Ashamed and scared, I had run from it, struggling to stay ahead of its grasp.

I had been living in fear for the last five years, hoping that my past wouldn't catch up with me and prevent me from moving forward professionally and socially, and terrified that the hundreds, maybe even thousands, of violent people that I helped create would seek me out and hurt me or my children. During my time in the movement, it was a standard and encouraged practice to vilify anyone who left the movement as a "race traitor." Leaving was also an open invitation for a brutal assault or murder. A case in point was Martell's 1987 vicious attack on Angie Streckler, the former skinhead whose near-lifeless body was left battered and beaten beneath a swastika that was drawn on her wall with her own blood.

In that moment, I felt as though the heavens had split and embraced me in beams of redemptive light, and I immediately knew what I had to do.

I tore after my former nemesis. I spotted him as he was leaving the building. For the first time, I ran toward something in these school halls instead of away from it. "Mr. Taylor!" I cried. "Hold on, please."

He turned, his smile abruptly fading as he recognized me.

"Excuse me. Do you remember me, Mr. Taylor?"

"You're hard to forget," he said, his voice holding back any emotion.

"I want to tell you…tell you I'm sorry," I said, catching my breath. "All those terrible things I said. What I did. My hatred. I made your life miserable when I attended school here. I'd take it back if I could. I'm not going to make excuses for myself. But I want you to know I'm not that person anymore."

He met my gaze, studying me, looking so deeply into my eyes I felt like he saw my soul. After a short time, with a slight nod, he held out his hand. "I'm glad to hear it, Mr. Picciolini." And in a brief moment, his words deciphered what my eyes had been too blind to see: "True freedom from our demons requires great amounts of sacrifice and pain. I believe you know what I'm talking about. It's your responsibility now to tell the world what healed you. Welcome back."

Tears stung my eyes as our hands connected, and I looked down to see hands that were once squeezed into fists longing to lash out now locked in mutual respect.

The concept was pure. Simple. True. I had to deal with my own pain before I could begin to repair the damage I'd done to others. I had to fully expose myself to the light so that the evil I'd once paid tribute to could be washed away once and for all.

In ancient Norse mythology—something Hitler and the Nazis borrowed heavily from and bastardized to justify their corrupt concept of the ultimate "white warrior"—there existed the idea of a symbolic series of apocalyptic events referred to as *Ragnarök*, a great battle amongst the warring Viking gods that would ultimately result in the violent destruction of the tainted world they lived in, so that a new and fertile one might resurface in its place. How fitting that this same concept could help heal me. Scorch the infested earth where my roots had once lain rotting so that new life could be fertilized and grow from its ashes.

The notion to reflect and repair myself from the inside, so that I could destroy the demons that had haunted me for so long, inspired me—lit a fire.

At eighteen, I'd stood on stage in a cathedral in Germany, cries of "Heil Hitler!" punctuating the roar of thousands of European skinheads shouting the name of my band.

At that very moment, I was responsible for the electricity in the air, the adrenaline coursing through throbbing veins, the sweat pouring down shaved heads.

Absolute devotion to white power pulsated through the crowd on that misty March evening in 1992. I imagined then it must have been how Hitler felt when he led his armies on his mission to dominate the world.

I'd talked about how laws favoring blacks were taking white jobs, and how we were overburdened with taxes used to support welfare programs. I believed that neighborhoods of law-abiding, hardworking white families were being overrun with minorities and their drugs. Gays—a threat to the propagation of our species—were demanding special rights. Our women were being conned into relationships by minorities. Clearly the white race was in peril.

Or so I was taught to believe.

It began with a benign intention. I yearned to feel something more, to do something noble, and I came up with a convenient plan to fulfill those needs. Oftentimes, the results were mundane, non-toxic. Sometimes even glorious. Other times, things went terribly wrong.

When I took thoughtless actions to "protect the ones I loved," selfish justice collided with social justice. I tried to absolve myself from my own pain, ingesting any medicine I believed could rid myself of that burden. My bloated ego clouded my judgment. And with that choice to circumvent my pain, rather than to deal with it in a more rational manner, came daunting consequences and responsibilities. Some people choose to abstain from the choice altogether and run, only to have it chase them forever, others cave under the weight of it, and the remaining few abuse the momentum that sometimes results from their decisions. I believe that an enlightened person finds the balance between the passion in his heart and the reason in his mind. Not the destructive decision to redefine the reality you're facing as something suiting you but also toxic to those around you.

The truth was my parents never lost jobs to any minorities. They struggled by the skin of their teeth to make good like most Americans do. To own their own businesses and support their families through hard work. To settle down in suburbia and claim their slice of the American pie. And when I chose to foolishly venture out into the darkness on my own, on a mission to demand respect rather than earn it, I was running from something. I didn't know it then, but I recognize now that I was running from my own fear of failure.

I was convinced being a warrior meant destroying the "enemy," battling anyone unlike me at any given moment, and spreading fear throughout the community. When in truth, it's weakness that carries a bloody sword, and real strength comes from being willing to fail. Repeatedly. To learn from your mistakes. To be vulnerable and honest and accept that you just don't know. To be human.

From that stage in Weimar, swastika flags littered the old German cathedral everywhere I looked. Crooked crosses glistened on skin, covered clothes, hung on banners.

I was up on stage to make sure nobody forgot who I was.

What power.

What *ignorance*.

When I look back on that time, I can barely breathe. How could I have been so stupid? So unfeeling about the pain I so readily inflicted on innocent people? All in the name of belonging and acceptance.

Sure, some of my irrational behavior was nothing more than the natural rebellious nature of an insecure teenager looking for a way to be heard. I looked around me and saw people like my parents working hard and not enjoying life. I didn't want that to be me some day. I didn't want to be ordinary. I was sure I was destined for something greater. Like weakness, failure wasn't an option. So when an opportunity to become more presented itself to me, I grabbed it without thinking of the consequences of that decision.

After tasting that success, I became ravenous for power and recognition. I wanted something that made me feel my hot blood coursing through my veins.

Music had that effect. And through white power music I met people who I thought cared about me, who I thought were like me. I was no longer a kid without a place to belong. Instead, I believed I was leading others on a valiant mission.

I confused hate and intimidation with passion, fear with respect.

Our words to each other were about honor. But when we spoke to the outside world, it was all deception. A bait-and-switch. A flimflam. Lies were our defense—our truth. To survive this Orwellian mindset, we had to constantly close our eyes and master the art of perjury. The lie and the truth had to taste the same.

The French have a saying called *l'appel du vide*, "the call of the void." It describes that tiny voice in your head that even the most rational people might hear, that taunts you to jerk the steering wheel into oncoming traffic, or the feeling when you look over the edge of a steep precipice and become gripped with the fear of falling, but the terrifying impulse to throw yourself off the edge still beckons. In the five years after I left the movement, I heard that nagging little voice constantly, always whispering in my ear to find a way to kill what I'd helped create. But I was frightened of the consequences and I didn't know how or where to start. It wasn't until I began to realize that the road to recovery started with me that I no longer wanted to silence that urge, hoping that my own figurative demise would somehow kill all the literal evil I'd helped create.

This stark realization was the beginning of a new life for me. Once I'd reached the point of finally letting go completely, that's when change began to take hold. So, when I finally felt the pavement end and I reached the edge of that cliff, I had no interest in stopping to evaluate. I wasn't scared anymore. After seven years of not being honest with myself, I grew too tired to juggle the lies and hide the fears. I'd been committing suicide in daily increments. It was time to face the truth. I stepped hard on the gas and drove off that metaphorical cliff. I floored it, content that the demons inside of me were falling to their death. And only then, when I'd allowed that painful, symbolic death to occur—the rusted hunk of my former self burning on the sharp rocks below—only then could I stand and watch the renascent phoenix raise itself up from the wreckage and spread its wings.

With a more positive view of life, my depression quickly began to fade. The next few years flew by in a flash. IBM hired me on full-time and I had a successful career in marketing and operations. While employed there, I jumped at an opportunity to take advantage of their educational assistance. In 2001, I enrolled at DePaul University, one of two colleges I'd originally been denied entrance to while still in alternative school, and once again found myself a student. But this time, I welcomed it. I threw myself into my studies. While school had once been the bane of my existence, I now cherished every moment of it. I met students from all walks of life and bonded with them on levels I'd never let myself believe existed. Professors opened my mind with new ideas and theories. An endless world awakened. I embraced the diversity and graduated not only as a student of life, but with a nearly perfect 3.98 grade point average and a double major in international business and international relations.

The high point of my college education came when I visited the United Nations as part of a global conference focused on the Millennium Development Goals. I learned about the horrific, all-too-common exploitation and trafficking of women and children, worldwide hunger, the AIDS pandemic, and the ravages of poverty and social class discrimination. The whole experience made me realize how much work there was to be done all over the world to make life fair for people of all races, religious beliefs, genders, and sexual preferences.

Despite our tumultuous relationship, Lisa and I are once again friends. I am so fortunate to have had her as a partner in raising our children. She is an incredibly dedicated mother and a caring human being. Together we have raised two respectful and precious young men with many talents to share with the world.

Through all of this, I honored my pledge to myself to be there for my kids. I seldom dated because I reserved my free time for them. I accompanied my boys to all their school functions and parent-teacher conferences, helped them with homework and school projects, and was there when they kicked their first soccer ball.

The only thing that filled me with as much joy as my time with my children was meeting Britton. The love of my life. Like me, she worked for IBM, but halfway across the country in a Dallas sales center. We communicated with each other about work regularly before meeting in person. It wasn't a case of love at first sight. It was love *before* first sight as we got to know each other through emails and phone calls. My main concern was she would take one look at the old tattoos I'd been covering up with long sleeves, see the evidence of my past, and run. I knew hatred and prejudice were alien concepts to her and I didn't believe she could ever love anyone with a history like mine.

But she is an amazing woman and saw beyond the mistakes I'd made as a misguided youth to the man I had become. When we finally met in person after months of getting to know each other long distance, it was better than any Hollywood meeting ever filmed. We ran into each other's arms and kissed before saying a single word. We will never stop kissing, stop loving, stop growing, and experiencing life together.

Within eight months of that first embrace, Britton moved to Chicago, insisting on living in her own place so we could properly introduce her into the boys' lives over time, and both be sure that it was the best situation for all of us. We married three years later. This time it wasn't a teenage marriage. We weren't playing at being grown-ups. This was the real thing. Two souls working together to support, honor, and cherish one another.

I reconciled with my parents. I know having me as their son was not easy. I tested them to their limits and now that I am a parent myself, I understand why they made the sacrifices they did. I was an obnoxiously arrogant, selfish, spoiled brat and never appreciated all the supportive and selfless acts of sacrifice they made for me until I was faced with those same challenges myself. They loved me and did what they believed was right at the time to provide a better life for me and my brother, and I respect them for that.

After all I had done, all the pain and misery I caused, the hate I spread, the downright evil I perpetrated across the U.S. and even into Canada and Europe, I felt so incredibly fortunate to have a college education, an incredible wife, two terrific sons, a good relationship with my parents at last, and a life I could be proud of.

But in one second, everything changed.

25

SINS OF THE BROTHER

My brother Alex. Buddy.

Sweetest guy you'll ever meet. And he loved me. I was his cool older brother. When he was little, he'd wait for me to get home from school. He'd follow me around the house, singing when I sang, dancing when I danced. He'd beg to come down to my apartment when I was fifteen and he was five so he could hang out with me. He wanted to go everyplace I went, do everything I did. But he was too young and I was too selfish.

"Buddy, when I'm older, will I be strong like you?"

"Yes," I'd say. "You'll be stronger."

"Will you teach me, Buddy? I want to be tough and beat people up, too."

"If that's what you want," I'd laugh.

He'd smile and I'd throw my arms around him, pretending to wrestle.

I never lost interest in him, but as I got increasingly involved in the white supremacist movement and then got married and had kids of my own, I had less and less time to share with him.

Sometimes this made him sad, and he'd fight back tears welling up in his eyes when I said, "Nah, can't take you with me this time, Buddy. Next time."

Christian and Buddy, 1985

Next time seldom came. He knew it'd be that way, but still, he'd smile and say, "Okay. Promise?"

I'd promise.

But we both knew it was unlikely.

When he got older, he stopped pretending "sometime" would come. He became angry with me. Resentful I'd left him behind. Betrayed. Deserted. His tone of voice had not been one of understanding when he was fourteen years old and confided in my mom that I was more a distant relative than a brother. He wanted his brother back. His Buddy. Though he'd never ask or let me know that himself.

But whether I was there for him or not, he was still influenced by me, his big brother. Like younger brothers are.

So he started misbehaving about the time he reached high school. Hanging out with negative influences. Gangs. Earned himself a reputation like I had. Although his was different. I was known as defiant, tough, someone who wouldn't back down. A leader.

Buddy, on the other hand, was a follower. You could count on him to go along with whatever was going down. And he'd take the fall if someone needed to. He'd seen me go through petty arrests and trials. It was no big deal. Life went on. Consequences could be dealt with.

Like me, he drank. But more than I had and not to be sociable, but to get drunk. Unlike me during my skinhead days, he got into drugs. He spent time in jail for marijuana and illegal firearm possession. It was a small amount of weed, insignificant, but the gun was enough to get him locked up. The judge sentenced him to do community service since it was his first offense, but Buddy wanted to prove he was tougher than me and demanded jail time instead. I didn't understand why he'd ask for such a stupid thing. I'd done my share of community service. It wasn't hard. Jail was. I worried about his choices, wrote to him and visited when he was locked up. Tried to reconnect, to find out what was going on with him. How I could help. I knew he still maintained friendships with people who were in street gangs like the Latin Kings. That worried me. He assured me he wasn't in a gang, but I knew hanging out with gang members—whether he was officially a member or not—would lead to more trouble. Violence. Danger.

Despite his gang friends, jail time, misbehavior, Buddy was a good kid. Sweet through and through. A warm heart. He was like a big teddy bear. No longer the tubby little boy I used to wrestle with as a child, he was now thick, solid. A man. You could depend on Alex for a smile and a good time.

When I moved back into my parents' basement after the divorce, I became more concerned about his choices. I tried talking to my parents, telling them where it would all lead. But they dismissed me, not having the courage to stand up to him, the same way they had feared me.

I had arguments with my brother about the path he was on, lecturing him even though I knew there was no way my words would penetrate. My efforts to point out that nothing good would come of the lifestyle he was leading only made him more angry. "Who the fuck are you to talk?" he'd say. "You aren't my parent. It's not like you even remembered I existed until now. You can't come back after all this time and expect to jump right in and be my brother again."

"Buddy, these guys you're hanging with are bad news," I warned.

"My name is Alex. I ain't your buddy," he'd say.

Other times he'd throw it in my face that I'd been way worse than him at his age and laugh it off. The laugh was bitter, leaving a chill around my heart.

"And look at what happened to me," I'd say. "My wife left me. I nearly lost my kids. Everything that mattered to me disappeared. And I wasted seven years of my life throwing it all away. You want that to happen to you? Open your eyes. Please, Buddy, see what's ahead."

"Fuck you."

After a while, I gave up trying to reach my brother. It only made him act out more. Besides, who needed the aggravation? Life got in the way. Work. Classes to attend. Two little boys to raise.

One night he was out driving around in a shady neighborhood with a couple of his gangbanger friends trying to buy a dime bag of weed. None of them were aware that a month before, blood had been shed between two rival gangs in that area—one black and one Latino. Guns were fired in a drive-by. That sort of bad business.

When the black kids on the corner saw the unfamiliar van my brother was in cruise down their block that dark night—driven by a young Mexican male—they thought the vehicle was full of rival gang members rolling up on them.

They opened fire.

The driver, my brother's friend Flaco, was shot in the spine.

Another bullet grazed my brother across the abdomen. A second one hit his groin, cutting through his femoral artery.

The other two passengers with them ducked in the back seat of the vehicle, escaping injury.

Seriously wounded himself, Flaco managed to drive to the hospital. The two in the back seat jumped out of the car and fled.

Flaco didn't make it in time. My brother—my Buddy—was pronounced dead on arrival. He was a month shy of his twenty-first birthday.

What followed—the arrest, arraignment, trial, and the ultimate acquittal of the person who allegedly murdered my brother—is perhaps another book. One I'm not yet ready to write. The guilt over the actions of my own misspent youth that may have ultimately led my brother to his end is still too overwhelming.

I felt then, as I do now, that I am to blame. I wish I'd been more involved in his life, more insistent he stay away from gangs and violence. More of a role model. He'd been following in my footsteps.

But more than that, I felt that somehow his death was retribution for all the violence and hate I'd projected into the world, for the pain I'd inflicted on others because of the color of their skin, and my misplaced idea that by abusing them, I could be somebody.

My brother was killed because he was in a car with people whose skin color threatened a bunch of scared, ignorant kids with a different skin color.

My brother's death was on me.

At the funeral, old racist friends of mine, my brother's friends, even family members who'd never been involved in any racist or gang activity in their lives, came up to me to see if I was going to seek revenge. They urged me to. Hungered for it, even. The score had to be settled.

To say I was dumbfounded is an understatement. Full of guilt and regret, the last thing I wanted was to keep the cycle of violence going.

It had to stop with me—with Buddy. I would never again be part of that world of hate. Never again live in a world where the color of someone's skin, the object of someone's love or faith, would inspire violence or judgment.

My brother had paid for my sins.

I would spend the rest of my life atoning for them.

EPILOGUE

Hᴏᴡ ʜᴀs ᴍʏ ᴀᴛᴏɴᴇᴍᴇɴᴛ ɢᴏɴᴇ? After seven years with IBM, I returned to the music business and the world of entrepreneurship. I served as general manager and executive producer of JBTV, an iconic, Emmy Award-winning music television program that helps expose the world to talented emerging artists. I am a writer, teacher, record label owner and artist manager, representing bands based on the strength of their music and character.

While I was earning my bachelor's degree from DePaul University, I had an extraordinary opportunity to work as a rapporteur for the United Nations' 57th Annual Conference on Civil Society and the Millennium Development Goals. As a result, I was able to produce an informational short film, hoping to inspire people to come together in peace to work on serious global issues like poverty and hunger, AIDS, and to promote gender equality in developing countries. As my final assignment before graduation, I wrote a twenty-page thesis detailing my involvement in the white power movement and my ultimate de-radicalization from violent, far-right wing extremism. Ten years later, that project became this book.

In 2008, I was invited to write an opinion editorial for the popular music magazine, *Alternative Press*, where I denounced my seven years of hate. The publication of that piece was pivotal for me, as it was the first time I'd openly spoken about my past in a large public forum. I urged readers to heed my story and find ways to make the world a better place. A world that promoted inclusion and equality for everyone.

For years after, I volunteered as a coach for my sons' soccer teams and encouraged all the young athletes I mentored to strive for integrity in what they do, both on and off the field.

On Dr. Martin Luther King Jr.'s birthday in 2010, I co-founded Life After Hate, a nonprofit organization striving to be an agent of change for those struggling with hate. By sharing our unique perspectives on empathy and compassion, and by promoting basic human goodness, we aspire to be a shining beacon of hope for those who feel mired by racism and prejudice. Leadership within the organization is made up entirely of reformed white power skinheads—both male and female. By and large, some of the kindest and most courageous people I know.

And I have written this book, acknowledging the dark legacy I've left behind, knowing that toxic weeds may still be sprouting from the infected seeds that I planted all those years ago. Knowing that there may be retaliation both from the racists I helped create who are still strong in my country, and from law enforcement, who still have me in their files; hoping that it will keep others—even one person—from making the same selfish and uneducated decisions I made, from going down that dark, evil path of racism and supporting the ignorant belief that anyone is better than anyone else solely based on their race, gender, religion, or sexual preference.

While regrets over my past still haunt me, I have made meaningful changes in my life and can now look in the mirror without seeing a monster staring back at me. I graduated from DePaul and married Britton, the most understanding and loving woman on the planet, someone who has never known a racist moment. Every day, I thank the gods of fate and destiny for letting my path join with a woman of her strength, character, intelligence, empathy, and loving nature.

I am the father to my sons I wished my own father had been to me. I have attended every one of their soccer and football games, their school events, and parent-teacher conferences. Now that they are young adults, wiser than I ever was at their age, I still hold them accountable for their actions, unafraid to talk to them when they do something I know could harm them or someone else. And it was my role as a father that I credit the most for my transformation. It made me constantly question the path I was on, as it was certain to separate me from my sons by either death or imprisonment, as it did for many people I've known.

Once I took those first steps away from the movement and towards my children, each successive stride became easier. I took great pleasure in experiencing new things with my sons and not being concerned with the unjust barriers of race and prejudice that might have clouded those special moments. It evoked a tremendous amount of emotion in me to think about anyone hurting my children—or anyone else's for that matter—because they might be "different." And I paid close attention to those powerful feelings, envisioning the pain other parents of sons and daughters who I'd hurt along my journey might have felt.

In 1996, during what were some of the earliest and darkest days of my depression and fear after I'd left the movement, I turned to recreational drugs and alcohol to relieve my pain. But they only made my feelings of worth feel even thinner. Knowing that my drug use and sudden detachment from society after I closed my store had begun to destroy me, I grabbed a lifeline and decided to revert to the only thing I knew how to do well—perform music. I put together a little-known punk band called Random55 to try to keep my mind from shutting down. This time the lyrics were about heartbreak and loss and not about prejudice and hatred. I was fortunate enough during my time with Random55 to meet one of the heroes of my youth—the venerated Joan Jett.

An acquaintance I'd met through my record store the following year was a concert promoter at a club across town. She called me one afternoon when she had a last-minute cancellation from one of the bands she'd booked to open for a major headliner that night. She asked if we could help her out and fill the slot. We were thrilled. Before I could ask who the band was that we'd be supporting, she hung up. We packed our gear and booked it to the club. When we arrived at the venue, we were ecstatic to learn that Random55 would be the opening act for Joan Jett and the Blackhearts.

Shrouded by the excitement of the night, inside I was battling a solitary depression that all but incapacitated me and constantly made me question whether my life was worth living. Shortly before the doors of the venue opened that evening, as Joan wrapped up her sound check before heading to her dressing room, she noticed me sitting quietly backstage. She must have sensed that I was hurting, because she approached and put her arm around me.

"I saw your sound check earlier," she said. "You guys are good."

"Thank you," I replied. Suddenly becoming starstruck snapped me out of my funk.

"I think you have a bright future. What's your name?"

"Christian. My name's Christian Picciolini." Though I think she probably meant my band's name.

"Christian, I'm Joan." I laughed as we shook hands. Of course I knew her name. She put her arm around my shoulder again. "Get up there and warm up the crowd for me." I told her I would.

Backstage later that night, after her second encore, I mentioned to Joan that I had actually met her briefly once before when I was thirteen years old. It had been while she was filming the movie *Light of Day* with Michael J. Fox, which they'd partly shot in Blue Island.

"Thanks for making me feel old," she joked. "Why were you so sad earlier? You guys played a great show to a sold-out crowd. You should be happy."

I told her that I'd been going through a rough patch. "You know, relationships, work, that kind of stuff," I replied.

"Well, cheer up. Things will only get better if you let them." Her voice was kind and caring. "We've actually got a tour coming up in the winter. If you guys aren't busy, I'd love it if you and the band would come along and be our support act for a few of those shows."

To this day, those gigs remain some of the highlights of my life. And throughout that tour, Joan continued to shower me with empathy.

Her words and actions helped save my life. During those dark and confusing days, when I often contemplated whether it was worth living, it was her kindness that lifted my spirits when I needed it most.

All human beings have a need for compassion and possess the ability to give it. To empathize—or to put yourself in someone else's shoes and allow yourself to understand the pain they feel are feeling, to humanize them—is the most important thing we can do. We all share the ability to laugh, to enjoy life, and to love. To process pain and loss and fear. Arbitrary things like skin color or sexuality have no effect on these and other wonderful human abilities.

I am far from perfect. I know I never will be perfect. I will stumble, I may even fall, but for the rest of my life, I will continue to pick myself up and strive to honor all people and try to be of service to that which will benefit mankind.

I am my father. My mother. My grandparents. My brother. My wife. My children. My friends. I am part of everyone I have ever met and they are part of me.

We are part of each other. Bound together by the fact that we are human beings. What becomes of the human race is everyone's responsibility, and when one of us fails, we all do. When one of us refuses to be part of what is wrong with the world, the world becomes brighter for all of us.

I urge you to recognize that and to honor it in your actions and decisions.

Be part of the good in the world. Part of the ever-growing community that seeks fairness, justice, and compassion. We all have the ability to *make good happen* if we just try.

You are me, and I am you.

Peace to us all.

STORAGE
BOX
Be
Kind

ACKNOWLEDGMENTS

THIS BOOK WOULD NOT HAVE BEEN POSSIBLE without the extraordinary support of a number of people, beginning with my incredible wife Britton, the rock on which my new life has been built. Although I began to take my first few steps toward my transformation before I met you, Britton, you've been the support I have needed to continue to move forward every day. Your wisdom and rational mind are a much-appreciated ballast to my frequent risk-taking and impulsive decisions. You are my partner and best friend, and I am forever grateful for being a part of your life. I can only hope my endless love for you offers some consolation for my numerous preoccupations.

I can't say enough to acknowledge my sons, Devin and Brandon, the catalysts for the awakening from my slumber. Words cannot express how immensely proud I am of these fine young men. May they remember that all people are imperfect, and that through our imperfections we become part of the same family—the human race. If I could impart any wisdom to them it is this: Follow your dreams and let your words and actions reflect your true heart. Make sure everything you do benefits peace and promotes acceptance, caring, and equality for everyone. I love you both so much.

Random street art, Chicago (artist unknown)

I want to express my love and gratitude to my parents, Anna and Enzo Picciolini. I owe them both so much for refusing to turn me away when I needed their help the most. Looking back, I fully recognize that they sacrificed their time with me because they loved me and wanted to make a better life for me and Alex than they'd had, and I respect them for that. I thank them for doing their best and for being good and decent people who truly care and love with all their heart.

Thanks to Zia Lina, to whom I owe all my creative and artistic ambitions. To Zia Mary, whose arms I remember being held in and whose melodies sang me to sleep. She was the friend I needed growing up. I owe my sense of adventure, my street savvy, and inventiveness to Zio Nando. To you I say, sometimes it takes a bunch of wrong turns in life to eventually stumble back on the right path. These three were my real heroes when I was growing up, and I owe much of my inspiration to them. I hope they continue to influence those around them with their positive presence and caring natures.

I owe a great deal to my indelible memories of Nonno Michele, the grandfather I so admired as an impressionable child. He not only built tables and chairs, but also helped build me. And where would I be without Nonna Nancy, who will forever remain in our hearts as the foundation of our family. I miss her toughness, her delicious meatballs, and her constant concern for my untied shoelaces.

My old friend Mike W., who passed too early in life to fully complete his own transformation, showed me that actions truly speak louder than words, even if the actions are those of two misguided, troublemaking kids. He taught me through his unselfish actions that loyalty and support for family and friends are things you uphold first and ask questions about later. From him I learned that having someone you can trust and rely on makes you strive to become a better person yourself, so you can become someone they can trust and rely on when they need you.

To Sarge, my old friend, it was me who drank all your beer that night. I hope you are finally free. Rest in peace, fella.

Peace, love, and gratitude go to my extended Life After Hate family—some of the most remarkable and transformed human beings on this planet—Angela King, Frankie Meeink, Tony McAleer, T.J. Leyden, Tim Zaal, Robert Örell, and Sammy Rangel. Thank you for your continued human goodness, your kindness, and your daily inspiration. Live and love.

Joan Jett, what can I say? You are as awe-inspiring to me today as the first day I heard your voice and music all those years ago. What you said to me in 1996, old friend, struck a chord, and I have never forgotten it. You are an amazing woman and an inspiring human being. On behalf of all those you've touched and stood shoulder to shoulder with over the decades: thank you.

Many thanks to Nora Flanagan, the coolest and most tattooed English teacher I know. If not for her friendship and invariable nudging, this book may never have been completed.

To my editor and my friend Michael Mohr. I'm so grateful we finished this journey together. Your invaluable insight and constant encouragement every time I threw my exhausted hands up pushed me to become a better writer and a better person. You also taught me to "kill my darlings" and, in the process, made me love the art of writing. Thank you.

Jill Bailin, my proofreader extraordinaire, I may not be as cool as your client Hunter S. Thompson, but I'm likely just as grateful as he was to have had the pleasure to work with you. You were the perfect exclamation point to my giant run-on sentence of a manuscript. I couldn't have asked for anyone better to bring this baby home.

To all those supporters and friends who came together and helped me fund the initial pressing of this book, I could not have done this without you. Thank you for believing in me.

And lastly in mention but always first in my heart, this book is for Alex. My brother. My Buddy. The greatest regret in my life is not being there for you when you needed me. You inspired me to write about my story and your tragic death showed me that life is something to be respected, cherished and remembered, never taken for granted or forgotten—no matter how dark some of the memories might be. We have not been the same since you left us.

ABOUT THE AUTHOR

CHRISTIAN PICCIOLINI is an award-winning television producer, a visual artist, and a reformed extremist. His work and life purpose are born of an ongoing and profound need to atone for a grisly past, and to make something of his time on this planet by contributing to the greater good.

After leaving the violent hate movement he was part of during his youth, he began the painstaking process of rebuilding his life. While working for IBM, Picciolini earned a degree from DePaul University and later began his own global entertainment media firm.

In 2010 and 2011, he was nominated for three regional Emmy Awards for his role as executive producer of JBTV, one of America's longest-running music television programs. He has worked as an adjunct professor at the college level, and as the community partnerships manager for Threadless.

Most notably, in 2010 he co-founded Life After Hate, a nonprofit dedicated to helping others gain the knowledge necessary to implement long-term solutions that counter all types of racism and violent extremism.

An explorer by nature, Picciolini loves to learn new things and thrives on challenging himself with "positive disruptive thinking." He values kindness, sincerity, and respect for all people, and believes that small ideas can change the world.

Christian Picciolini (Photo by Mark Seliger)

If you, or someone you know, is in the dark, lonely world that racism takes you to, ExitUSA can help.

No judgment. Just help. There is life after hate.

Find out more at:
www.exitusa.org